THE ANNOTATED MOTHER GOOSE

BRAMHALL HOUSE · NEW YORK

The
ANNOTATED
Mother Goose

NURSERY RHYMES OLD AND NEW, ARRANGED AND EXPLAINED

BY

WILLIAM S. BARING-GOULD
&
CEIL BARING-GOULD

ILLUSTRATED BY
WALTER CRANE, RANDOLPH CALDECOTT,
KATE GREENAWAY, ARTHUR RACKHAM,
MAXFIELD PARRISH, AND EARLY
HISTORICAL WOODCUTS

With Chapter Decorations by E. M. Simon

This book is for our daughter, Judy, and our son, Bill.

Acknowledgments

The Authors wish to acknowledge the generosity and assistance of: Frederick Warne and Co., Ltd., for permission to reproduce Illustrations from the following books: MOTHER GOOSE, OR THE OLD NURSERY RHYMES illustrated by Kate Greenaway; BABY'S OPERA illustrated by Walter Crane; RANDOLPH CALDECOTT'S FIRST COLLECTION OF PICTURES AND SONG; THE HEY DIDDLE DIDDLE PICTURE BOOK illustrated by Randolph Caldecott; The British Museum, for permission to reproduce some of the pictures from TOMMY THUMB'S PRETTY SONG BOOK; The American Antiquarian Society, for permission to reproduce illustrations from their edition of MOTHER GOOSE'S MELODY; the executor of the Arthur Rackham Estate for permission to reproduce a number of the artist's illustrations in MOTHER GOOSE, THE OLD NURSERY RHYMES, published by William Heinemann Ltd.; and Justin Schiller for his kindness in lending MOTHER GOOSE IN PROSE by L. Frank Baum, so that the Maxfield Parrish illustrations can grace these pages.

W. CRANE

Table of Contents

. . . smooth stones from the brook of time,
worn round by constant friction of tongues
long silent.

ANDREW LANG

Here Mother Goose on Winter Nights

The old and young she both delights.

SCOTCH CHAPBOOK OF 1817

CHAPTER I

All About "Mother Goose"

They are the beloved heritage of Nobody-Really-Knows how many countries or how many centuries.

Here in America we are likely to lump them all together under a single heading and call them the "Mother Goose" rhymes.

Our cousins the British refer to them, more accurately, as nursery rhymes—or "melodies," or "songs," or "jingles."

Still others, in Sweden, Finland, Denmark, Switzerland, France, Italy, Spain, and other parts of Europe, know them simply as the "folk" rhymes of children.

What exactly are they?

Some, undoubtedly, *are* rhymes that were created by just plain "folk"—rhymes to be repeated by their children while playing active games, from knee-dandling to skip-rope, from hoop-rolling and ball-bouncing to seesaw and the ride on the rocking-horse.

Akin to these are the counting-out rhymes, like "Eena, Meena, Mina, Mo," whose purpose, even to-

1. There is a tradition in England that some of these counting-out rhymes may be relics of formulas used by the druids in choosing human sacrifices.

2. Never originally intended for the nursery. We must expect some earthiness, not to say ribaldry—not to say plain vulgarity—in the earliest versions of some of the rhymes. In the seventeenth and eighteenth centuries, adults were far less squeamish about what was fit for children's ears than they are today.

day, is to designate which of a group of children shall be singled out as "It."**1**

Then there are the rhymes that are supposed to help young children to learn numbers, letters, and designations—the toe-counting and the feature-naming rhymes, to begin at the very beginning (from the child's point of view) and the somewhat later (again, from the child's point of view) "A Was an Archer" and "A for the Ape" and all the other alphabet rhymes.

Other "Mother Goose" rhymes are lullabies, others are prayers, others are drinking and love songs.**2**

Still other "Mother Goose" rhymes are riddles and "catches" and tongue twisters. Still others are charms and incantations, proverbs in verse and weather lore in doggerel. Still others are simple humor—often nonsense humor—pleasantly packaged as a verse, often in the limerick form. And still others are fragments of ballads commemorating actual occurrences of at least local importance.

Finally, there are those rhymes which well may be, as many earnest scholars insist they are, "political diatribes, religious philippics, and popular street songs, embodying comedies, tragedies and love episodes of many great historical personages, lavishly interspersed with English and Scotch folklore flung out with dramatic abandon."

We are quoting here from *The Real Personages of Mother Goose,* by Katherine Elwes Thomas, published in Boston in 1930 by Lothrop, Lee & Shepard Co.

Later in the same volume Miss Thomas writes:

"These political satires, written with a merciless keenness of scintillating thrust and bloodletting, in the directness of their lunge at the heart of people and events, embody through many notable reigns the vices and foibles of humanity upon the throne and about the court of England.

"The lines of Little Bo-Peep and Little Boy Blue, which to childish minds have only quaint charm of meaning, which suggest but the gayest of blue skies and rapturous-hearted creatures disporting in daisy-pied meadows, hold in reality grim import. Across all this nursery lore there falls at times the black shadow of the headsman's block, and in their seeming lightness are portrayed the tragedies of kings and queens, the corruptions of opposing political parties, and stories of fanatical religious strife that have gone to make world history.

"Love, politics and religion are the three inexhaustible themes upon which the changes are incessantly rung. The caustic wits of many ages, kings, courtiers, scholars, dilettante lords and ladies of high degree have contributed to this wonderful collection of unrivaled brilliance. Long-forgotten plays, mummings and masques abound in the familiar verses. . . ."

This is all very exciting, and much of it is true—but some students may, perhaps, have been a little overzealous in reading meaning into rhymes where no meaning was ever intended.

Consider, if you will, what John Bellenden Ker was able to make of:

> There was an Old Woman
> Liv'd under a Hill,
> And if she isn't gone
> She lives there still.

"The point of this distich," Ker wrote in *An Essay on the Archaeology of Popular English Phrases and Nursery Rhymes,* published in 1834, expanded in 1837 and again in 1840, "seems to be a reproach to the friars with their mass, chanting, and other solemnities as carried on for the means of filling their bellies, and implies, if they are not well paid, they would not be at the trouble of performing merely for religious or conscientious motives."

One would almost think that Ker lived in the seventeenth century, when the frenzied cry was, "No Popery! No Popery! No Popery!"—when the House of Commons resolved (on April 29, 1678) that the House, "taking into serious consideration the dangers arising to this kingdom from the restless endeavours of priests and Jesuits, and other Popish recusants, to subvert the true religion planted amongst us, and reduce us again under the bondage of Roman superstition and idolatry . . . do therefore think it requisite to apply some remedy to this growing evil."

No serious scholar doubts that many of the "priests and Jesuits" of seventeenth-century England were grossly corrupt, but the remedies taken against the Catholic laymen seem, today, to have been drastic: it was high treason, or a crime at least, for any Catholic to convert anyone to the Church of Rome, to come to court, or to London, or (unless a tradesman) within ten miles of London, to practice law or medicine, or hold any government office, or to act as executor, administrator, or guardian.3

Attempts like Ker's to find latent meaning in the beloved old rhymes have of course been protested. The editors of an edition of *Songs for the Nursery*, published by Darton and Clark of Holborn Hill, early struck out against such prejudiced (and preposterous) interpretations, and Iona and Peter Opie, the distinguished editors of *The Oxford Dictionary of Nursery Rhymes,* have more recently called Ker's essay "probably the most extraordinary example of misdirected labour in the history of English letters."

*　　*　　*　　*
　*　　*　　*
*　　*　　*　　*

How ancient can some of the "Mother Goose" rhymes actually be said to be?

In James Orchard Halliwell's great nineteenth-century collection, *The Nursery Rhymes of England,* and its "sequel," *Popular Rhymes and Nursery Tales,* no *manuscript* source goes farther back than the reign of Henry VIII.

But the Reverend Sabine Baring-Gould (1834-1924), an acknowledged authority on the songs and sagas of Iceland,4 was convinced that "Jack and Jill" could be traced back to "the Eddaic Hjuki and Bil. . . . Hjuki, in Norse, would be pronounced Juki, which would readily become Jack; and Bil, for the sake of euphony, and in order to give a female name to one of the children, would become Jill."5

The anonymous author of the Preface to *Mother Goose's Melody* (c. 1765)—and he may have been,

3. Until very recently, some nursery rhyme books could still, with justice, be accused of intolerance toward Catholics. Witness this rhyme in a book published in both Britain and the United States in the year 1925:

> *A penn'orth of bread to feed the Pope,*
> *A penn'orth of cheese to choke him,*
> *A pint of beer to wash it down,*
> *And a good old faggot to burn him.*

It was perhaps in retaliation to such shocking bias as this that Frank Scully undertook a drastic rewriting of the old rhymes for the eyes and ears of Catholic children. See his *Blessed Mother Goose* (Hollywood: House-Warven, 1952).

4. He was also an enthusiastic British and Continental folklorist, a novelist, and a hymn writer, best remembered today for his "Onward, Christian Soldiers" and "Now the Day Is Over."

5. The quotation is from *Curious Myths of the Middle Ages* (1866).

in reality, a very jocular author indeed—explained to his young readers that "the custom of singing these songs and lullabies to children is of great antiquity: It is even as old as the time of the ancient Druids. Charactatus, King of the Britons, was rocked in his cradle in the Isle of Mona, now called Anglesea, and turned to sleep by some of these soporiferous sonnets."

It is going back much too far to say that many of the rhymes as we know them today are anywhere near as ancient as that, but there can be little doubt that a few of them at least were well known when Shakespeare was a boy, that perhaps a quarter of them were current during the reign of Charles I (1625-49), and that others were added during the Commonwealth, under the Cromwells, and the subsequent reigns of Charles II, James II, William and Mary, Anne, and George I.

And now it is time to consider "Old Mother Goose" herself, as a personality, and to inquire who she might have been.

She might have been the Queen of Sheba. Or so some scholars seriously contend.

Not so, say other scholars.

She might have been Bertha, the Queen Bertha who died in 783, the wife of Pepin and the mother of the great King Charlemagne. Or she might have been another Bertha—wife of Robert II of France ("Robert the Pious," c. 970-1031).

Unhappily, these two Berthas have become almost inextricably confused.

Both, however, seem to have been connected in the public mind with that common barnyard fowl, the goose.

One Bertha—most probably the mother of Charlemagne—was known to her subjects by a name derived from the size, or possibly the shape, of her foot: she was *La Reine Pédauque* (or *Pédance*), otherwise *Berthe au grand pied,* "Queen Goose-foot," or "Goose-footed Bertha."

The second Bertha—and this is unquestionably the wife of Robert the Pious—was so closely related to her husband that on his marriage to her, he was excommunicated from the Catholic Church. The result of this near-incestuous union (it was whispered) was the birth of a monster—a creature with the head of a goose.

In more pleasant French legendry, "Goose-footed Bertha" is represented as incessantly spinning, with hordes of children clustered about her, listening to her stories.[6]

Certainly the name "Mother Goose"—as a teller of nursery *tales* rather than the supposed author of the well-known *rhymes*—is French, and goes back to the year 1650, when, as Andrew Lang discovered, Loret's *La Muse Historique* was published. The volume contains the line, *Comme un conte de la Mère Oye*—"Like a Mother Goose story."

Perhaps the German *Fru Gode* or *Fru Gosen* also contributed something.

But the popularity of "Mother Goose"—again, as a teller of *tales*—dates from 1697, in which year Charles Perrault[7] published, under the name of his ten-year-old son, Perrault d'Armancourt, a collection of fairy tales called *Les Contes de la Mère l'Oye (Tales of My Mother Goose)*. The book contains eight stories: "Little Red Riding Hood," "Bluebeard," "The Sleeping Beauty," "Puss in Boots," "Cinderella," "Little Tom Thumb," and two other tales less well known today.

In England, the phrase "Mother Goose"— again, as a teller of *tales*—was probably first used in a book of fairy tales published by J. Pote of Charing Cross in March, 1729.

But now it is time for the New World to put in its claim.

"Mother Goose," many American scholars stoutly maintain, was Elizabeth Foster Goose (or Vergoose or Vertigoose)[8] of Charleston and Boston. Elizabeth

6. From this arose the French custom of referring to any tall tale as one told "at the time when good Queen Bertha spun."

7. Charles Perrault was a member of the French Academy, a stout champion of the moderns against the ancients, and a brother of Claude Perrault, who was not only a doctor of medicine but an architect, and designed the colonnade of the Louvre.

8. The name "Vergoose" or "Vertigoose" comes from the French word *vert*—meaning a "green" goose, that is, a young goose, a gosling.

was the daughter of William and Ann Foster of Charleston, where she was born on April 5, 1665. On July 5, 1692, when she was twenty-seven years of age, she became the wife of Isaac Goose of Boston, aged about fifty-five. Isaac had been married before, and Elizabeth found herself a stepmother to ten children by that previous marriage. She herself bore Isaac six others: Elizabeth, Elizabeth (again), Ann, Isaac, Ann (again), and Peter.[9]

Elizabeth Goose—the surviving daughter of that name—was married in 1715, by no less a divine than the famous Cotton Mather, to a scholarly but somewhat waggish young man named Thomas Fleet, who (some say) had quietly sailed from Bristol, England, after taking a leading part in the riots occasioned there by the Jacobite uprising,[10] to establish, in Boston, on Pudding Lane, a printshop whose sign was the Crown and Heart, to which was later added a crest in the form of a bird bearing a letter in its beak.

Soon, Thomas and Elizabeth Fleet had a baby, and before too long they had produced six other little Fleets.

Like many another grandmother, Elizabeth Goose, it is said, culled her memory for rhymes that would "lull" the little ones. Thomas Fleet, listening to her lullabies—"until [he] was almost driven distracted by them," says *The Oxford Dictionary of Nursery Rhymes*—determined to publish them, perhaps out of "malice and spite and spleen, to be revenged on his wife's mother." He did publish them, it is alleged, in a book (more likely a broadside) printed in 1719, under the title of *Songs for the Nursery, or Mother Goose's Melodies*.

Whether or not such a book or broadside was ever actually published is a bibliographic mystery; indeed, it has been called "the most elusive 'ghost' volume in the history of American letters."

The late John Fleet Eliot of Boston, a great-grandson of Thomas and Elizabeth Fleet, stated[11] that the late Edward A. Crowinshield, also of Boston, had once examined a fragmentary copy of *Songs for the*

9. The first Elizabeth lived only fifteen days, and so the next child—happily, a girl—was given the same name. The first Ann also died young.

10. The Reverend Edward Everett Hale, in his introduction to the 1905 edition of *The Only True Mother Goose Melodies,* stated that Fleet had been born in Norwich, and implied a possible connection with the rhyme that begins "The Man in the Moon came tumbling down / And ask'd his way to Norwich . . . .

11. Under the pseudonym of "Requiescat" in the Boston *Transcript,* issue of January 14, 1860.

12. Crowinshield had died eleven months before Eliot referred to his supposed discovery.

13. The Holmes-was-an-American theory was originated and stoutly upheld by the late Christopher Morley.

Nursery in the library of the American Antiquarian Society at Worcester, Mass.[12]

But no records of the book or broadside appear in that library's catalogue; repeated advertisements and researches have failed to bring it to light; and no other copy has ever been found elsewhere.

William A. Wheeler, who produced in 1869 his own edition of "Mother Goose"—he is described by the editors of *The Oxford Dictionary of Nursery Rhymes* as an "ardent publicist"—thought that the volume must have been "mislaid, or overlooked, or lost, or destroyed," but it is perhaps more reasonable to suppose that the late Edward A. Crowinshield of Boston was mistaken; he was engaged in other research at the time, he told John Fleet Eliot, and so he simply jotted down the title.

Isaac Goose died on November 29, 1710, at the age of seventy-three. "Mother Goose," if she *was* Mother Goose, died late in 1756 or early in 1757, and was reputedly put to rest in the Old Granary Burying Ground, although no headstone is there.

True or not, it is a pleasant story, and it would be cheering to Americans to think that "Mother Goose," like Sherlock Holmes,[13] may have been an American.

*   *   *   *

It would hardly be fair to end this chapter without acknowledging that the "Mother Goose" rhymes have their detractors as well as their champions.

As early as 1641 George Wither was protesting that many of the rhymes were unfit for childish ears. He was followed, in the first half of the nineteenth century, by Sarah Trimmer and Samuel Goodrich.

In 1925 Mrs. Winifred Sackville Stoner, Jr., once a child prodigy who "used a typewriter" at the age of three, tried to attack Mother Goose constructively by promulgating informative jingles, rhymes that "represent life." Example:

> Every perfect person owns
> Just two hundred and six bones.

In 1937 Professor Allen Abbott urged nursery rhyme reform, as did Geoffrey Hall in 1949-50. And in 1952 Geoffrey Handley-Taylor of Manchester, England, published a brief biography of the literature of nursery rhyme reform in which he wrote that:

"The average collection of 200 traditional nursery rhymes contains approximately 100 rhymes which personify all that is glorious and ideal for the child. Unfortunately, the remaining 100 rhymes harbour unsavoury elements. The incidents listed below occur in the average collection and may be accepted as a reasonably conservative estimate based on a general survey of this type of literature.

  8 allusions to murder (unclassified),
  2 cases of choking to death,
  1 case of death by devouring,
  1 case of cutting a human being in half,
  1 case of decapitation,
  1 case of death by squeezing,
  1 case of death by shrivelling,
  1 case of death by starvation,
  1 case of boiling to death,
  1 case of death by hanging,
  1 case of death by drowning,
  4 cases of killing domestic animals,
  1 case of body snatching,
21 cases of death (unclassified),
  7 cases relating to the severing of limbs,
  1 case of the desire to have a limb severed,
  2 cases of self-inflicted injury,
  4 cases relating to the breaking of limbs,
  1 allusion to a bleeding heart,
  1 case of devouring human flesh,
  5 threats of death,
  1 case of kidnapping,
12 cases of torment and cruelty to human beings and animals,
  8 cases of whipping and lashing,
  3 allusions to blood,
14 cases of stealing and general dishonesty,
15 allusions to maimed human beings and animals,
  1 allusion to undertakers,
  2 allusions to graves,
23 cases of physical violence (unclassified),
  1 case of lunacy,
16 allusions to misery and sorrow,

1 case of drunkenness,
4 cases of cursing,
1 allusion to marriage as a form of death,
1 case of scorning the blind,
1 case of scorning prayer,
9 cases of children being lost or abandoned,
2 cases of house burning,
9 allusions to poverty and want,
5 allusions to quarrelling,
2 cases of unlawful imprisonment,
2 cases of racial discrimination.

ROUND about, round about,
　　Magotty Pye ;
My Father loves good Ale,
　　And fo do I.

"Expressions of fear, weeping, moans of anguish, biting, pain and evidence of supreme selfishness may be found in almost every other page."

Let the poet Walter de la Mare speak in defense of poor Old Mother Goose. Her rhymes, he wrote,[14] "free the fancy, charm tongue and ear, delight the inward eye, and many of them are tiny masterpieces of word craftsmanship—of the latest device in rhythm, indeed—the 'sprung'! Last, but not least, they are not only crammed with vivid little scenes and objects and living creatures, but, however fantastic and nonsensical they may be, they are a direct short cut into poetry itself. How any child who was ever delightedly dandled to their strains can have managed to grow up proof against their enchantment, and steadily and desperately more and more matter-of-fact and prosaic, is a question to which I can find no satisfactory answer."

We hope that you, the present reader, will agree with him. And now on to the rhymes themselves.

14. In his introduction to *Nursery Rhymes for Certain Times* (London: Faber & Faber, Ltd., 1956).

CHAPTER II

The Pretty Songs of Tommy Thumb

Little Tommy Thumb,
With his little Pipe & Drum,
Is come to give you a Dance;
And Lovechild so Taper,
Will show you a Caper,
Dunoyer brought over from France.
She is pleas'd that you look,
Into her little Book,
And like her Songs so well
That her Figures you know,
Before you can goe,
And Sing them
Before you can spell.

In the year 1744, or thereabouts, the London publisher, Mary Cooper, brought out at least two, and perhaps three or more, little volumes—a mere three inches by one and three-quarters inches in size—which she titled *Tommy Thumb's Pretty Song Book* —"for the Diversion of all Little Masters and Misses." Price, sixpence a volume.

No copy of Volume I of the *Song Book,* or the third or more volumes, if such were ever published, has yet been discovered, but there does exist a single copy of Volume II. It is a treasured possession of the British Museum, and it would be difficult to estimate its worth.

Tommy Thumb's Pretty Song Book, Vol. II, is generally agreed to be the earliest known book of nursery rhymes, and it contains in all thirty-eight of them, many old favorites, some now suppressed, some now forgotten. Each of the rhymes is illustrated with a rude woodcut, and some of the longer rhymes with two.

Actually, of course, many of the rhymes in *Tommy Thumb's Pretty Song Book* must have been printed, in one form or another, long before 1744.

Librarians at the Bodleian and the British Museum Libraries told Katherine Elwes Thomas that the first collected editions of the "Mother Goose" rhymes were published in England as early as 1620, and followed by reprints in 1648. And the *original* publication of many of the rhymes may have been in the form of handbills—generally printed on coarse single sheets of paper—brought out as early as 1600, many of them by the Printing Press of Pye Corner in London.[1]

Up to the present time, however, no student has been able to locate copies of any of these reputed publications.

Here, then, are the "pretty songs" of Tommy Thumb. They appear here exactly as they appeared there, well over two hundred years ago, except that we have inserted an occasional comma, apostrophe, or question mark, and changed the old English ſ to *s* for the convenience of the modern reader.

[1]. Bath, Bristol, and Edinburgh are three other British cities in which various of the rhymes are believed by some to have been composed and first printed.

To these we have added five rhymes from three other children's books published in the next fifteen or so years. First, there is the famous "House That Jack Built," which made its original appearance in *Nurse Truelove's New-Year's-Gift; or the Book of Books for Children,* published in 1755 by John Newbery, about whom we shall read more later. Next come three rhymes—including "Little Boy Blue"—whose earliest appearance was in *The Famous Tommy Thumb's Little Story-Book,* published by Stanley Crowder and Benjamin Collins around the year 1760. The chapter ends with "Jacky Nory" from *The Top Book of All, for Little Masters and Misses,* which Crowder and Collins, joined by one R. Baldwin, brought out about the same time.

« 1 »

Little Robin[2] red breast,[3]
Sitting on a pole,
Niddle, Noddle,
Went his head,
And Poop went his Hole.[4]

2. "Robin" is a name in two senses: In England it is a bird allied to the nightingale, and it a diminutive of "Robert" (without the capital R, it is also a word that means lout or bumpkin).

"The Christian names given to birds deserve a notice," the great nineteenth-century collector of nursery rhymes, James O. Halliwell, wrote. "Thus we have Jack Snipe, Jenny Wren, Tom Tit, Robin Redbreast, Poll Parrot, Jill Hooker, Jack Curlew, Jack Nicker, and King Harry for a goldfinch. . . . A starling is always Jacob, a sparrow is Philip, a raven is Ralph, and the consort of the Tom Tit rejoices in the euphonic name of Betty! Children give the name of Dick to all small birds, which, in nursery parlance, are universally Dickey-birds." And: "A magpie is Madge," William A. Wheeler added in 1869.

3. The robin's red breast, it is said, was produced by the blood of Jesus. When He was on His way to Calvary, a robin picked a thorn from His temple. A drop of Christ's blood fell on the robin's breast and turned it forever red.

Another legend has it that the robin used to carry dew in its beak to refresh sinners

parched in hell. The scorching heat turned the bird's feathers red. John Greenleaf Whittier referred to this legend when he wrote:

He brings cool dew on his little bill,
And lets it fall on the souls of sin;
You can see the mark on his redbreast still,
Of fires that scorch as he drops it in.

4. This is the *second* rhyme in the earliest existing book of nursery rhymes (the first, "Lady Bird, Lady Bird," seemed to us to be more at home in our twelfth chapter). It is a crude little jest which later editors were quick to refine:

> *Little Robin Redbreast*
> *Sat upon a rail;*
> *Niddle noddle went his head,*
> *Wiggle waggle went his tail.*

> *Little Robin Red-breast*
> *Sat upon a hirdle,*
> *With a pair of speckled legs,*
> *And a green girdle.*

As hero, and sometimes as victim, the robin appears in many nursery rhymes, and we give here three of the shorter ones:

> *Little Bob Robin,*
> *Where do you live?*
> *Up in yonder wood, sir,*
> *On a hazel twig.*

> *Pit, pat, well-a-day,*
> *Little Robin flew away;*

« 2 »

The Moon shines Bright,
The Stars give a light,
And you may kiss
A pretty girl
At ten a clock at Night.**5**

« 3 »

Sing a Song of Sixpence,**6**
A bag full of Rye,**7**
Four and twenty**8**
Naughty boys,**9**
Bak'd in a Pye.**10**

When the pie was opened,
The birds began to sing;
Was not that a dainty dish,
To set before the king?

The king was in his counting-house,**11**
Counting out his money;
The queen was in the parlor,
Eating bread and honey.

The maid was in the garden,
Hanging out the clothes,
There came a little blackbird,
And snapped off her nose.**12**

Where can little Robin be?
Gone into the cherry tree.

Little Robin Redbreast
Came to visit me;
This is what he whistled,
Thank you for my tea.

5. This is the original version of the later, better known:

When I was a little boy
*   My mammy kept me in,*
Now I am a great boy
*   I'm fit to serve the king;*
I can handle a musket,
*   And I can smoke a pipe,*
And I can kiss a pretty girl
*   At twelve o'clock at night.*

6. Scholars have seen supposed references to this nursery rhyme in *Twelfth Night*—*Come on, there is sixpence for you; let's have a song;* and in Beaumont and Fletcher's *Bonduca* (1614)—*Whoa, here's a stir now! Sing a song of sixpence!*

7. *A pocket full of rye* in most later versions. It is possible that "a pocket full" was once a specific measurement in recipes, as "a table-spoonful of sugar."

8. We shall find that "four and twenty" is one of the numbers most frequently met with in "Mother Goose" rhymes. It is, of course, a "double dozen" and the number 12 is rich in associations, traditions, and superstitions.

9. Later *Four and twenty blackbirds*. Theories about this rhyme abound: the "blackbirds" are the twenty-four hours in a day, "the king" is the sun, and "the queen" is the moon, for example. On the other hand, Katherine Elwes Thomas identified the king as Henry VIII, the queen as Katherine, and the maid as Anne Boleyn; the "blackbirds" were four and twenty manorial deeds baked in a pie—as in "Little Jack Horner" (Rhyme 50). Still another theory holds that this song celebrates the printing of the first English Bible—the "black-birds" being the letters of the alphabet set in pica type ("baked in a pie").

10. According to Iona and Peter Opie, the editors of *The Oxford Dictionary of Nursery Rhymes,* an Italian cookbook of 1549, trans-lated into English in 1598, actually contains a recipe "to make pies so that birds may be alive in them and flie out when it is cut up." They continue: "This dish is further referred to (1723) by John Nott, cook to the Duke of Bol-

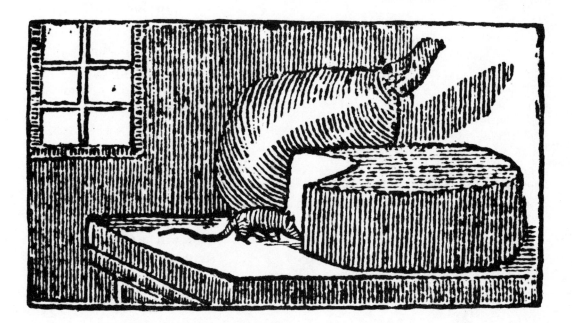

27

ton, as a practice of former days, the purpose of the birds being to put out the candles and so cause a 'diverting Hurley-Burley amongst the Guests in the Dark.' "

11. A "counting-house" was the house or office used to conduct the business of an establishment—much referred to in *The Merry Wives of Windsor*.

12. Later versions provide happy endings:

> *They sent for the king's doctor,*
> *Who sewed it on again,*
> *He sewed it on so neatly,*
> *The seam was never seen.*

Or:

> *But there came a Jenny Wren*
> *And popped it on again.*

13. This old catch was printed as early as 1714 in a work called *The Academy of Compliments*.

In the 1810 edition of *Gammer Gurton's Garland*, this version appeared:

> *Pillycock, pillycock, sate on a hill,*
> *If he's not gone—he sits there still.*

"Pillycock" is a vulgar word whose meaning may easily be guessed, and this version of the rhyme has been suppressed.

In *The Tragedy of King Lear*, first published in 1608, Shakespeare has Edgar say (Act III, Scene 4, lines 74-5) :

> *Pillicock sat on Pillicock-hill:*
> *Halloo, halloo, loo, loo!*

« 4 »

There was an Old Woman
Liv'd under a Hill,**13**
And if she isn't gone,
She lives there still.**14**

Baked apples she sold,
And cranberry pies,
And she's the old woman
That never told lies.**15**

« 5 »

Little Tom**16** Tucker**17**
Sings for his supper;**18**
What shall he Eat?
White bread and Butter;
How will he Cut it,
Without e're a Knife?
And how will he be Married,
Without e're a Wife?**19**

« 6 »

When I was a little boy,
I wash'd my
Mother's Dishes.
I put my finger in my
Ear, and pull'd out
Little fishes.

My Mother call'd me
Good boy,
And bid me pull out more,
I put my Finger
In my Ear,
And pull'd out fourscore.**20**

« 7 »

When I was a little boy,
I liv'd by my self,**21**
And all the Bread
And Cheese I got,
I hid upon my shelf.

Did Shakespeare know the "Pillicock" version of "There Was an Old Woman"? Or did
the "Pillycock" version of the nursery rhyme
stem from Edgar's line in *Lear*? Those are
questions that cannot be answered today.

14. "There Was an Old Woman" is a fine example of "the self-evident proposition." This,
like the Spoonerism, the Wellerism, and the
Irish Bull, was a recognized form of the humor
of speech, and one that was much loved by our
forefathers; we shall meet with it often in
"Mother Goose" rhymes.

The whimsical editor of *Mother Goose's
Melody* (c. 1765) added to this rhyme the
"maxim": "This is a self-evident Proposition,
which is the very Essence of Truth. 'She lived
under a hill, and if she is not gone she lives
there still.' Nobody will presume to contradict
this."

15. The second verse did not appear in
Tommy Thumb's Pretty Song Book, but was
added to the rhyme as it appeared in *The
Only True Mother Goose Melodies* (c. 1843).

16. Usually, in later versions, "Tommy." In
Songs for the Nursery (1805) the would-be

29

bridegroom's name is given as "Little Johnny Stutter."

17. *Tom Tucker* is an exceedingly ancient English and Scottish phrase which means a person who grasps all, or who stuffs himself at the expense of others. Katherine Elwes Thomas saw in this rhyme a shaft leveled at Thomas, Cardinal Wolsey (1475?-1530), chief minister of Henry VIII, a scornful man who compelled bishops to tie his shoelaces and forced dukes to hold basins of water while he washed his hands.

18. "To sing for one's supper" has long been a proverbial phrase. It comes from the wandering performers who entertained at English inns and taverns. These troubadours literally sang for their suppers, and nursery rhyme literature contains many of their songs.

19. The editor of *Mother Goose's Melody* (c. 1765) added the "maxim," attributed to *Puftendorff*: "To be married without a wife is a terrible thing, but to be married with a bad wife is something worse; however, a good wife that sings well is the best musical instrument in the world."

The Rats, and the Mice,
They made such a strife,
I was forc'd to go to
London, to buy me a Wife.

The Streets were so
Broad, and the Lanes
Were so narrow,
I was forc'd to bring
My Wife home,
In a Wheelbarrow.**22**

The Wheelbarrow broke,
And give my Wife a fall,
The duce**23** take
Wheelbarrow, Wife & all.**24**

« 8 »

Hickere, Dickere Dock,**25**
A Mouse ran up the Clock,
The Clock Struck One,
The Mouse fell down,
And Hickere Dickere Dock.**26**

« 9 »

Mistress Mary,
Quite contrary,
How does your
Garden grow?
With Silver Bells,**27**
And Cockle Shells,**28**
And so my Garden grows.**29**

20. According to the English chronicler John Aubrey (1627-97), the first verse of this nursery rhyme was originally "an old filthy Rhythme used by base people":

When I was a young Maid, and
wash't my Mother's dishes,
I putt my finger in my - - - - and
pluck't-out little Fishes.

The second verse was most probably added by a seventeenth-century play, *Love without Interest, or The Man too hard for the Master.* There are several later versions of the rhyme:

When I was a little boy,
I washed my mammy's dishes,
Now I am a great big boy
I roll in golden riches.

When I was a little boy,
I washed my mother's floor;
Now I am a man of wealth,
And drive a coach and four.

21. Compare the opening lines of the ballad, "The Foggy, Foggy Dew," popularized in recent years by the folk singer Burl Ives:

When I was a bach'lor
I lived all alone . . . .

22. Another phrasing familiar from several ballads, especially "In Dublin's Fair City," also known as "Sweet Molly Malone":

Through streets wide and narrow
She wheeled her wheelbarrow . . . .

23. Read "deuce," meaning "the devil." In the popular mythology of both the Celts and the Teutons there were certain hairy wood-demons called by the former "Dus" and by the latter "Scrat." Our common names of "deuce" and "Old Scratch" are plainly derived from these.

24. This nursery rhyme may have come originally from an old Scottish song, sung to the tune of "John Anderson My Jo." The editor of the later *Mother Goose's Melody* added his usual maxim to this rhyme: "Provide against the worst, and hope for the best."

25. Where did this curious phrase come from? It is, perhaps, an onomatoplasm—an attempt to capture, in words, a sound; in this case, the sound of a ticking clock, most likely a grandfather's clock. But the editors of *The*

Oxford Dictionary of Nursery Rhymes suggest another origin: They point out that the shepherds of Westmorland once used "Hevera" for "eight," "Devera" for "nine," and "Dick" for "ten" in counting the numbers of their flocks. The rhyme form is a very popular one—that of the limerick.

26. The editor of *Mother Goose's Melody* added to this rhyme the maxim: "Time stays for no man." Edward F. Rimbault, in his *Nursery Rhymes with the Tunes to Which They Are Still Sung* (1864) seems to have been the first to publish the additional verses:

> *The clock struck three,*
> *The mouse ran away.*
> *The clock struck ten,*
> *The mouse came again.*

27. There is a small tree called the "silverbell," with snowy white flowers which grow two to four in a cluster. But it is far more likely that this line refers to the onetime custom of hanging silver bells on the branches of trees, to tinkle whenever the wind blew.

28. Used, perhaps, to form the garden paths.

29. Today the last line is usually given as, *And pretty maids all in a row,* but there are many other variants: *Sing cuckolds all in a row; And cowslips all in a row; With lady bells all in a row; And columbines all in a row.*

"Mistress Mary" is popularly supposed to have been Mary, Queen of Scots (1542-87). "In this case," say the editors of *The Oxford Dictionary of Nursery Rhymes*, "the 'pretty maids' might be the renowned 'Four Marys' [Mary

« 10 »

There was an Old Woman,
And she sold
Puddings and Pyes.
She went to the Mill,
And the Dust
Flew into her Eyes.
Hot Pyes, and cold
Pyes, to sell,
Wherever She goes,
You may follow her
By the Smell.**30**

« 11 »

Blow, Bobby, Blow,
Can you make a Horseshoe?
Yes Master that I can,
As well as any
Little Man.**31**

« 12 »

Nauty Pauty,
Jacky Dandy,
Stole a piece of
Sugar Candy,
From the Grocer's
Shoppe Shop,
And away did
Hoppe Hop.**32**

« 13 »

Robbin and Bobbin,
Two great Belly'd Men,
They eat more Victuals
Than threescore Men.[33]

« 14 »

Taffy was born
On a Moon Shiny Night,
His Head in the Pipkin,[34]
His Heels upright.[35]

« 15 »

My Mill grinds
Pepper, and Spice,
Your Mill grinds
Rats, and Mice.[36]

« 16 »

Bah, Bah a black Sheep,
Have you any Wool?
Yes merry have I,
Three Bags full,
One for my Master,
One for my Dame,
One for my little Boy
That lives in the lane.[37]

Beaton, Mary Seaton, Mary Fleming, and Mary Livingston], her ladies-in-waiting, and it has even been stated that the 'cockleshells' were the decorations upon a particular dress she was given by the Dauphin."

30. This is the first of twelve verses in a broadside ballad of 1675, "The Old Pudding-pye Woman." The editors of *The Oxford Dictionary of Nursery Rhymes* note that the old woman is described in the succeeding verses "as having nauseous personal habits," and there is a warning at the end against buying her "pudding-pyes" (custard pies). A version of this rhyme appears in the later *Mother Goose's Melody*, with the maxim: "Either say nothing of the absent, or speak like a friend."

31. There are many variants of this old rhyme, but the version best known today is:

Robert Barnes, fellow fine,
Can you shoe this horse of mine?
Yes, good sir, that I can,
As well as any other man.
There's a nail, and there's a prod,
And now, good sir, your horse is shod.

32. Other versions of this rhyme begin "Handy spandy, Jack-a-Dandy" and "Namby-pamby, Jack-a-Dandy." The latter is particularly interesting, because the rhyme as it appears here was written in 1725 by the English poet and musical composer Henry Carey (1697-1743) to introduce his *Namby Pamby or a Panegyric on the New Versification.*
"Namby Pamby" was the nickname bestowed by Carey (and by Alexander Pope) on the poet Ambrose Phillips, and the *Panegyric*

was intended to ridicule the "soft and sickly," sugar candy style of Phillips's verse.

33. A later version goes:

Robin the Bobbin, the big-bellied Ben,
He ate more meat than fourscore men;
He ate a cow, he ate a calf,
He ate a butcher and a half,
He ate a church, he ate a steeple,
He ate the priest and all the people!

Katherine Elwes Thomas identified "Robin the Bobbin, the big-bellied Ben" with Henry VIII, who in a sense did "eat churches and priests," but the much later printing of even the earliest-known version of this rhyme makes such an identification unlikely.

34. His head in a cooking pot.

35. *Taffy,* the Welsh pronunciation of "Davy," David, became a nickname given the Welshman by the Englishman, as "Sawney" or "Sandy"—from the name Alexander—became a nickname for the Scotsman.

On St. David's Day, the first of March, baiting the Welsh was customary on the Welsh-English border and in other parts of England. "The Rabbles," says an early eighteenth-century chapbook, would hang out "a Bundle of Rags in representation of a Welshman mounted on a red Herring with a Leek [a Welsh national symbol] in his Hat."

Says the Welsh captain Fluellan in Shakespeare's *Henry the Fifth* (Act V, Scene 1, lines 5-10): "The rascally, scald, peggarly, lousy, pragging knave, Pistol . . . he is come to me, and prings me pread and salt yesterday [St. David's Day], look you, and pid me eat my leek."

From this manner of humiliating the Welshman on the first of March comes our expression "to eat the leek" or "to eat one's leek," meaning to retract something under compulsion.

This "nursery rhyme" undoubtedly originated as a taunting verse shouted at Welshmen on St. David's Day.

36. Another "taunting" rhyme, this one probably shouted by one child at another. Clifton Johnson, in his book *What They Say in New England: A Book of Signs, Sayings, and Superstitions* (Boston: Lee and Shepard, 1896), has collected a large number of American "taunts," some of which will be found in the notes to Rhyme 802.

« 17 »

Girls and Boys,
Come out to play,
The Moon does shine,
As bright as Day,**38**
Come with a Hoop,**39**
Come with a Call,
Come with a good will,
Or not at all.**40**
Loose**41** your supper,
And loose your Sleep,
Come to your Play fellows
In the Street,
Up the Ladder
And down the Wall,
A halfpenny Loaf
Will serve us all.
You find milk
And I'll find flour,
And we'll have a pudding
In half an hour.**42**

« 18 »

As I went by a Dyer's door,
I met a lusty Taunymoor,**43**
Tauny hands, & Tauny face,
Tauny Peticoats,
Silver lace.

« 19 »

Piss a Bed,
Piss a Bed,
Barley Butt,
Your Bum is so heavy
You can't get up.**44**

« 20 »

Lyer Lyer Lickspit,
Turn about the
Candlestick,
What's good for Lyers?
Brimstone and Fire.**45**

37. Katherine Elwes Thomas reads into this rhyme a complaint of the common people—the "little Boy That lives in the lane"—against the amount of wool that went to the King—"my Master"—and the overrich nobility—"my Dame."

The rhyme has changed little in two hundred years. Rudyard Kipling used it as the basis for his 1888 short story, "Baa, Baa, Black Sheep." The editor of the later *Mother Goose's Melody* appended his usual maxim: "Bad habits are easier conquered today than tomorrow."

38. This "call to play" was by no means new when it appeared for the first time in an existing nursery rhyme book in *Tommy Thumb's Pretty Song Book*. As the editors of *The Oxford Dictionary of Nursery Rhymes* point out, it may be found in "dance books of 1708, 1719, and 1728, in satires of 1709 and 1725, and in a political broadside of 1711 . . . . "

39. Not the rolling kind is meant here, but a "whoop."

40. The rhyme as given in *Tommy Thumb's Pretty Song Book* ends here.

41. Read "Lose." In modern versions, generally given as "Leave."

42. Skippers, hop-scotchers, ball-bouncers and rope-jumpers who still sing this rhyme as an accompaniment to their game sometimes add here: "With salt, mustard, vinegar, pepper . . . . "

In the later *Mother Goose's Melody*, the final couplet is given as:

But when the Loaf is gone, what will you do?
Those who eat must work—'tis true.

The editor added the ancient proverb: "All work and no play makes Jack a dull boy," which modern quipsters have emended to: "All work and no play makes jack."

43. An old word for "blackamoor," a Negro.

44. This is one of the old nursery rhymes which has been suppressed. Another—from which we have deleted one especially objectionable line—also appeared in *Tommy Thumb's Pretty Song Book*:

Blackamoor, Taunymoor,
- - - - - - - - - -,

Your Father's
A Cuckold,
Your Mother told me.

45. Like Rhyme 15, this is a taunt, directed against someone who has been caught in a falsehood.

46. In more modern versions, the first line of this rhyme is usually given as: "Tell Tale Tit."

47. A horrible warning to tattletales of what might be done to them, to which the editor of the later *Mother Goose's Melody* appended the maxim: "Point not at the faults of others with a foul finger."

48. Modern versions of course begin: *Who killed Cock Robin?*

49. Only the first four verses appear in *Tommy Thumb's Pretty Song Book.*

50. The fact that "shovel" is supposed to rhyme here with "Owl" is an indication that "Cock Robin" may go back to the fourteenth century, when the pronunciation of "shovel" was "shouell."

« 21 »

Spit Cat, Spit,**46**
Your tongue shall be slit,
And all the Dogs
In our Town,
Shall have a Bit.**47**

« 22 »

Who did kill Cock Robbin?**48**
I, said the Sparrow,
With my bow & Arrow,
And I did kill Cock Robbin.

Who did see him die?
I, said the Fly,
With my little Eye,
And I did see him die.

And who did catch his blood?
I, said the Beetle,
With my little Dish,
And I did catch his blood.

And who did make his shroud?
I, said the Fish,
With my little Needle,
And I did make his shroud.**49**

Who'll dig his grave?
I, said the Owl,
With my pick and shovel,**50**
I'll dig his grave.

Who'll be the parson?
I, said the Rook,
With my little book,
I'll be the parson.

Who'll be the clerk?
I, said the Lark,
If it's not in the dark,
I'll be the clerk.

Who'll carry the link?**51**
I, said the Linnet,

I'll fetch it in a minute,
I'll carry the link.

Who'll be chief mourner?
I, said the Dove,
I mourn for my love,
I'll be chief mourner.

Who'll carry the coffin?
I, said the Kite,
If it's not through the night,
I'll carry the coffin.

Who'll bear the pall?
We, said the Wren,
Both the cock and the hen,
We'll bear the pall.

Who'll sing a psalm?
I, said the Thrush,
As she sat on a bush,
I'll sing a psalm.

Who'll toll the bell?
I, said the Bull,
Because I can pull,
I'll toll the bell.

All the birds of the air
Fell a-sighing and a-sobbing,
When they heard the bell toll
For poor Cock Robbin.[52]

« 23 »

We are all a dry,
With drinking on't;
We are all a dry,
With drinking on't;
The Piper kissed
The Fidler's Wife,
And I can't Sleep,
For thinking on't.[53]

51. "Link" here means "torch"—the Lark did not want to be the clerk (pronounced "clark") in the dark.

52. Some scholars believe that "Cock Robin" may be a metrical rendering of some early myth, perhaps the Norse tale of the death of Balder, the god of summer sunlight, the incarnation of the life principle, slain by Hoder at the instigation of Loki.

The resurrection of "Cock Robin" in the mid-eighteenth century is due, other scholars say, to the identification of "Cock Robin" with Sir Robert Walpole, First Earl of Orford (1676-1745). The rhyme as a whole should then be taken as an allegorical description of the intrigues which attended the downfall of Walpole's ministry—popularly known as the Robinocracy—in 1742.

53. This is a very old song, which Robert Burns borrowed for his poem, "My Love, She's But a Lassie Yet," published in 1790 in the collection called the *Scots Musical Museum*.

54. A former English gold coin, so called because first minted (1663) from Guinea gold. It was issued until 1817.

55. This rhyme at first appears to be mere nonsense, but its meaning is clarified by a story-in-verse discovered by the editors of *The Oxford Dictionary of Nursery Rhymes* in the volume *Vocal Harmony*, published around 1806:

Heighho! who's above?
Nobody's here but me, my love.
Shall I come up and say how do?
Aye, marry, and thank you to.
Where's your governess? She's a-bed.
Where's the key? Under her head.
Gently trip and bring it here,
And let me in to you, my dear.
The dog will bark, I dare not stir.
Take a halter and hang the cur.
No, no. Why, why?
'Cause not for a guinea my dog should die.

56. Only the first two verses appear in *Tommy Thumb's Pretty Song Book*; the third was first printed by James O. Halliwell in 1842. In most later versions the rhyme words of the third and last lines of each verse are triplicated: *And the Ball was made of Lead, Lead, Lead* .... Katherine Elwes Thomas associated *the Drake* of this rhyme with Sir Francis Drake —an explanation *The Oxford Dictionary of Nursery Rhymes* calls "fanciful."

« 24 »

The Dog will bark,
I dare not to stir,
Take a Halter
And Hang up the Cur.
No, No. Why, Why?
I would not for a Guinea[54]
My Dog should die.[55]

« 25 »

There was a little Man,
And he had a little Gun,
And the Ball was made of Lead.
He went unto the Brooke,
To shoot at a Duck,
And he hit her
Upon the Head.

Then he went home,
Unto his Wife Joan,
To bid her a good fire make,
To roast the Duck,
That swam in the Brook,
And he would go fetch
Her the Drake.[56]

The drake was a swimming
With his curly tail;
The little man made it his mark!
He let off his gun,
But he fir'd too soon,
And the duck flew away with a quack.

« 26 »

Here comes a lusty Wooer,
My A Dildin my A Daldin,
Here comes a lusty Wooer,
Lilly bright and shine, A.

Pray who do you wooe for,
My A Dildin my A Daldin,
Pray who do you wooe for,
Lilly bright and shine, A.

For your fairest Daughter,
My A Dildin my A Daldin,
For your fairest Daughter,
Lilly bright and shine, A.

Then there she is for you,
My A Dildin my A Daldin,
Then there she is for you,
Lilly bright and shine, A.

« 27 »

There was a Mad Man,
And he had a Mad Wife,
And they lived in a Mad town,
They had three Children
All at a Birth,[57]
And they were Mad
Every One.

The Father was Mad,
The Mother was Mad,
The Children all Mad besides,
And they all got
Upon a Mad Horse,
And Madly they did ride.[58]

They rode by night and they rode by day,
Yet never a one of them fell,
They rode so madly all the way,
Till they came to the gates of hell.

Old Nick[59] was glad to see them so mad,
And gladly let them in:
But he soon grew sorry to see them so merry,
And let them out again.

57. Multiple births were viewed with some suspicion by our ancestors. It was thought, for example, that the mother of twins had been guilty of having intercourse with two men, and the mother of triplets with three.

58. Only the first two verses appear in *Tommy Thumb's Pretty Song Book*; the others are later additions.

59. Among many theories, it is thought by some that we owe "Old Nick" as a name for the devil to the Florentine statesman, Niccolo Machiavelli (1469-1527), who set forth his unscrupulous principles in his famous treatise *Il Principe* (*The Prince*).

60. The beginning we know best today is:

There was a man of our town,
And he was wondrous wise . . . .

but other versions begin: "There was a man of "Thessaly" or "Thessary" or "Thistleworth" or "Nineveh" or "Newington." There is also a ballad, printed c. 1562, which begins: "There

« 28 »

There was a Man so Wise,**60**
He jumpt into
A Bramble Bush,
And scratcht out both his Eyes.
And when he saw,
His Eyes were out,
And reason to Complain,**61**
He jumpt into a Quickset Hedge,**62**
And Scracht them in again.**63**

« 29 »

We will go to the Wood,
Says Robbin, to Bobbin,
We will go to the Wood,
Says Richard, to Robbin,
We will go to the Wood,
Says John all alone,
We will go to the Wood,
Says every one.

What to do there?
Says Robbin, to Bobbin,
What to do there?
Says Richard, to Robbin,
What to do there?
Says John all alone,
What to do there?
Says every one.

We will shoot at a Wren,
Says Robbin, to Bobbin,
We will shoot at a Wren,
Says Richard, to Robbin,
We will shoot at a Wren,
Says John all alone,
We will shoot at a Wren,
Says every one.

She's down, she's down,
Says Robbin, to Bobbin,
She's down, she's down,
Says Richard, to Robbin,
She's down, she's down,

dwelt a man in Babylon . . . . " It is likely that it is this ballad and not the nursery rhyme that Sir Toby quotes in *Twelfth Night*, but this has suggested to some commentators another connection between Shakespeare and "Mother Goose."

61. Or: "With all his might and main."

62. A hedge composed of living shrubs or trees, especially hawthorn.

63. Katherine Elwes Thomas identified the man "so Wise" with the Reverend Dr. Henry Sacheverell (1674?-1724) of St. Saviour's Church, Southwark, who preached a famous sermon at Derby on August 15, 1709, and another at St. Paul's on November 5th of the same year. In both he declared that the Established Church was "in danger from the Papists on the one hand & Fanatics on the other, from these her professed Enemies & other false Bretheren," and he ended both sermons with an impassioned appeal to all true Churchmen to rally and defend the faith.

Reaction to the Reverend Dr. Sacheverell's two sermons was the wildest excitement. In Parliament, the great Marlborough arose and advised the people to ignore the divine's warning. Upon the 13th of December, 1709, Sacheverell was brought before the House of Lords and formally accused of seditious libel. At the close of his impeachment, he was found guilty.

Says John all alone,
She's down, she's down,
Says every one.

Then pounce, then pounce,
Says Robbin, to Bobbin,
Then pounce, then pounce,
Says Richard, to Robbin,
Then pounce, then pounce,
Says John all alone,
Then pounce, then pounce,
Says every one.

She is dead, she is dead,
Says Robbin, to Bobbin,
She is dead, she is dead,
Says Richard, to Robbin,
She is dead, she is dead,
Says John all alone,
She is dead, she is dead,
Says every one.

How shall we get her home?
Says Robbin, to Bobbin,
How shall we get her home?
Says Richard, to Robbin,
How shall we get her home?
Says John all alone,
How shall we get her home?
Says every one.

We will hire a Cart,
Says Robbin, to Bobbin,
We will hire a Cart,
Says Richard, to Robbin,
We will hire a Cart,
Says John all alone,
We will hire a Cart,
Says every one.

Then Hoist, Hoist,
Says Robbin, to Bobbin,
Then Hoist, Hoist,
Says Richard, to Robbin,
Then Hoist, Hoist,

His offending sermons were ceremoniously burned in front of the Royal Exchange, London, and he was prohibited from preaching for a three-year period. Figuratively, he indeed seemed to have "jumpt into A Bramble Bush, and scracht out both his Eyes."

However: shortly after his impeachment, the man "so Wise" was publicly restored to favor and appointed to high honors as Rector of St. Andrews. He had, so to speak, "scracht his Eyes in again." The editor of the later *Mother Goose's Melody* added a maxim, ascribed to *Wiseman's New Way to Wisdom*, to this rhyme, reading: "How happy it was for the man to scratch his eyes in again, when they were scratch'd out! But he was a blockhead, or he would have kept himself out of the hedge, and not been scratch'd at all."

64. The second, fifth, sixth, and last four verses given here are later additions. In *Gammer Gurton's Garland*, however, the rhyme ends after *Then Hoist, Hoist . . . .* with the couplet:

*So they brought her away, after each pluck'd
   a feather,
And when they got home, shar'd the booty
   together.*

In all four kingdoms of the British Isles, it is a tradition to hunt the wren on St. Stephen's Day, December 26th, and this rhyme was perhaps chanted by the "Wren Boys" after the kill had been made. They would then go from house to house, carrying the dead wren on a branch decorated with gay, streaming ribbons.

Stopping in front of each house they would sing:

God bless the mistress of this house,
A golden chain around her neck,
And if she's sick or if she's sore,
The Lord have mercy on her soul.

Then, in salute to the master of the house, they would sing:

The wren, the wren, the king of all birds,
On Saint Stephen's day was caught in the furze,
Up with the kettle and down with the pot,
And give us our answer and let us be gone.

The master of the house was then supposed to take a careful look at the bird to make sure it was a wren and not, perhaps, a sparrow, after which he would give alms to the singers. There is an old tradition that the first Christian missionaries to Britain were offended because the pagan druids showed great respect for the wren, "the king of all birds." The missionaries ordered that the wren be hunted and killed on the morning of Christmas Day. The custom was later transferred to the morning of the following day, December 26th.

Says John all alone,
Then Hoist, Hoist,
Says every one.

She's up, she's up,
Says Robbin, to Bobbin,
She's up, she's up,
Says Richard, to Robbin,
She's up, she's up,
Says John all alone,
She's up, she's up,
Says every one.

How shall we dress her?
Says Robbin, to Bobbin,
How shall we dress her?
Says Richard, to Robbin,
How shall we dress her?
Says John all alone,
How shall we dress her?
Says every one.

We'll hire seven cooks,
Says Robbin, to Bobbin,

We'll hire seven cooks,
Says Richard, to Robbin,
We'll hire seven cooks,
Says John all alone,
We'll hire seven cooks,
Says every one.

How shall we boil her?
Says Robbin, to Bobbin,
How shall we boil her?
Says Richard, to Robbin,
How shall we boil her?
Says John all alone,
How shall we boil her?
Says every one.

In the brewer's big pan,
Says Robbin, to Bobbin,
In the brewer's big pan,
Says Richard, to Robbin,
In the brewer's big pan,
Says John all alone,
In the brewer's big pan,
Says every one.**64**

65. We shall meet other "accumulative rhymes," as they are properly called, in these pages, but none more widely known than "The House That Jack Built."

The accumulative device is to be found in prose as well as in poetry, as in the nursery tale of "The Old Woman and Her Pig": "The cat began to kill the rat, the rat began to gnaw the rope, the rope began to hang the butcher ...and so the old woman got home that night."

Although "The House That Jack Built" first appeared in print in 1755, the rhyme is probably very old. James O. Halliwell thought that the reference to "the priest all shaven and shorn" attested to its antiquity. There are similar rhymes in many European languages, and some scholars think that the rhyme stems from a Hebrew chant first printed in 1590.

66. Katherine Elwes Thomas identified "Little Boy Blue" with Thomas, Cardinal Wolsey (see also notes to Rhyme 5). Wolsey was the son of a well-to-do Ipswich butcher, and, as a boy, he undoubtedly did look after his father's flocks.

The editors of *The Oxford Dictionary of Nursery Rhymes*, on the other hand, find this identification "unlikely." Perhaps, they think, the well-known nursery rhyme stems from the words of Edgar in *King Lear* (Act III, Scene 6, lines 41-4):

> *Sleepest or wakest thou, jolly shepherd?*
> *Thy sheep in the corn;*
> *And for one blast of thy minikin mouth,*
> *Thy sheep shall take no harm.*

Boy Blue is also a character met with in A. A. Milne's *When We Were Very Young*.

67. One is irresistibly reminded of the immortal Lewis Carroll (Charles Lutwidge Dodgson, 1832-98) and his:

> *The sun was shining on the sea,*
> *Shining with all his might:* ...
> *And this was odd, because it was*
> *The middle of the night.*

In the early years of the twentieth century, when many "Mother Goose" books became anthologies of poetry rather than true collections of nursery rhymes, Carroll-Dodgson gave his permission for "The Walrus and the Carpenter" to be included in several of them.

68. Archaic: *likewise, also.*

« 30 »

This is the house that Jack built.

This is the malt
That lay in the house that Jack built.

This is the rat,
That ate the malt
That lay in the house that Jack built.

This is the cat,
That killed the rat,
That ate the malt
That lay in the house that Jack built.

This is the dog,
That worried the cat,
That killed the rat,
That ate the malt
That lay in the house that Jack built.

This is the cow with the crumpled horn,
That tossed the dog,
That worried the cat,
That killed the rat,
That ate the malt
That lay in the house that Jack built.

This is the maiden all forlorn,
That milked the cow with the crumpled horn,
That tossed the dog,
That worried the cat,
That killed the rat,
That ate the malt
That lay in the house that Jack built.

This is the man all tattered and torn,
That kissed the maiden all forlorn,
That milked the cow with the crumpled horn,
That tossed the dog,
That worried the cat,
That killed the rat,
That ate the malt
That lay in the house that Jack built.

This is the priest all shaven and shorn,[65]
That married the man all tattered and torn,

That kissed the maiden all forlorn,
That milked the cow with the crumpled horn,
That tossed the dog,
That worried the cat,
That killed the rat,
That ate the malt
That lay in the house that Jack built.

This is the cock that crowed in the morn,
That waked the priest all shaven and shorn,
That married the man all tattered and torn,
That kissed the maiden all forlorn,
That milked the cow with the crumpled horn,
That tossed the dog,
That worried the cat,
That killed the rat,
That ate the malt
That lay in the house that Jack built.

This is the farmer sowing his corn,
That kept the cock that crowed in the morn,
That waked the priest all shaven and shorn,
That married the man all tattered and torn,
That kissed the maiden all forlorn,
That milked the cow with the crumpled horn,
That tossed the dog,
That worried the cat,
That killed the rat,
That ate the malt
That lay in the house that Jack built.

« 31 »

Little Boy Blue,[66] come blow your horn,
The cow's in the meadow, the sheep in the corn:
But where is the little boy tending the sheep?
He's under the hay-cock fast asleep.
Will you wake him? No, not I,
For if I do, he's sure to cry.

« 32 »

Three children sliding on the Ice
   Upon a Summer's Day,[67]
As it fell out they all fell in,
   The rest they ran away.

Oh! had those Children been at School,
   Or sliding on dry Ground,
Ten Thousand Pounds to one Penny,
   They had not then been drown'd.

Ye Parents who have children dear,
   And eke[68] ye that have none,
If you would keep them safe abroad
   Pray keep them all at home.[69]

« 33 »

The Sow came in with a Saddle,
The little Pig rock'd the Cradle,
The Dish jump'd a top of the Table,
To see the Pot wash the Ladle;
The Spit that stood behind the Door
Call'd the Dishclout a dirty Whore;[70]
Odsplut,[71] says the Gridiron,
Can't ye agree,
I'm Head Constable,
Bring 'em to me.[72]

« 34 »

I'll tell you a Story,
   Of Jacky Nory,[73]
Will you have it now or anon?
   I will tell you another,
   Of Jack and his Brother,
And my Story's done.

69. This burlesque ballad, sung to the tune "Chevy Chase" or "Lady's Fall," dates back to the middle of the seventeenth century, and may have been occasioned by the fire of February 1633, which destroyed much of London Bridge. Its publication in the later (c. 1765) *Mother Goose's Melody* led to its being ascribed to Oliver Goldsmith, and it has also been ascribed to John Gay (1685-1732), of *Beggar's Opera* fame.

The editor of *Mother Goose's Melody*, Goldsmith or another, added a most inelegant "maxim" to this rhyme: "There is something so melancholy in this song, that it has occasioned many people to make water. It is almost as diuretic as the tune to which John the coachman whistles to his horses." This the editor attributed to *Trumpington's Travels.*

70. This couplet was of course refined in later versions:

The Spit that stood behind a Bench
Call'd the Dishclout dirty Wench . . . .

Then:

The spit that stood behind the door
Threw the pudding-stick on the floor.

71. "Odd's-bobs" in later versions. "Odsplut" is a variant of "ods blud," which in turn is a contraction of the oath "God's blood."

72. The "Note" affixed to this rhyme by the editor of *Mother Goose's Melody* reads: "If [the Gridiron] acts as constable in this case, the cook must surely be the Justice of the Peace."

73. *Jacky Nory*—sometimes *Jack a Nory*—also goes by many other names in variants of this rhyme, used to discourage children who beg, "Tell me a story."

Good people all, of every sort,
  Give ear unto my song;
And if you find it wondrous short,
  It cannot hold you long.

OLIVER GOLDSMITH

CHAPTER III

And a Melody of Twenty-five Others

John Newbery (1713-67), the London publisher whose name we in America honor today by attaching it to the John Newbery Award for the best children's book of the year, specialized in juvenile literature.

Sometime before his death, he published *Mother Goose's Melody: or Sonnets for the Cradle;* some scholars think as early as 1760, others five or even six years later.

Oliver Goldsmith (1730?-74), that eccentric but lovable poet, dramatist, and novelist, is known to have been a constant writer for Newbery between 1762 and 1767,[1] and the Preface, at least, of the *Melody* was probably written by Goldsmith. It is signed as "By a very Great Writer of very Little Books"—a line that sounds like Goldsmith—and it quotes the song "There Was an Old Woman Toss'd in a Blanket," one of Goldsmith's favorite ditties and a song he often sang to amuse children.[2]

All in all, it is highly likely that Goldsmith edited the *Melody* for Newbery, writing not only the Preface but many of the jesting "Notes and Maxims,

1. Newbery published *The History of Little Goody Two Shoes,* generally ascribed to Goldsmith, in 1765.

2. According to Dr. Sam Johnson, Goldsmith also sang it on the night of January 29, 1768, to console himself on the poorly received opening of his play, *The Good Natur'd Man.*

3. A strange way of putting it.

4. Interestingly enough, Thomas had married a granddaughter of Thomas and Elizabeth Fleet, and so was related, on the distaff side, to old "Mother Goose" herself.

5. Later versions would have you believe that the old woman was tossed in a "basket."

6. In later versions, the poor old dear is tossed "ten," "nineteen," "fifty," "seventy," even "ninety-nine" times as high as the moon. We'll settle for seventeen—a mere 4,060,570 miles.

7. The earliest printed version of this song available to us today appears (just as it is given here) in the Preface to Newbery's *Melody.* The Preface writer says:

"When [Henry V of England] turned his arms against France, he composed a march to lead his troops to battle, well knowing that music has often the power of inspiring courage, especially in the minds of good men. Of this his enemies took advantage, and, as our happy nation, even at that time, was never without a faction, some of the malcontents adopted words [of the rhyme] to the king's own march, in order to ridicule his majesty, and to show the folly and impossibility of his undertaking.... Here the king is represented as an old woman, engaged in a pursuit and the most absurd and extravagant imaginable; but when he had routed the whole French army at the battle of Agincourt, taking their king and the flower of the nobility prisoners, and with ten thousand men only made himself master of their kingdom; the very men who had ridiculed him before, began to think nothing was too arduous for him to surmount, they therefore cancelled the former sonnet, which they were now ashamed of, and substituted this in its stead, which you will please to observe goes to the [same tune as the king's march]."

"So vast is the prowess of Harry the Great,
He'd pluck a hair from the pale fac'd moon;

Historical, Philosophical and Critical" which embellish the little volume.

"Mother Goose" rhymes—"the most celebrated Songs and Lullabies of the good old Nurses, calculated to amuse Children and to excite them to sleep"**3** make up the first part of the *Melody.* There are fifty-two of them in all, but a large number of these had been printed earlier, and we have already encountered them; some we shall meet later.

The second part of the *Melody* contains songs "of that sweet Songster and Nurse of Wit and Humour, Master William Shakespeare"—a fact that some scholars think gives color to the impression that Shakespeare was among the wits who secretly penned a number of the rhymes that may possibly be political pasquinades.

No copy of the first edition of the *Melody* is known to exist, but the volume was reprinted, in 1786, by Isaiah Thomas of Worcester, Mass., and sold at his bookstore in that city.**4** No complete copy of this 1786 printing has been found, to date. The earliest known perfect copy, one of a printing made in 1794, is in the library of the American Antiquarian Society at Worcester. From this copy, William H. Whitmore (in 1889), W. F. Prideaux (in 1904), and Frederick G. Melcher (in 1945) produced facsimile editions, Whitmore's with a long and scholarly historical introduction.

Here, now, are the rhymes added by Newbery and Goldsmith to the rising tide of "Mother Goose" melodies.

« 35 »

There was an old woman toss'd in a blanket,**5**
Seventeen times as high as the moon;**6**
But where she was going no mortal could tell,
For under her arm she carried a broom.
Old woman, old woman, old woman, said I!
Whither, ah whither, ah whither so high?
To sweep the cobwebs from the sky,
And I'll be with you by and by.**7**

« 36 »

There was a little man,
Who wooed a little maid;
And he said, little Maid, will you wed, wed, wed?
I have little more to say,
So will you aye or nay,
For the least said is soonest men-ded, ded, ded.**8**

Then replied the little Maid,
Little Sir, you've little said
To induce a little Maid to wed, wed, wed;
You must say a little more,
And produce a little Ore,**9**
E'er I make a little Print in your Bed, Bed, Bed.**10**

Then the little Man reply'd,
If you'll be my little Bride,
I'll raise my Love Notes a little higher, higher,
    higher;
Tho' my offers are not meet,
Yet my little Heart is great,
With the little God of Love all on Fire, Fire, Fire.

Or a lion familiarly take by the tooth,
    And lead him about as you lead a baboon.
All princes and potentates under the sun,
Through fear into corners and holes away run
    While no dangers nor dread his swift prog-
        ress retards,
    For he deals about kingdoms as we do our
        cards.

"When this was shown to his majesty he smilingly said that folly always dealt in extravagancies, and that knaves sometimes put on the garb of fools to promote in that disguise their own wicked designs. 'The flattery in the last (says he) is more insulting than the impudence of the first, and to weak minds might do more mischief, but we have the old proverb in our favor—*If we do not flatter ourselves, the flattery of others will never hurt us.*'"

The only trouble with this story is that there doesn't seem to be a word of truth in it; the whole thing is probably merely a Goldsmithian whimsey.

8. Possibly the origin of the well-known proverb: "Little said is soon amended" (literary); "Least said, soonest mended" (colloquial).

9. Katherine Elwes Thomas identifies this "little man" with Philip II of Spain (1527-1598), once again (he was the husband of Mary I, "Bloody Mary," Queen of England from 1553 until her death in 1558) seeking to ally Spain with England by a marriage to its Queen. The Queen—or coy "little maid"—in that case would be Elizabeth I (1533-1603), "whose taunting reply," Miss Thomas writes, "shows that she comprehends perfectly that it is covetousness for her nation's gold that prompts this wooing . . . ."

10. In later versions, this line was "refined" to read: "Ere I to the church will be led, led, led."

11. In the *Melody*, this line is followed by an asterisk and the footnote: "He who borrows is another man's slave, and pawns his honor, his liberty, and sometimes his nose for payment. Learn to live on a little, and be independent." This good advice the editor attributed to *"Patch* on Prudence."

12. *Betty Winckle,* in virtually all later versions of this rhyme, becomes *Betty Pringle,* though no one seems to know quite why. Perhaps Betty Pringle, in her day, corresponded to Betty Boop—or Betty Coed.

13. This rhyme is titled "A Dirge" in the *Melody*, and the editor offers this "explanation": "A dirge is a song made for the dead; but whether this was made for Betty Winckle or her pig, is uncertain; no notice being taken of it by Cambden, or any of the famous antiquarians." This is attributed to Walt's *System of Sense*.

14. With "trenchers" followed by "dishes," it is natural to think that a trencher here means a board or wooden platter on which to carve or serve food. (We are all familiar with the phrase, "a good trencherman," meaning a hearty eater.) But the intended meaning is quite different. "Trenchers" in this rhyme denote clogs or wooden boots, and "dishes" the high, iron-heeled shoes once worn by countrywomen when working around a farmstead.

15. So reads the rhyme in the *Melody*, but a "bawn," especially in Ireland, means an enclosure of mud or stone walls around a house

Then the little Maid reply'd,
Should I be your little Bride,
Pray what must we have for to eat, eat, eat?
Will the Flame that you're so rich in
Light a Fire in the Kitchen,
Or the little God of Love turn the Spit, Spit, Spit?
Then the little man he sigh'd
And, some say, a little cry'd,
For his little Heart was big with Sorrow, Sorrow,
    Sorrow;
As I am your little Slave,
If the little that I have
Be too little, little, little, we will borrow, borrow,
    borrow.**11**

Then the little Man so gent,
Made the little Maid relent,
And sent her little Heart a think-king, king, king.
Tho' his Offers were but small,
She took his little All,
She could have but the Cat and her Skin, Skin, Skin.

« 37 »

Little Betty Winckle**12** she had a Pig,
It was a little Pig and not very big;
When he was alive he liv'd in Clover,
But now he's dead, and that's all over;
Johnny Winckle, he
Sat down and cry'd,
Betty Winckle she
Laid down and dy'd;
So there was an End of one, two, and three,
Johnny Winckle He,
Betty Winckle She,
And Piggy Wiggie.**13**

« 38 »

Trip upon Trenchers,
And dance upon Dishes,**14**
My mother sent me for some Bawn, some Bawn:**15**
She bid me tread lightly
And come again quickly,
For fear the young Men should do me some Harm.
Yet didn't you see,
Yet didn't you see,
What naughty tricks they put upon me;
They broke my Pitcher,
And spilt the Water,
And huffed**16** my mother,
And chid her Daughter,
And kiss'd my Sister instead of me.**17**

or castle, and, hence, the fortified outwork of a castle. The word intended here (and so it appears in later versions of this rhyme) is "barm," the yeast formed on brewing liquors.

16. The word "huffed" here simply means "bullied." But you would not be far wrong in thinking that "Trip upon Trenchers" stems from a ribald song. In David Herd's *Scots Songs and Ballads*, two manuscript volumes in the library of the British Museum, parts of which were published in 1776, the rhyme reads:

> I'll Trip upon Trenchers, I'll dance upon
> dishes;
> My mither sent me for barm, for barm!
> And thro' the kirk yard I met wi' the laird,
> The silly poor body could do me no harm.
> But down i' the park, I met with the clerk,
> And he gied me my barm, my barm!

17. In the *Melody*, this rhyme is titled "A Melancholy Song." The *Melody* adds: "What a succession of misfortunes befell this young girl! But the last circumstance was the most affecting, and might have proved fatal." This is attributed to Winslow's *View of Bath*.

18. For generations, "Cross Patch" has been a colloquial name for an ill-natured person; originally, for a peevish fool.

19. In later versions, the last line is often moralized: "And let good temper in." The *Melody* adds: "A common case, this, to call in our neighbors to rejoice when all the good liquor is gone." This the editor attributes to Pliny.

20. Usually, in later versions, "my mother's."

21. Our ancestors preferred to spell "Jill" this way, since they lacked the "J." In many nursery rhymes the phrase *Jack and Gill* may be read "lad and lass." A modern child might say, "But I don't *want* to be my Daddy's boy," or "I don't *want* to be Mommy's good girl."

22. The Melody adds the maxim: "Those arts are the most valuable which are of the greatest use."

23. Rather like saying "a sophisticated young matron of Podunk." For five hundred years, Gotham, a village near Nottingham, has been considered a town of fools. Its reputation perhaps started when King John (1340-1399) ex-

53

pressed his intention to pass through the town. In those days, any road over which the king passed was forever after a public road, and the villagers (like many suburbanites today) disliked the idea of their main street becoming a public highway. To convince the king's outriders that everyone in Gotham was mad, and that the king should therefore take a different route, the villagers one and all played the fool. Some tried to drown an eel in a pond; others dragged carts to the roof of a barn "to shade it from the sun"; still others tried to trap a cuckoo (and so have perpetual summer) by building a hedge around it—hence our slang word "cuckoo" for crazy.

The "foles of gotyam" are mentioned in a manuscript of about 1450, and the earliest existing collection of Gothamite tales is dated 1630; it contains twenty stories and has been reprinted repeatedly. One tale has it that a man of Gotham rode to market on horseback with two bushels of wheat. So that his horse should not carry too heavy a burden, the man placed the sacks of wheat on his own back.

At the beginning of the 1800's, Washington Irving applied the name "Gotham" to New York City, and, oddly enough, it stuck.

24. The *Melody* adds: "It is long enough. Never lament the loss of what is not worth having." This it attributes to *Boyle*. Like "I'll Tell You a Story of Jacky Nory" (Rhyme 34), "Three Wise Men of Gotham" was a device used to discourage children who beg, "Tell me a story."

25. Iron and steel, in the folklore of all nations, are powerful charms. Swearing by the point of a knife would undoubtedly carry special weight.

26. The *Melody* adds: "The only instance of a miller refusing toll, for which the cat has just cause of complaint against him." This is attributed to *Coke* upon Littleton.

27. This refrain is very old, going back at least to the sixteenth century.

Shakespeare in *The Merchant of Venice* (Act III, Scene 2, lines 70-1) writes:

Let us all ring fancy's knell;
I'll begin it,—Ding, dong, bell.

And in *The Tempest* (Act I, Scene 2, lines 402-4), Ariel sings:

« 39 »

Cross Patch[18] draw the Latch,
Sit by the Fire and spin;
Take a cup and drink it up,
Then call your Neighbors in.[19]

« 40 »

I won't be my Father's Jack,
I won't be my Father's[20] Gill,[21]
I will be the Fiddler's Wife,
And have Music when I will.
 T'other little tune,
 T'other little tune,
 Prithee, Love, play me
 T'other little tune.[22]

« 41 »

Three wise men of Gotham[23]
They went to Sea in a Bowl,
And if the Bowl had been stronger
My Song had been longer.[24]

Sea-nymphs hourly ring his knell:
Hark! now I hear them,—Ding-dong, bell.

Katherine Elwes Thomas believed that the rhyme as we know it today originated in Bristol, a city which had the reputation, in the seventeenth and eighteenth centuries, for tolling a bell on every occasion under the sun, "grave or gay, national or civic, important or of no import whatever."

28. The *Melody* adds the maxim: "He that injures one threatens an hundred." In recent years, some critics of the nursery rhyme have taken particular objection to "Ding, Dong, Bell," claiming that it has influenced children to drown cats. A "reformed" version in *New Nursery Rhymes for Old* (1949) reads:

Ding dong bell,
Pussy's at the well.
Who took her there?
Little Johnny Hare.
Who'll bring her in?
Little Tommy Thin.

What a jolly boy was that
To get some milk for pussy cat
Who ne'er did any harm,
But played with the mice in his father's
    barn.

29. There is no room here for a discussion of family names and their derivation, but we might point out that it was natural to call a worker in metals—a smith—and his descendants, even though they did not happen to be workers in metal, by the name Smith. A worker in gold might well become "Goldsmith." A moneylender, a banker, might become "Gold" or "Gould." Other names that may have arisen in the same way are "Gardner" and "Potter."

30. The last line is another onomatoplasm, an attempt to find words that sound like the object being described, in this case, a nail being driven into a horseshoe. We might add that a "ticktack" is a device that makes a tapping or rattling sound on a window, once a necessity for any well-equipped Hallowe'en prankster. "Tick-tack-too" or "tick-tack-toe" is also another name for the grand old paper-and-pencil game, Noughts and Crosses.

31. The refrain is exceedingly ancient. A line in a play by Thomas Preston, *Cambises King of Percia*, printed in 1569, implies that it was a tune played for dancing.

32. There seems to be no reason to doubt that even before the reign of Henry VIII, it was the custom to dub those in and about the

court with ridiculous nicknames, generally of
animals. A violent epidemic of this kind of
nicknaming seems to have swept over the
court during the reign of Elizabeth I. *The Cat*
of this line, some scholars think, was Elizabeth
herself, called "The Cat" from the manner in
which she played with her Cabinet as if the
ministers were so many mice.

As for *the Fiddle*, Katherine Elwes Thomas
has written that: "At the supposedly sedate
age of forty-eight, 'the Cat' was frequently to
be caught sight of in her apartments spiritedly
dancing to the music of her beloved fiddle."

The expression, other scholars say, refers to:
1) Catherine of Aragon, called Catherine la
Fidèle (1485-1536), daughter of Ferdinand and
Isabella of Spain, wife of Henry VIII of England, mother of Mary I of England, divorced
1533, introduced into Shakespeare's *Henry
VIII*; 2) Catherine II, Catherine the Great,
Empress of Russia, 1729-96; 3) Caton, a supposed governor of Calais, called Caton le fidèle; 4) the game of *cat*, or trap-ball, and the
fiddle music provided by some of the old-time
inns where the game used to be played.

33. This line, too, has been connected by
some scholars with Elizabeth I, through the
elaborate charades that she caused to be
played at Whitehall and at Hampton Court.
Other theories about the rhyme, stemming
mostly from this line, are that: 1) it is connected with the worship of Hathor, the Egyp-
tian goddess of love, sometimes represented as
having a cow's head; 2) it refers to various
constellations, Taurus and Bull and Canis
Minor, for example; 3) it describes the pe-
riodic flight of the Egyptians from the rising
waters of the Nile.

James O. Halliwell thought that he could
trace this rhyme back at least to the ancient
Greeks, but it appears that he was being
hoaxed. John Bellenden Ker, as we might expect from what we learned of him in our first
chapter, thought that the rhyme tells of Papist
priests urging the laboring classes to work
harder.

The editors of *The Oxford Dictionary of
Nursery Rhymes* call "High Diddle, Diddle"
"probably the best-known nonsense verse in
the language," and add significantly that "a
considerable amount of nonsense has been
written about it."

« 42 »

There was an old Woman
Liv'd under a Hill,
She put a mouse in a Bag,
And sent it to Mill:
The Miller did swear
By the point of his Knife,[25]
He never took Toll
Of a Mouse in his Life.[26]

« 43 »

Ding dong Bell,[27]
The Cat is in the Well,
Who put her in?
Little Johnny Green,
Who pulled her out?
Little Tommy Stout.
What a naughty Boy was that,
To drown Poor Pussy Cat,
Who never did any Harm,
And kill'd the Mice in his Father's Barn.[28]

« 44 »

Is John Smith[29] within?
Yes, that he is.
Can he set a Shoe?
Aye, marry two.
Here a Nail, and there a Nail,
Tick, tack, too.[30]

« 45 »

High diddle, diddle,[31]
The Cat and the Fiddle,[32]
The Cow jump'd over the Moon;[33]
The little Dog laugh'd[34]
To see such Craft,[35]
And the Dish ran away with the Spoon.[36]

« 46 »

Cock a doodle doo,[37]
My Dame has lost her Shoe;

My Master's lost his Fiddle Stick,
And knows not what to do.

Cock a doodle doo,
What is my dame to do?
Till master finds his fiddling stick
She'll dance without her shoe.

Cock a doodle doo,
My dame has found her shoe,
And master's found his fiddling stick,
Sing doodle doodle doo.

Cock a doodle doo,
My dame will dance with you,
While master fiddles his fiddling stick,
For dame and doodle doo.**38**

34. "The Little Dog," say those scholars who hold to an Elizabethan origin of this rhyme, was Robert Dudley, Earl of Leicester (1532?-1588). Elizabeth for a time thought of marrying him. "I cannot live without seeing him every day," she told De Foys, the French ambassador to her court. "He is like my little lap-dog . . . ." Says the *Melody* at the end of the rhyme: "It must be a little dog that laugh'd for a great dog would be ashamed to laugh at such nonsense."

35. Usually, "To see such sport," but the above is the earliest printed version.

36. To some, another reason for identifying the rhyme with Elizabeth I and her court—and an interesting one. "The Dish" was, it is said, the formal title given to the courtier honored by being detailed to carry certain golden

dishes into the state dining room. "The
Spoon," always a beautiful young woman of
the court, was the lady selected to be taster at
the royal meals—a precaution many kings and
queens then took to keep from being poisoned
by their loving subjects.

The particular "Dish" and "Spoon" supposed to have been referred to here were Edward, Earl of Hertford, and Lady Katherine
Grey, sister of the famous Lady Jane Grey
(1537-54, great-niece of Henry VIII, wife to
the son of the Duke of Northumberland, who
persuaded Edward VI to name her as his successor; unwillingly proclaimed queen, 1553,
she was imprisoned after nine days and Mary
I became queen). Edward and Lady Katherine
were secretly married. As soon as Elizabeth
discovered this, she had the couple confined
to the Tower of London. There they existed
for seven years, and there two children were
born to them.

37. Another onomatoplasm, and a very ancient one—an attempt, in words, to "mocke
the cockes," to reproduce their crow at dawn.
One of Johnny Hart's finest "B.C." comic

« 47 »

There was an old Man
In a Velvet Coat,
He kiss'd a Maid
And gave her a Groat;**39**
The Groat it was crackt,
And would not go,**40**
Ah, old Man, d'you serve me so?**41**

« 48 »

Jack and Gill**42**
Went up the Hill,**43**
   To fetch a Pail of Water;**44**
Jack fell down
And broke his Crown,
   And Gill came tumbling after.**45**

Up Jack got, and home did trot,
   As fast as he could caper,
To old Dame Dob, who patched his nob,
   With vinegar and brown paper.

When Gill came in, how she did grin,
  To see Jack's paper plaster;
Dame Dob, vexed, did whip her next
  For causing Jack's disaster.**46**

« 49 »

There were two birds sat on a Stone,
  Fa, la, la, la, lal, de;
One flew away and then there was one,
  Fa, la, la, la, lal de;
The other flew after,
And then there was none,
  Fa, la, la, la, lal, de;
And so the poor Stone
Was left all alone,
  Fa, la, la, la, lal de.
One of the birds then back again flew,
  Fa, la, la, la, lal de;
T'other came after, and then there were two:
  Fa, la, la, la, lal de.

strips shows the attempt of a prehistoric cock to find a better crow. He tries "Crag-a-battle she" and "Snock-a-docka baa," but ends, in the final panel, with "Cock a doodle doo" and the comment, "You can't beat the old standards."

38. The earliest existing version of the first verse of this very popular nursery rhyme—in a nursery rhyme book—is that given here, from *Mother Goose's Melody*, with the maxim: "The cock crows us up in the morning, that we may work for our bread, and not live upon charity or upon trust; *for he who lives upon charity shall be often affronted, and he that lives upon trust shall pay double.*"

But a version of two lines from the rhyme appeared in 1606 in a black-letter pamphlet titled *The Most Crvell and Bloody Murther committed by an Innkeeper's Wife, called Annis Dell, and her Sonne George Dell, Foure yeeres since.* The pamphlet tells the harrowing story of a little girl about four who witnessed the murder of her three-year-old brother. The murderers, to prevent the child from naming them, cut the tongue from her head. Three years later, it is said, the poor dumb

59

child heard a cock crow and miraculously re-gained her speech, her first words, repeated after a friend, being:

Cocka doodle dooe,
Peggy hath lost her shoe.

39. An English silver coin, worth fourpence, issued from the time of Edward III to Charles II, and later as "maundy money"—coins struck for alms to be distributed on Maundy Thursday, the Thursday of Holy Week.

40. Could not be spent.

41. The editor of the *Melody* added the maxim: "If the coat be ever so fine that a fool wears, it is still but a fool's coat."

42. The woodcut which illustrated this rhyme in the *Melody showed,* not a girl and a boy, but two *boys.* John Bellenden Ker thought that "Jack and Gill" here designated two priests, and Katherine Elwes Thomas identified the pair with Cardinal Wolsey and his coadjutor, Bishop Tarbes.

Said one t'other—
How do you do?
 Fa, la, la, la, lal de;
Very well, thank you,
And How are you?
 Fa, la, la, la, lal de.**47**

« 50 »

Little Jack Horner[48]
Sat in a Corner,
   Eating of Christmas Pye;
He put in his Thumb,
And pull'd out a Plum,[49]
   And [said] what a good Boy was I.[50]

« 51 »

   Who comes here?
     A Grenadier.[51]
   What do you want?
     A Pot of Beer.
   Where is your Money?
     I've forgot.
     Get you gone
   You drunken Sot.[52]

43. Miss Thomas interpreted this line as a reference to the journey to France taken by Wolsey and Tarbes to arrange the marriage of Mary Tudor to the French monarch.

44. To Ker, the real meaning of the "Pail of Water" was "The burial perquisite (one of the principal bonuses of the priests at that time), and water is here used in the meaning of fee, and sounds (in early Saxon) as we pronounce water." Miss Thomas thought that the *Pail of Water* meant "nothing less . . . than the holy water of the popeship then boldly intrigued for by Wolsey."

We have noted, in Chapter I, that at least one authority, the Reverend Sabine Baring-Gould, thought "Jack and Gill" a rhyme of great antiquity. According to Lewis Spence also (*Myth and Ritual,* 1947), some ancient mystic ceremony may be traced in this rhyme, for "no one in the folk-lore sense climbs to the top of a hill for water unless that water has special significance."

45. The editors of *The Oxford Dictionary of Nursery Rhymes* have written that the rhyme of *after* with *Water* may indicate that this rhyme originated in the first half of the seventeenth century.

It has been said that "Jack and Gill" is mentioned several times in Shakespeare. In *Midsummer Night's Dream* (Act III, Scene 2, line 461), Puck says: *Jack shall have Jill, Naught shall go ill . . . .* And Berowne in *Love's Labour's Lost* (Act V, Scene 2, line 882), says: *Our wooing doth not end like an old play; Jack hath not Jill.* But these passages do not refer to the nursery rhyme at all: as noted in Rhyme 40, "Jack" and "Gill" (or "Jill" or "Jille") were synonyms for "lad" and "lass"—from the fifteenth century on.

The rhyme as given in the *Melody* ends here, with a maxim: "The more you think of dying, the better you will live"—attributed to Aristotle.

46. As many as fourteen verses were later added to "Jack and Gill." The second and third verses above are those most commonly found in "Mother Goose" books today.

47. The editor of the *Melody* added: "This may serve as a chapter of consequence in the next new book of logic."

In Charles Kingsley's *The Water Babies* (1863) the last of the Gairfowl croons a version of this old song to herself.

48. While the *Melody* is the earliest known nursery rhyme book in which "Little Jack Horner" is to be found, a version of the rhyme was printed as early as 1720 in the ballad by Henry Carey titled "Namby Pamby" (see notes to Rhyme 12):

> *Now he sings of Jacky Horner*
> *Sitting in the Chimney-corner*
> *Eating of a Christmas-Pie,*
> *Putting in his Thumb, Oh fie!*
> *Putting in, Oh fie! his Thumb*
> *Pulling out, Oh, Strange! a Plum.*

49. A persistent legend states that the original *Jack Horner* was *Thomas* Horner, steward to Richard Whiting, last of the abbots of Glastonbury Cathedral. At the time of the Dissolution, when Henry VIII was taking over all the Church property he could get his royal hands on, the abbot is said to have sent his steward to London with a Christmas gift intended to appease the king: a pie in which were hidden the deeds to twelve manorial estates. On the

« 52 »

Jack Sprat[53]
Could eat no Fat,
His Wife could eat no Lean;[54]
And so, betwixt them both,
They lick'd the platter clean.[55]

« 53 »

What care I how black I be,[56]
Twenty Pounds will marry me;
If Twenty won't, Forty shall,[57]
I am my Mother's bouncing Girl.[58]

« 54 »

When I was a little Boy
    I had but little Wit,
'Tis a long Time ago,
    And I have no more yet;
Nor ever, ever shall,
    Until that I die,
For the longer I live,
    The more Fool am I.[59]

journey, Thomas Horner is alleged to have opened the pie and extracted one deed—that to the fine manor of Mells (a plum indeed!) There his descendants live to this day. As for Abbot Whiting, he was tried (with Thomas Horner sitting on the jury!), found guilty of having secreted gold sacramental cups from the profane touch of the king, and consequently hanged, beheaded, and quartered.

50. The editor of the *Melody* here appended a note he attributed to *Bentley on the Sublime and Beautiful:* "Jack was a boy of excellent taste, as should appear by his pulling out a plum; it is therefore supposed that his father apprenticed him to a mince pie maker, so that he might improve his taste from year to year; no one standing in so much need of good taste as a pastry cook."

51. Originally, a soldier who threw hand grenades. The "nursery rhyme" was probably, to begin with, a drinking song, bellowed in Stuart times by soldiers in alehouses soon after the formation of the first Grenadier units.

52. A version of this rhyme—as in the case of "Little Jack Horner"—was printed c. 1720 in Henry Carey's ballad "Namby Pamby":

Now he acts the Grenadier,
Calling for a Pot of Beer:
Where's his money? He's forgot:
Get him gone, a Drunken Sot.

The maxim added to this rhyme by the editor of the *Melody* reads: "Intemperance is attended with diseases, and idleness with poverty."

53. Originally, "Jack Prat"—a sixteenth- and seventeenth-century name for a dwarf.

54. John Bellenden Ker found in "Jack Sprat" another opportunity to attack the Catholic clergy. "Jack Sprat Could eat no Fat" he took to mean "in the doctrine of the priests, it is righteous to cheat the last farthing."

Katherine Elwes Thomas read into the lines a reference to Charles I (1600-49) and his wife Henrietta Maria (1609-66), daughter of Henry IV of France and sister to Louis XIII. Henrietta Maria was unpopular with the English because she was, of course, a Roman Catholic. The English also seem to have regarded her, with some reason, as a seeker after spoil and plunder, a grasper at "fat" bits. The later reference to "licking the platter clean" Miss Thomas took to mean Charles's attempt to meet the cost of his war with Spain by demanding large supplies from his first Parliament, mostly Puritans, who would appropriate only £140,000. Charles in a rage dissolved Parliament and raised the needed sums by a revival of the hated system of "benevolences" and the quartering of soldiers in private houses.

55. A version of this rhyme appeared in print as early as 1639, in John Clarke's collection of proverbs, and it was paraphrased twenty years later to poke fun at an Archdeacon Pratt and his wife Joan. Its earliest appearance in print, more or less as we know it today, was in 1670.

The editor of the *Melody* appended to "Jack Sprat" the maxim: "Better go to bed supperless, than rise in debt."

56. It seems that men, not necessarily gentlemen, preferred blondes many years B.L.—Before (Anita) Loos. This lass indicates that she has had the misfortune to be born a brunette.

57. Or: Make the dowry big enough, and you'll see a lot of those fellows coming around.

« 55 »

A long tail'd Pig, or a short tail'd Pig,
Or a Pig without any Tail;
A Sow Pig, or a Boar Pig,
Or a Pig with a curling Tail.
Take hold of the Tail and eat off his Head;
And then you'll be sure the Pig hog is dead.**60**

« 56 »

Bow, wow, wow,
Whose Dog art thou?
Little Tom Tinker's Dog,**61**
Bow, wow, wow.

« 57 »

Robin and Richard
Were two pretty Men,**62**
They lay in Bed
  'Till the Clock struck Ten:
Then up starts Robin
  And looks at the sky,
Oh! Brother Richard,
  The Sun's very high;
You go before
  With the Bottle and Bag,
And I will come after
  On little Jack Nag.**63**

« 58 »

I wou'd, if I cou'd,
If I cou'dn't how cou'd I?**64**
I cou'dn't, without I cou'd, cou'd I?
Cou'd you, without you cou'd, cou'd ye?
Cou'd ye, cou'd ye?
Cou'd you, without you cou'd, cou'd ye?**65**

« 59 »

Piping hot, smoking hot,
What I've got,
You know not,
Hot hot Pease, hot, hot, hot;
Hot are my Pease, hot.**66**

According to *London Lickpenny*, the cries most heard in the fifteenth century were "Hot Pease!" "Hot fine Oatcakes!" "Whiting, maids, whitings!" "Hot codlings!" (see Rhyme 831), "Maribones!" Maribones!" "Have you any Old Boots?" and "Buy a Mat!"—"with a general hullabaloo," Walter de la Mare adds, "of 'What d'ye lack? What d'ye lack?' and an occasional bawling of 'Clubs' to summon the tag, rag and bobtail to a row."

"Of singing cries, nowadays," Walter de la Mare continues, "we may still hear in the sunny London streets the sweet and doleful strains of Won't you buy my sweet blooming lavender: Sixteen branches a penny! And in the dusk of November the muffin-man's bell. Besides these, we have Rag-a'-bone! Milk-o! Any scissors to grind? Clo' props! Water-creeses!"

58. Pronounced, of course, "gal." The editor of the *Melody* added the maxim: "If we do not flatter ourselves, the flattery of others would have no effect."

59. This rather sad little rhyme appeared in print as early as 1684 as "a New Catch." Some commentators have thought it worth comparing with the Clown's song in *Twelfth Night* and the Fool's song in *King Lear*.

The editor of the *Melody* added to this rhyme his usual maxim: "He who will be his own master, has often a fool for a scholar."

60. This was the cry of the "pig pye man," who, in the eighteenth century, hawked in the streets of English cities pigs made of paste, with their bellies filled with currants and two currants placed for eyes in their heads. Katherine Elwes Thomas, however, saw in the first three lines of this rhyme raps at the Cavalier and the Roundhead, and in the fourth line a thrust at Charles II, termed both "a fat pig" and "Curly Locks" by some of his enemies.

The custom of crying one's wares in the street is a very ancient one, and one that has inspired many other nursery rhymes, among them "Piping Hot, Smoking Hot" (Rhyme 59), "If I'd As Much Money As I Could Spend" (Rhyme 118), "Diddle, Diddle, Dumpling, My Son John" (Rhyme 129), "Hot Cross Buns" (Rhyme 351).

61. In later versions, "I am my master's dog ..." The editor of the *Melody* added: "Tom Tinker's dog is a very good dog, and an honester dog than his master." Tinkers—itinerant menders of pots and pans—were often gypsies, who traditionally had a bad reputation for honesty.

62. In later versions, "Alfred and Richard" and "two lazy men."

63. The editor of the *Melody* commented: "What lazy rogues are these to lie in bed so long, I daresay they have no clothes to their backs; for *Laziness clothes a man with rags*."

64. Titled, in the *Melody*, "A Logical SONG; or the CONJUROR'S Reason for not getting Money," this nonsense is probably the refrain of an old ballad.

65. The editor of the *Melody* added the note: "This is a new way of handling an old argument, said to be invented by a famous senator; but it has something in it of Gothic construction." This the facetious man attributed to *Sanderson*.

66. This is another street vendor's cry, as the editor of the *Melody* indicated by the note he added, attributed to *Huggleford on Hunger*: "There is more music in this song, on a cold frosty night, than even the Syrens were possessed of, who captivated Ulysses; and the effects stick closer to the ribs."

Then let us sing merrily,

Merrily now,

We'll live on the custards that come from the cow.

CHAPTER IV

Simple Simon and Nancy Cock

Between the Newbery edition of *Mother Goose's Melody* in 1760, or thereabouts, and the publication, in 1784, of Joseph Ritson's collection, *Gammer Gurton's Garland,* several other books appeared which contributed to the "Mother Goose" rhymes some of those we know the best and love the most today.

A chapbook published by Cluer Dicey and Richard Marshall in 1764 introduced the tale of "Simple Simon,"[1] into which Katherine Elwes Thomas read the romantic story of the ascension of James VI of Scotland to the throne of England as King James I.

"Upon a spring night in the year 1603 a travel-stained horseman dashed to Holyrood Palace, spurring his steed the long way from London by relay, that he might be the first to bear the great tidings...." she begins her chapter breathlessly.

1. Boyd Smith in his *Mother Goose* (1919) states that a tale of Simple Simon formed one of the chapbooks of the Elizabethan era, but there is no existing evidence to prove this.

2. "Why did the little moron put his father in the icebox?" "Because he wanted cold pop." The reader will find a generous collection of Little Moron stories in B. A. Botkin's *A Treasury of American Folklore* (New York: Crown Publishers, Inc., 1944), pp. 461-64.

3. In later nursery rhyme books, she is often called Nancy *Cook*.

4. It was supposedly "Nurse Love-child," tired of looking after naughty children, who made the collection of "pretty songs" for good little Nancy Cock. And sometimes, in English nursery literature, "Nurse Love-child," like our American "Mother Goose," was credited with actually having composed the jingles. Mary Cooper even went so far as to commercialize the old lady; the last page of *Tommy Thumb's Pretty Song Book* carried this advertisement for *The Child's Plaything*, another Cooper-published volume:

> The Childs Plaything
> I recommend for Cheating
> Children into learning
> Without any beating.
>
> N. Lovechild.
>
> Sold by M. Cooper.
> Price one Shilling.

5. To the editors of *The Oxford English Dictionary*, "Simple Simon" is simply an old name for "a natural, a silly fellow." But to Katherine Elwes Thomas, as we have seen, Simple

But Simple Simon seems to us more a remote ancestor of the Little Moron about whom we told so many stories in the early 1940's.[2]

Then, about the year 1780, the London publisher John Marshall brought out an important volume titled *Nancy Cock's Pretty Song Book for all Little Misses and Masters.*

Like "Tommy Thumb," "Nancy Cock"[3] would seem to have been an accepted nursery character. At the end of the *Song Book*, Marshall printed "Some account of Nancy Cock, and our good Friend Nurse Love-child."[4] According to this account, Nancy Cock, while not a child of the richest family in town, was certainly the best girl in the village.

She "would not tell a fib could she have got her belly full of custards by it," was the handsome tribute paid to Nancy by Marshall himself—or by the true but today unknown editor of her *Song Book.*

« 60 »

Simple Simon met a pieman,
    Going to the fair;
Says Simple Simon to the pieman,
    Let me taste your ware.

Says the pieman to Simple Simon,
    Show me first your penny;
Says Simple Simon to the pieman,
    Indeed I have not any.

Simon was the seventeenth-century English-man with a Scottish king, James I, *the pie-man*. England is *the fair; your ware* "the glittering titles of nobility for which history records a marvelously quick and plentiful sale"; and *Show me first your penny* "the genuinely stern Scotch demand" for money for such titles. Perhaps the *thistle* of the last verse, a Scottish plant, helped to inspire this interpretation.

These four stanzas are the ones most often found in "Mother Goose" books, but there are many other "Simple Simons." Here are some of them:

Simple Simon went to town
  To buy a piece of meat;
He tied it to his horse's tail,
  To keep it clean and sweet.

He went to catch a dickey-bird
  And thought he could not fail,
Because he had got a little salt,
  To put upon his tail.

He went to ride a spotted cow,
  That had got a spotted calf,
She threw him on the ground,
  Which made the people laugh.

Then Simple Simon went a-hunting,
  For to catch a hare,
He rode a goat about the street,
  But he could not find one there.

He went for to eat honey,
  Out of the mustard-pot,
He bit his tongue until he cried,
  That was the good he got.

He went to take a bird's nest,
  Was built upon a bough;
A branch gave way, and Simon fell,
  Into a dirty slough.

He went to shoot a wild duck,
  But the wild duck flew away;
Says Simon, "I can't hit him,
  Because he will not stay."

Once Simon made a great snowball,
  And brought it in to roast,
He laid it before the fire,
  And soon the ball was lost.

He went to slide upon the ice,
  Before the ice would bear;
Then he plunged in above his knees,
  Which made poor Simon stare.

He washed himself with a blackening-ball,
  Because he had no soap;

Simple Simon went a-fishing,
  For to catch a whale;
All the water he had got
  Was in his mother's pail.

Simple Simon went to look
  If plumbs grew on a thistle;
He pricked his finger very much,
  Which made poor Simon whistle.**5**

« 61 »

Old Father Greybeard,
  Without tooth or tongue,
If you'll give me your finger
  I'll give you my thumb.
Go! you're a naughty boy,
  So is your brother;
If you give him your blockhead,
  He'll give you another.**6**

Then, then, said to his mother,
"I'm a beauty now, I hope!"
He went for water in a sieve,
But soon it all ran through;
And now poor Simple Simon
Bids you all adieu.

6. As the editors of *The Oxford Dictionary* of *Nursery Rhymes* say: "The significance of this, if any, is not apparent . . . ." It might be added, however, that *Greybeard* was the name given to a large stone bottle holding three or more gallons, its handle terminating in a druidic face. Greybeards were often used as repositories for some exceedingly curious charms and amulets.

7. *Old father Long-Legs* is the insect we know as the daddy longlegs, harvestman, or crane-fly, and this rhyme was formerly addressed to the creature by children cruel enough to pull off its legs. In some curious way, lines from this rhyme have become merged with those from "Goose-a, Goose-a, Gander" (see Rhyme 89).

« 62 »

Old father Long-Legs
Can't say his prayers:
Take him by the left leg,
And throw him down stairs.
And when he's at the bottom,
Before he long has lain,
Take him by the right leg,
And throw him up again. **7**

« 63 »

O rare Harry Parry!
When will you marry?
When Apples and Pears are ripe; **8**
I'll come to your Wedding,
Without any Bidding, **9**
And lie with your Bride all Night. **10**

« 64 »

I had a little husband,
    No bigger than my thumb; **11**
I put him in a pint-pot **12**
    And there I bid him drum. **13**
I bought a little horse
    That galloped up and down;
I bridled him, and saddled him
    And sent him out of town.
I gave him a pair of garters
    To garter up his hose,
And a little silk handkerchief,
    To wipe his snotty nose. **14**

« 65 »

There was a lady lov'd a swine,
    Honey, quoth she,
Pig-hog, wilt thou be mine?
    Hoogh, quoth he.

I'll build thee a silver stye,
    Honey, quoth she,
And in it thou shall lye;
    Hoogh, quoth he.

Pinn'd with a silver pin,
    Honey, quoth she,
That thou may go out and in,
    Hoogh, quoth he.

Wilt thou have me now,
    Honey? quoth she,
Hoogh, hoogh, hoogh, quoth he,
    And went his way.**15**

« 66 »

Up hill and down dale;
Butter is made in every vale;
And if that Nancy Cock
Is a good girl,**16**
She shall have a spouse,
And make butter anon,

8. That is, when the harvest is in.

9. This rhyme is probably of Welsh origin. It was the custom in Wales, until recently, to hold a "bidding" ceremony on wedding days. Friends and relations would present the bride and groom with sums of money for setting up housekeeping.

10. "And dance and sing all night" in later versions.

11. The "little husband," according to Katherine Elwes Thomas, was Philip II of Spain, husband to Queen Mary I of England. There is no doubt that Philip was "a small, meagre man, much below the middle height, with thin legs, a narrow chest, and the timid shrinking air of an habitual invalid," but it is a little ridiculous to find, as Miss Thomas does, a reference to Philip in virtually every "Mother Goose" rhyme which has in it "a little man."

12. John Bellenden Ker "explained" this jingle as having strong religious significance. The simile of putting the husband in *a pint-pot* is held to be a thrust at Mary's Catholicism, since "pint-pot," according to Ker, was at that time a common expression "for the fine-fund of money accruing from the penalties imposed by the confessors."

13. An American version of the first verse goes:

I had a little brother,
  No bigger than my thumb;
I put him in the coffee pot—
  He rattled like a drum.

14. Needless to say, this line quickly became "To wipe his pretty nose."

15. Only two verses of "The Lady and the Swine" appeared in *Nancy Cock's Pretty Song Book*, with a somewhat different wording than that given here. This is the fuller, better-known version, as it appeared in the later *Gammer Gurton's Garland*. It is thought that this song was originally composed by students at St. John's College, Oxford, for Twelfth Night revels, and Richard Brome incorporated it into his comedy, *The English Moor*, published in 1658.

Before her old grandmother
Grows a young man.
Then let us sing merrily,
Merrily now,
We'll live on the custards that
  come from the cow.

« 67 »

Taffy was a Welshman,**17**
  Taffy was a thief;
Taffy came to my house,
  And stole a piece of beef;
I went to Taffy's house,
  Taffy wasn't home,**18**
Taffy came to my house,
  And stole a marrow bone.**19**
I went to Taffy's house,
  Taffy was in bed,
I took the marrow bone
  And beat about his head.
Taffy was a Welshman,
  Taffy was a sham,
Taffy came to my house,
  And stole a leg of lamb;

I went to Taffy's house;
  Taffy was away,
I stuffed his socks with sawdust
  And filled his shoes with clay.
Taffy was a Welshman,
  Taffy was a cheat,
Taffy came to my house,
  And stole a piece of meat ;
I went to Taffy's house,
  Taffy was not there,
I hung his coat and trousers
  To roast before a fire.

« 68 »

Drunk or sober, go to-bed Tom,
  Go to-bed Tom,
  Go to-bed Tom,
Drunk or sober, go to-bed Tom,
  T'other pipe,
  And t'other pot;
  Then to-bed, Tom,
  Then to-bed, Tom,
Drunk or sober, go to-bed Tom.**20**

16. This line is obviously out of rhyme. Henry Carey quoted this song in part in 1725, and his wording indicates that in the original version the fourth line may have contained an indelicacy that has not come down to us.

17. See Chapter II, Note 35.

18. Or:

  I went to Taffy's house,
    Taffy wasn't in,
  I jumped upon his Sunday hat,
    And poked it with a pin.

19. The rhyme as given in *Nancy Cock's Pretty Song Book* ends here; the other verses are later additions.

20. A shorter version, given in many later books of nursery rhymes, goes:

    Go to bed, Tom,
    Go to bed, Tom,
    Drunk or sober,
    Go to bed, Tom.

Both versions seem to be words written to a bugle call, and this is almost certainly a military song, chanted while drinking and accompanied by a drumming of fists on the table.

With my wing wang waddle oh,
Jack sing saddle oh,
Blowsey boys bubble oh,
Under the broom. . . .

CHAPTER V

Gammer Gurton's Garland

Joseph Ritson, in his time, was a celebrated and painstaking antiquarian.[1] He was also a highly eccentric and extremely irascible man.

Ritson was born on October 2, 1752, at Stockton-upon-Tees, Durham, and was bred to the legal profession. But he was far more interested in English poetry than he was in English law. By 1782 he had published a quarto pamphlet in which he launched a vicious attack on the *History of English Poetry*, written between 1774 and 1781 by Thomas Warton (1782-90), who was made poet laureate of England in 1785.

Warton had stated—quite correctly—that the Elizabethan poet and dramatist Christopher Marlowe (1564-93) had died from a wound given him by his own dagger turned against him by a drinking companion. Unfortunately for Warton, he had added that this wound was in *Marlowe's bosom*.

Nowhere could Ritson find any confirmation of this. Addressing Warton in his quarto pamphlet, Ritson wrote: "Your propensity to corruption and falsehood seems so natural, that I have been sometimes tempted to believe you often substitute a lie in the place of a fact without knowing it. How else

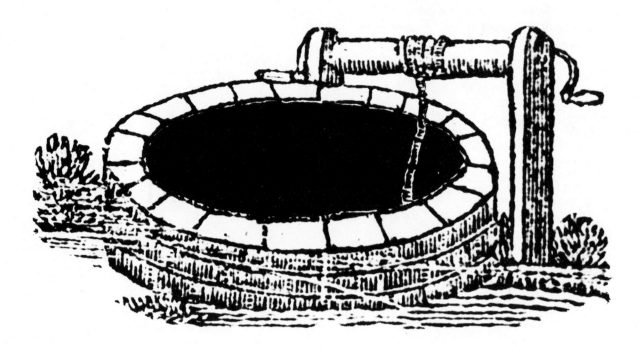

R. CALDECOTT

you came to tell us that Marlowe was stabbed in the bosom I cannot conceive."

Ritson had purchased a copy of Newbery's *Mother Goose's Melody* in 1781, and shortly afterward he was collecting rhymes of the same kind and urging his nephew to do likewise. Ritson's collection, titled *Gammer Gurton's Garland*, was first published in 1784, reprinted c. 1799 and again in 1810, seven years after his death, when his publishers produced a much enlarged edition containing two supplements (Parts III and IV) that added fifty-five rhymes to Ritson's original seventy-nine.

The full title of this edition is *Gammer Gurton's Garland: or, the Nursery Parnassus;*[2] *A Choice Collection of Pretty Songs and Verses,* FOR THE AMUSEMENT OF ALL LITTLE GOOD CHILDREN WHO CAN NEITHER READ NOR RUN. The printers were "Harding and Wright, St. John's-square" for "R. Triphook,

37, St. James's Street." The foreword reads: "Parts I and II were first collected and printed by a literary gentleman deceased,**3** who supposed he had preserved each piece according to its original idiom; an opinion not easily refuted, if worth supporting. Parts III and IV are now first added."

A contributor to Parts III and IV of this 1810 edition was probably Francis Douce,**4** and Douce in turn probably drew upon *Infant Institutes,* essentially a spoof of Shakespearean comment in terms of a "learned" essay on nursery rhymes, ascribed to the Reverend B. N. Turner "of Denton Co., Linc., and of Wing Co., Rutland," a close friend of Dr. Sam Johnson.**5**

But, again, enough of bibliography—on to the rhymes.

R. CALDECOTT

« 69 »

There was a frog liv'd in a well,
   Kitty alone, Kitty alone,**6**
There was a frog liv'd in a well,
   Kitty alone and I.
There was a frog liv'd in a well,
And a farce**7** mouse in a mill,
   Cock me cary, Kitty alone,
   Kitty alone and I.

This frog he would a wooing ride,
   Kitty alone, Kitty alone,
This frog he would a wooing ride,
   Kitty alone and I.
This frog he would a wooing ride,
And on a snail he got astride,
   Cock me cary, Kitty alone,
   Kitty alone and I.

He rode till he came to my Lady Mouse hall,
   Kitty alone, Kitty alone,
He rode till he came to my Lady Mouse hall,
   Kitty alone and I.
He rode till he came to my Lady Mouse hall,
And there he did both knock and call,
   Cock me cary, Kitty alone,
   Kitty alone and I.

1. "He would have walked from London to Oxford to collate a manuscript, or correct an error," wrote Robert Chambers, the Scottish author and publisher (1802-71) in his famous *Book of Days.*

2. *Parnassus* comes from the Greek mountain of that name, the supposed home of Apollo and the Muses. Hence it has come to mean the domain of poetry.

3. Ritson, of course.

4. See Chapter XII, Note 28.

5. *Infant Institutes* was in existence in 1797, although the original printing may have been made some years earlier.

6. In other versions, "Cuddie alone." The nursery rhyme, as set down by Ritson, most probably stems from a ballad, "A moste Strange weddinge of the frogge and the mowse," "licensed by the Stationers to Edward White, 21 November 1580." Here the refrain is:

   Humble-dum, humble dum,
   tweedle, tweedle twine.

This suggests that the ballad was originally a spinning song, "Humble-dum" representing the humming of the wheel and "tweedle twine" the twiddling and twining of the thread.

7. "Farce"—merry.

Quoth he, Miss Mouse, I'm come to thee,
　Kitty alone, Kitty alone,
Quoth he, Miss Mouse, I'm come to thee,
　Kitty alone and I.
Quoth he, Miss Mouse, I'm come to thee,
To see if thou can fancy me,
　Cock me cary, Kitty alone,
　Kitty alone and I.

Quoth she, answer I'll give you none,
　Kitty alone, Kitty alone,
Quoth she, answer I'll give you none,
　Kitty alone and I.
Quoth she, answer I'll give you none,
Until my uncle Rat come home,
　Cock me cary, Kitty alone,
　Kitty alone and I.

And when her uncle Rat came home,
　Kitty alone, Kitty alone,
And when her uncle Rat came home,
　Kitty alone and I.
And when her uncle Rat came home,
Who's been here since I've been gone?
　Cock me cary, Kitty alone,
　Kitty alone and I.

Sir, there's been a worthy gentleman,
　Kitty alone, Kitty alone,
Sir, there's been a worthy gentleman,
　Kitty alone and I.
Sir, there's been a worthy gentleman,
That's been here since you've been gone,
　Cock me cary, Kitty alone,
　Kitty alone and I.

The frog he came whistling through the brook,
　Kitty alone, Kitty alone,
The frog he came whistling through the brook,
　Kitty alone and I,
The frog he came whistling through the brook,
And there he met with a dainty duck,
　Cock me cary, Kitty alone,
　Kitty alone and I.

The duck she swallow'd him with a pluck,
  Kitty alone, Kitty alone,
The duck she swallow'd him with a pluck,
  Kitty alone and I.
The duck she swallow'd him with a pluck,
So there's an end of my history book,
  Cock me cary, Kitty alone,
  Kitty alone and I.[8]

« 70 »

Can you make me a cambrick shirt,[9]
  Parsley, sage, rosemary and thyme,[10]
Without any seam or needle work?
  And you shall be a true lover of mine.

Can you wash it in yonder well,
  Parsley, sage, rosemary and thyme,
Where never spring water, nor rain ever fell?
And you shall be true lover of mine.

Can you dry it on yonder thorn,
  Parsley, sage, rosemary and thyme,
Which never bore blossom since Adam was born?
  And you shall be a true lover of mine.

Now you have ask'd me questions three,
  Parsley, sage, rosemary and thyme,
I hope you'll answer as many for me,
  And you shall be a true lover of mine.

Can you find me an acre of land,
  Parsley, sage, rosemary and thyme,
Between the salt water and the sea sand?
  And you shall be a true lover of mine.

Can you plow it with a ram's horn,
  Parsley, sage, rosemary and thyme,
And sow it all over with one pepper corn?
  And you shall be a true lover of mine.

Can you reap it with a sickle of leather,
  Parsley, sage, rosemary and thyme,
And bind it up with a peacock's feather?
  And you shall be a true lover of mine.

8. Much better known today is the more recent version of this old song that begins:

A frog he would a-wooing go,
  Heigh ho! says Rowley,
A frog he would a-wooing go,
Whether his mother would let him or no.
  With a rowley, powley, gammon and
    spinach,
  Heigh ho! says Anthony Rowley.

9. In earlier days, a man who asked a girl to make him a shirt was, in effect, asking for her hand in marriage. If the girl made him the shirt, she signified that she would accept him as a suitor.

10. These herbs were all thought to have magical and medicinal properties. The refrain perhaps stems from a witch's incantation or from a housewife's recipe.

R. CALDECOTT

79

When you have done and finish'd your work,
   Parsley, sage, rosemary and thyme,
Then come to me for your cambrick shirt,
   And you shall be a true lover of mine.[11]

« 71 »

Says t'auld man tit oak tree,[12]
Young and lusty was I when I kenn'd thee;
I was young and lusty, I was fair and clear,
Young and lusty was I mony a lang year,
But sair fail'd am I, sair fail'd now,
Sair fail'd am I sen kenn'd thou.

« 72 »

I'll sing you a song:
The days are long,
The woodcock and the sparrow:
The little dog he has burnt his tail,
And he must be hanged tomorrow.[13]

« 73 »

There was an old woman, and what do you think?
She liv'd upon nothing but victuals and drink;
And tho' victuals and drink were the chief of her
   diet,
This plaguy old woman cou'd never be quiet.
She went to the baker, to buy her some bread,
And when she came home, her old husband was
   dead;
She went to the clerk to toll the bell,
And when she came back her old husband was
   well.[14]

« 74 »

There was a little Guinea-pig,
Who, being little, was not big,[15]
He always walked upon his feet,
And never fasted when he eat.

When from a place he ran away,
He never at that place did stay,

R. CALDECOTT

11. Ritson in 1794 called this "a little English song sung by children and maids." Scholars have traced it to a tale in the fourteenth-century *Gesta Romanorum*, later set down in Germany by the brothers Grimm, in which a king vows to marry any maid who can make him a shirt from three square inches of linen. Its first appearance in print as a ballad—attributed by some to James I of Scotland—was in a black-letter broadside of about 1670 titled *The Wind hath blown my Plaid away, or, A discourse betwixt a young Woman and the Elphin Knight.*

And when he ran, as I am told,
He ne'er stood still for young or old.

He often squeak'd and sometimes vi'lent,
And when he squeak'd he ne'er was silent;
Tho' ne'er instructed by a cat,
He knew a mouse was not a rat.

One day, as I am certify'd,
He took a whim and fairly dy'd;
And as I'm told by men of sense,
He never has been living since.

« 75 »

A man of words and not of deeds[16]
Is like a garden full of weeds;[17]
And when the weeds begin to grow,
It's like a garden full of snow;[18]
And when the snow begins to fall,
It's like a bird upon the wall;
And when the bird away does fly,
It's like an eagle in the sky;
And when the sky begins to roar,
It's like a lion at the door;
And when the door begins to crack,
It's like a stick upon your back;
And when your back begins to smart,
It's like a penknife in your heart;
And when your heart begins to bleed,
You're dead, and dead, and dead, indeed.[19]

« 76 »

Here stands a fist,
   Who set it there?
A better man than you,
   Touch him if you dare.[20]

« 77 »

A little old man and I fell out,
How shall we bring this matter about?
Bring it about as well as you can,
Get you gone, you little old man![21]

12. Titled, in the *Garland*, "The Old Man and the Oak. A North Country Song."

13. In his fascinating book, *The Coasts of Illusion* (New York: Harper & Brothers, 1924), Clark B. Firestone has written: " . . . domestic animals which had killed or maimed persons were regularly tried in the criminal courts of ancient Greece and medieval Europe, [while] ecclesiastical courts long exercised jurisdiction over smaller animal offenders. . . . From the ninth to the nineteenth century, there is a record of 144 successful prosecutions of animals, vermin included, and these are thought to be only a fraction of the total number of such litigations . . . ."

The editors of *The Oxford Dictionary of Nursery Rhymes* note that: "On 25 May 1595, at Leyden, a dog, 'Troeveetie' by name, was hung by means of a string on a gallows in punishment after a proper trial . . . for accidentally inflicting a fatal injury of a child's finger. In 1714 Addison in *The Spectator* (11 Aug.) refers to the hanging of all the mastiffs of Syracuse because they had attacked a priest. And as late as 1771 a dog belonging to a Farmer Carpenter was on trial at Chichester." The editors surmise that it was from such practices that we got our expression "a hang-dog look."

The custom of executing animals is also reflected in:

Swing 'em, swang 'em, bells at Wrangham,
Three dogs in a string, hang 'em, hang 'em.

14. Note the close resemblance of the second stanza to "Old Mother Hubbard" (Rhyme 134), whose first existing appearance in print was not made until twenty-one years after "The Surprising Old Woman."

John Bellenden Ker found in this rhyme another opportunity to attack the Catholic Churchman: "The old woman is a corruption of Saxon Onwel-wije, the wafer consecrator, i.e., the hostmaker or priest. The lines are meant to imply that the same voice which conjures the bread out of the mouths of the industrious, is equally employed in mocking them for the folly of their pains."

15. This nonsense would seem to owe rather a lot to "Little Betty Winckle She Had a Pig" (Rhyme 37).

16. This rhyme—in later years sung as a ball-bouncing song—begins Part II of *Gammer Gurton's Garland*, with the title "A Man of Words."

17. This couplet in various forms is found in several early collections of proverbs, one of them dating back to 1659.

18. Or: "Then does the garden overflow . . . ."

19. This is one of the rhymes of which there are many versions. One begins:

> *There was a man of double deed*
> *Sowed his garden full of seed . . . .*

James O. Halliwell recorded a version which he said was a burlesque song on the battle of Culloden (1746) at which Prince Charles Edward Stuart of Scotland (1720-88), known as Bonnie Prince Charlie and the Young Pretender, was defeated by English troops:

> *Double Dee Double Day,*
> *Set a garden full of seeds . . . .*

20. This belligerency reminds one of schoolboy challenges that can be observed on "playgrounds" to this day: the custom of putting a stick on one's shoulder for the other boy to knock off, if he dares—and, especially, the custom of balling a hand into a fist and daring the other boy to "Smell that!"

There is also the challenge in which a boy places one fist on top of the other and says to his rival:

> *Club fist!*
> *Take it off or*
> *I knock it off.*

Or a boy who has secured a good position and means to hold it may say:

> *I'm the king of the castle,*
> *Get you down you dirty rascal.*

21. In 1911, Beatrix Potter, Mrs. William Heelis (1866-1943), best remembered today for *The Tale of Peter Rabbit* (1902), made use of this rhyme in *The Tale of Timmy Tiptoes*: "Down inside the woodpecker's tree, a fat squirrel voice and a thin squirrel voice sang this together." There are many versions of this rhyme, among them:

> *My grandfather's man and me coost out,*
> *How will we bring the matter about?*

« 78 »

Little boy, pretty boy, where was you born?
In Lincolnshire, master: come blow the cow's horn.
A halfpenny pudding, a penny pye,
A shoulder of mutton, and that love I.[22]

« 79 »

The man in the moon[23]
Came tumbling down,[24]
And ask'd his way to Norwich.[25]
He went by the south,
And burnt his mouth,
With supping hot pease porridge.[26]

« 80 »

O that I was where I would be,
Then would I be where I am not;
But where I am I must be,
And where I would be I can not.[27]

« 81 »

A diller,[28] a dollar,[29]
A ten o'clock scholar,
What makes you come so soon?
You us'd to come at ten o'clock,
And now you come at noon.

We'll bring it about as weel as we can,
And a' for the sake o' my grandfather's man.
My little old man and I fell out.
I'll tell you what 'twas all about;
I had money, and he had none,
And that's the way the row begun.

Moll-in-the-wad and I fell out,
And what do you think it was all about?
I gave her a shilling, she swore it was bad,
It's an old soldier's button says Moll-in-the-
    wad.

Mollie, my sister and I fell out,
And what do you think it was all about?
She loved coffee, and I loved tea,
And that was the reason we couldn't agree.

An even later version was used as a counting-out rhyme:

Me an' the minister's wife cast out,
And guess ye what it was all about?
Black puddin', dish clout,
Eiri orie, you're out.

22. There are many other versions, perhaps
the most interesting that given in *The Only
True Mother Goose Melodies* (c. 1843):

Little lad, little lad, where were you born?
Far off in Lancashire, under a thorn,
Where they sup butter-milk
With a ram's horn;
And a pumpkin scoop'd

With a yellow rim,
Is the bonny bowl they breakfast in.

This of course means that the *little lad* was
one of the Little People—and it is one of the
very rare mentions of fairies to be found in the
older nursery rhymes.

23. "Every one knows that the moon is in-
habited by a man with a bundle of sticks on
his back, who has been exiled thither for many
centuries, and who is so far off that he is beyond the reach of death," the Reverend Sabine
Baring-Gould wrote in *Curious Myths of the
Middle Ages* (1866). "He has once visited this
earth, if the nursery rhyme is to be credited,
... but whether he ever reached [Norwich] the
same authority does not state. The story as
told by nurses is, that this man was found by
Moses gathering sticks on a Sabbath, and that,
for this crime, he was doomed to reside in the
moon till the end of all things; and they refer
to Numbers xv. 32-36 . . . . "

24. In later versions, "Came down too soon."
It *does* make a better rhyme.

25. The county seat of Norfolk, England,
Norwich in the eleventh century, ranked with
London, York, and Bristol in ecclesiastical and
commercial importance. Today it is principally a grain market and a manufacturing
center.

26. In later versions, "With supping cold plum porridge." Frank Kidson, the editor of *75 British Nursery Rhymes* (1904) and *Children's Songs of Long Ago* (c. 1905), states that the melody to which this rhyme was sung is an old English air of the sixteenth or seventeenth century, "Thomas I Cannot."

27. This complaint, as the editors of *The Oxford Dictionary of Nursery Rhymes* note, is the only nursery rhyme that has made its way into *The Oxford Book of English Verse* (1939). The editor of that volume, Sir Arthur Quiller-Couch, presented a considerably more "literary" version:

> *O would I were where I would be!*
> *There would I be where I am not:*
> *For where I am I would not be,*
> *And where I would be I can not.*

28. Perhaps a shortened form of "dilatory." "Or again," say the editors of *The Oxford Dictionary of Nursery Rhymes*, "diller is a Yorkshire word for a schoolboy who is dull and stupid at learning."

29. Perhaps a shortened form of "dullard." Or "A diller, a dollar," taken together, may have some relation to "dilly-dally." In any case, it seems that teachers have been complaining about tardiness in their pupils for quite a long time.

30. "Enow"—enough.

31. In later versions, "Rowsty dowt" or "Hey, diddle dout" or "Diddle, diddle, doubt."

32. In later versions, "My candle is out."

33. Or "saddle my hog"—reminiscent of "The Sow Came in with a Saddle" (Rhyme 33).

34. Another version reads:

> *I'll saddle my cock,*
> *And bridle my hen . . .*

35. Here ends the rhyme as given in *Gammer Gurton's Garland*. The second verse is a later addition.

36. "Shod"—the old past tense of "shed" or "split," suggesting that the porridge was a *pease* porridge.

37. "Truckler's"—pedlar's.

38. Later versions read: "And one in a velvet

R. CALDECOTT

« 82 »

I am a pretty wench,
  And I come a great way hence,
And sweethearts I can get none:
  But every dirty sow,
  Can get sweethearts enow,**30**
And I, pretty wench, can get never a one.

« 83 »

I doubt, I doubt,**31**
  My fire is out,**32**
My little dame an't at home;
  Come, bridle my hog,**33**
  And saddle my dog,**34**
And fetch my little dame home.**35**
  Home she came,
  Tritty trot,
She asked for the porridge she left in the pot;
  Some she ate,
  And some she shod,**36**
And some she gave to the truckler's**37** dog;
  She took up the ladle and knocked its head,
  And now poor Dapsy dog is dead!

« 84 »

Hark, hark, the dogs do bark,
Beggars are coming to town;
Some in jags, and some in rags,
And some in velvet gowns.**38**

Some gave them white bread,
And some gave them brown,
And some gave them a good horse-whip,
And sent them out of town.**39**

« 85 »

I will tell my own daddy when he comes home,
What little good work my mommy has done,
She has earnt a penny, spent a groat,
And burnt a hole in the child's new coat.**40**

« 86 »

I had a little moppet,**41**
I put it in my pocket,
And fed it with corn and hay;
There came a proud beggar,
And swore he would have her,
And stole my little moppet away.

« 87 »

There was an old woman who lived in a shoe,**42**
She had so many children she didn't know what to
do,**43**
She gave them some broth without any bread;
She whipped them all soundly and put them to
bed.**44**

gown." Some scholars take this to be a reference to William III (1650-1702), king of England, Scotland and Ireland, 1689-1702, the son of William II of Orange, in which case the "beggars" would be the Dutchmen in his train. On the other hand, the "beggars" could well be, quite literally, beggars. The editors of *The Oxford Dictionary of Nursery Rhymes* quote from G. M. Trevelyan's *English Social History*: "All through the Tudor reigns, the 'beggars coming to town' preyed on the fears of dwellers in lonely farms and hamlets, and exercised the minds of magistrates, Privy Councilors and Parliaments."

39. The second verse does not appear in *Gammer Gurton's Garland*, but was added in the Kate Greenaway edition of *Mother Goose* (1881). See also Verse 124.

40. This little tattletale might well bear in mind what happened to "Tell Tale Tit" (Rhyme 21).

41. *Time, The Weekly Newsmagazine*, by repeatedly referring to any young child as a moppet, single-handedly brought into use again this eighteenth-century word for a baby or a doll.

42. The version here given is the one best known today, but there are many others. In *Infants Institute*, for example, the rhyme reads:

> There was an old woman and she lived in a shoe,
> She had so many children she didn't know what to do;
> She crumm'd 'em some porridge [gave them a very little porridge] without any bread;
> And she borrowed a beetle [a heavy wooden hammer], and she knoc'd 'em o' the head.

And there is the Scotch version:

> There was a wee bit wifie,
> Who lived in a shoe;
> She had so many bairns,
> She kenn'd not what to do.
> She haed to the market
> To buy a sheep head;
> When she came back,
> They were a' lying dead.
> She went to the wright,

R. CALDECOTT

To get them a coffin;
When she came back,
They were a' lying laughing.
She gaed up the stair,
To ring the bell;
The bell rope broke,
And down she fell.

Compare the above lines with some of those in

"Old Mother Hubbard" (Rhyme 134).

43. It is tempting to connect the "old woman" who "had so many children" with Elizabeth Goose of Boston, her ten stepchildren, her six children by Isaac Goose, and her (at least) seven grandchildren. But the jingle is far older than "Mother Goose." Some scholars hold that Parliament was the "old woman" who geographically lived in a "shoe" which was the British Isles, ruling the many "children" of the then far-flung Empire "upon whom the sun never sets."

44. Parliament indeed gave her children a bitter cup of broth "without any bread" in the cordially disliked person of James I of Scotland for their king. Having "whipped them all soundly," Parliament then "put them to bed" to sleep on the matter and digest it as best they could.

45. The second verse did not appear in *Gammer Gurton's Garland*, but is a later addition.
Here again we find John Bellenden Ker using a nursery rhyme to attack the Catholic clergy: "This pasquinade seems aimed at the three branches of the tonsured profession, viz.; the friar, the lawyer, and the regular clergyman, and refers to the share that each takes in the pillage of the countryman's property. At the end [of the first verse as given here] the

« 88 »

Come, let's to bed,
Says Sleepy-head;
Sit up a while, says Slow;
Hang on the pot,
Says Greedy-gut,
We'll sup before we go.

To bed, to bed,
Cried Sleepy-head,
But all the rest said, No!
It is morning now;
You must milk the cow,
And tomorrow to bed we go.[45]

« 89 »

Goose-a-goose-a, gander,
Where shall I wander?
Up stairs, down stairs,
In my lady's chamber;
There you'll find a cup of sack[46]
And a race[47] of ginger.[48]

« 90 »

Four and twenty tailors
    Went to kill a snail,
The best man among them
    Durst not touch her tail;
She put out her horns
    Like a little Kyloe cow,[49]
Run, tailors, run,
    Or she'll kill you all e'en now.[50]

« 91 »

John, come sell thy fiddle,
And buy thy wife a gown.
No, I'll not sell my fiddle,
For ne'er a wife in town.[51]

« 92 »

There was a lady all skin and bone;[52]
Sure such a lady was never known:

regular clergyman is made to say he thinks he is quite rogue enough to be entitled to the whole of the booty, and not to share with such inferiors as the other two are in his eyes."

46. "Sack"—*vin sec*—dry wine.

47. "Race"—root. The word is now obsolete except when it is used as it is here: as a root of ginger.

48. As noted in Rhyme 62, "Old Father Long-Legs" and the above rhyme have become in some curious way merged. Today we know the combination of the two as:

> Goosey, goosey, gander,
>   Whither shall I wander?
> Upstairs and downstairs
>   And in my lady's chamber.
> There I met an old man
>   Who would not say his prayers.
> I took him by the left leg
>   And threw him down the stairs.

To Katherine Elwes Thomas, however, the "old man who wouldn't say his prayers" was Cardinal Beaton, who, refusing to accord with the reformed doctrines of the Covenanters, was indeed thrown "down the stairs." Stabbed to death on reaching its foot, the cardinal's bleeding body was then hung from the ramparts of his Castle of St. Andrews.

49. *Kyloes* are the cattle of the Hebrides and the Scotch Highlands.

50. Tailors are traditionally a timid lot. The proverb "Nine tailors make a man" is well known, but "tailors" here is probably a corruption of "tellers," a *teller* being one stroke of the church bell at the time of a funeral. The custom was to toll the bell thrice for a child,

six times for a woman, and nine times for a man—hence, "nine tellers" meant (made) "a man." Alternatively, those who believe that "Clothes make the man" interpret the proverb as meaning that it takes nine tailors to make the really fine suit that in turn "makes the man." The only intention of the above verse may have been to poke fun at the weaving trade. On the other hand, it may reflect some of the genuine awe which superstitious people have had of the snail (see Rhyme 471).

51. This would appear to be the earliest "nursery rhyme" version of the later, longer:

> Jacky, come give me thy fiddle,
>   If ever you mean to thrive.
> Nay, I'll not give my fiddle
>   To any man alive.
> If I should give my fiddle,
>   They'll think that I've gone mad,
> For many a joyful day
>   My fiddle and I have had.

Actually, both verses would seem to have stemmed from a Scots folk song which Robert Burns collected and added to for *The Scots Musical Museum*, published by James Johnson in 1788, "Oh, Rattlin, Roarin Willie." According to Sir Walter Scott, in a note to *The Lay of the Last Minstrel*, Rattlin Roarin Willie was a real person, a "jovial harper" who lived in the seventeenth century in the Harwick and Langholm districts. He had the misfortune to murder a fellow fiddler who went by the name of "Sweet Milk," and was executed at Jedburgh.

52. This is the first of the verses in Part III of *Gammer Gurton's Garland*, the beginning of those added to the book by Ritson's pub-

87

lishers in 1810. They titled this song "The Gay Lady That Went to Church." This is the same as to say, "The Lady of Little Virtue That Went to Church."

53. The *Garland* here adds the note: "This line has been adopted in the modern ballad of *Alonzo and Fair Imogene*." It is also the refrain of even more modern ballads—many of them college songs, most of them ribald in the extreme.

54. And small wonder. Of course, the kindly old nurse who was lulling her charges to sleep with this "song for the nursery" screamed too at this point, thereby sending the children to bed terrorized. The "scare" device is common in both folk song and folk tale. At his lectures, Mark Twain could usually frighten many of his listeners with his telling of "The Golden Arm."

55. James O. Halliwell in 1844 gave a somewhat similar rhyme about Doctor *Foster*:

> *Doctor Foster went to Gloucester*
> *In a shower of rain;*
> *He stepped in a puddle,*

It happen'd upon a certain day,
This lady went to church to pray.

When she came to the church stile,
There she did rest a little while;
When she came to the church yard,
There the bells so loud she heard.

When she came to the church door,
She stopt to rest a little more;
When she came to the church within,
The parson pray'd gainst pride and sin.

On looking up, on looking down,
She saw a dead man on the ground;
And from his nose unto his chin,
The worms crawl'd out, the worms crawl'd in.**53**

Then she unto the parson said,
Shall I be so when I am dead:
O yes! O yes! The parson said,
You will be so when you are dead.
*Here the lady screams.***54**

« 93 »

Old Dr. Forster,
Went to Glo'ster,
To preach the word of God:
When he came there,
He sate in his chair,
And gave all the people a nod.**55**

« 94 »

Old woman, old woman, shall we go a shearing?
Speak a little louder, Sir, I'm very thick of hearing.

Old woman, old woman, shall we go a gleaning?
Speak a little louder, Sir, I cannot tell your meaning.

Old woman, old woman, shall we go a walking?
Speak a little louder, Sir, or what's the use of talking?

Old woman, old woman, shall I kiss you dearly?
Thank you, kind Sir, I hear you very clearly.**56**

« 95 »

Sing jig my jole, the pudding bowl,
The table and the frame,
My master he did cudgel me,
For kissing of my dame.**57**

« 96 »

Bell horses, bell horses,**58**
What time o' day?
One a clock, two a clock,
Time to away.**59**

« 97 »

O the little rusty, dusty, rusty miller:
I'll not change my wife for either gold or siller.**60**

« 98 »

The rose is red, the grass is green,
Save King George our noble king:**61**
Kitty the spinner,**62** will sit down to dinner,
And eat of the leg of a frog;
All good people look over the steeple,
And see the cat play with the dog.

Right up to his middle,
And never went there again.

Boyd Smith said of this version in 1920 that it describes an incident that actually happened to Edward I in his travels. The king's horse stuck so deep in the mud of a Gloucester street, it was said, that planks had to be laid on the ground before the animal could regain its footing. Edward, furious, vowed never to visit the city again.

Katherine Elwes Thomas, on the other hand, wrote that the rhyme describes the defeat of the Cavaliers, under Prince Rupert, by the Roundheads, under the Earl of Essex, at the battle of Newberry, which followed the siege of Gloucester.

56. The editors of *The Oxford Dictionary of Nursery Rhymes* write: "The fun of these lines is increased if the last question is asked very softly." The earliest-known version of the song from which this "nursery rhyme" derives is to be found in David Herd's *Scots Songs and Ballads* (1776).

57. In later versions, bowdlerized to "For speaking of my dame."

58. Perhaps the lead horse on a cart or wagon or coach, often, in England, decked with bells, especially on such festive occasions as May Day, and therefore called the "bell horse." Or the "bell horses" may have been race horses —in Stuart times, races were run for silver bells rather than for cups or trophies.

59. In the nineteenth century, this rhyme was used for starting children's races. It also seems to have been recited by children when blowing the seed off the heads of dandelions. There are many versions, and an additional couplet is later given:

The master is coming and what will he say?
He'll whip them, and drive them, and send
them away.

60. A dance tune and words that goes back to the early eighteenth century. Robert Burns based a poem on it: "Hey, the dusty Miller / And his dusty coat . . . ." which appeared, unsigned, in the *Scots Musical Museum* in 1788. There are many versions, an especially interesting variant being:

Margaret wrote a letter,
Seal'd it with her finger,

Threw it in the dam
For the Dusty Miller.
She has wrote a letter
With a Pen of siller,
Sealed it up and sent it
To the Dusty Miller.
O the dusty miller,
O the jovial carrier,
First he came to woo her,
Then he came to marry her.

Another jolly version ends with the rousing chorus:

Hey the dusty miller!
Ho the dusty miller!
Dusty was his coat,
Dusty was his color,
Dusty was the kiss
I got from the miller!
O the dusty miller
With the dusty coat,
He will spend a shilling
Ere he win a groat!
Hey the dusty miller . . . .

Perhaps *the dusty miller* of these verses was that same popular nursery-rhyme character, the jovial miller of Dee, whom we will meet in Rhyme 124.

61. In later-printed versions, "Serve Queen Bess our noble queen!"—which certainly makes a better rhyme.

62. Or "Jenny the spinner"—in either case, a spider.

63. In other versions, "Doctor Faustus," "The master," "John Smith" and (in Ireland) "John O'Gudgeon."

« 99 »

Doctor Foster[63] was a good man,
He whipped his scholars now and then,
And when he had done, he took a dance,
Out of England into France.
He had a brave beaver with a fine snout,
Stand you there out![64]

« 100 »

The cat sat asleep by the side of the fire,
The mistress snored loud as a pig:
John took up his fiddle, by Jenny's desire,
And struck up a bit of a jig.[65]

« 101 »

Little maid, pretty maid, whither goest thou?
Down in the forest[66] to milk my cow.
Shall I go with thee?[67]—No, not now;
When I send for thee, then come thou.

« 102 »

The cock's on the dunghill[68] a blowing his horn;
The bull's in the barn a threshing of corn;
The maids in the meadow are making of hay;
The ducks in the river are swimming away.[69]

« 103 »

Up street and down street, each window's made of
    glass;
If you go to Tom Tickler's house, you'll find a pretty
    lass:
Hug her, and kiss her, and take her on your knee,
And whisper very close: Darling girl, do you love
    me?[70]

« 104 »

As I was going up Pippen Hill,[71]
    Pippen Hill was dirty,
There I met a pretty Miss,
    And she dropt me a curtsy.

R. CALDECOTT

64. The version given here is a counting-out rhyme, but another version gives as the last two lines:

> *Out of France into Spain,*
> *Over the hills and back again.*

65. So ends the "nursery rhyme" version of this old song. But the lines above are the first of fifteen verses which first appeared in print in 1805 in *Whimsical Incidents, or, The Power of Music, a Poetic Tale by a near Relation of Mother Hubbard*, published by John Harris.

66. Or: "Down in the meadow . . ."

67. The editors of *The Oxford Dictionary of Nursery Rhymes* write: "This dialogue may not be so inconsequential as it appears. In some parts of England to ask a girl if one might go milking with her was considered tantamount to a proposal of marriage."

According to a manuscript in the British Museum, Henry VIII is said to have sung a song which began:

> *Hey, troly, loly, lo;*
> *Maid, whither go you?*
> *I go to the meadowe to mylke my cowe . . . .*

It's a pretty safe bet here that the intentions of the young man asking the questions were strictly dishonorable.

68. This became, in more polite versions, "The cock's on the wood pile . . . ."

69. This rhyme would seem to derive from a Wiltshire manuscript dated 1740:

> *The bull in the barn, thrashing the corn,*
> *The cock on the dunghill is blowing his*
> *   horn.*
> *I never saw such a sight since I was born!*

70. Certainly a pleasant way to while away an afternoon. But we suspect that our forefathers may have had a rather unpleasant word for men of Tom Tickler's profession—this has been called a "slum song."

71. "Pippin" or "Pepin" was the name of some very real-life Frankish mayors and later kings (see also Chapter VII, Note 6). And a pippin is an apple of many varieties. But your present editors have had no luck in trying to locate a Pippen Hill.

72. He was asking for about sixty cents a day —a sum that these days would keep very few girls happy.

73. Pronounced "clark" in the English fashion. This is "A 3 Voc. Catch"—an unaccompanied round for three voices, "with amusing effects produced by the catching up on one another's words by the respective singers." Its first appearance in print seems to have been in 1709 in a volume called *The Jovial Companions.*

74. The editors of *The Oxford Dictionary of Nursery Rhymes* have traced this quatrain back to a song of six verses beginning: "If all the world were Paper . . . ." This seems to have been well known in the time of Charles I, for it was published in 1641 in *Witt's Recreations,* a book of "ingenious conceites" and "merry medecines."

75. The Reverend Sabine Baring-Gould and other scholars have held that this rhyme was intended as a parody on the language used in ancient Jewish and medieval ecclesiastical services. An ode sung in synagogues on the first day of the Feast of Pentecost begins:

Could we with ink the ocean fill . . . .

A saying in the Talmud begins:

If all the seas were ink and all the rushes pens . . . .

The Koran contains the passage:

And were the trees that are in the earth pens,
and the sea ink with seven more seas to swell its tide,
The words of God would not be spent.

A somewhat similar passage is the last in the Gospel according to St. John:

But there are also many other things which Jesus did; were every one of them to be written, I suppose that the world itself could not contain the books that would be written.

And here is another nursery rhyme that is thought by many to parody ecclesiastical language:

If all the seas were one sea,
What a great sea that would be!
If all the trees were one tree,
What a great tree that would be!
If all the axes were one axe,
What a great axe that would be!
If all the men were one man,
What a great man that would be!

And if the great man took the great axe,
And cut down the great tree,
And let it fall into the great sea,
What a splish-splash that would be!

Little Miss, pretty Miss,
Blessings light upon you,
If I had half-a-crown a day,[72]
I'd spend it all upon you.

« 105 »

Barnaby Bright he was a sharp cur,
He always would bark if a mouse did but stir;
But now he's grown old, and can no longer bark,
He's condemn'd by the parson to be hang'd by the clerk.[73]

« 106 »

If all the world was apple-pie[74]
And all the sea was ink;
And all the trees were bread and cheese,
What could we do for drink?[75]

« 107 »

Old Mother Niddity Nod swore by the pudding-bag,
She would go to Stoken Church fair;[76]
And then old Father Peter, said he would meet her
Before she got half way there.

« 108 »

Little Brown Betty[77] lived at the Golden Can,[78]
Where she brew'd good ale for gentlemen;[79]
And gentlemen came every day,
Till little brown Betty she hopt[80] away.
She hopped upstairs to make her bed,
And she tumbled down and broke her head.

« 109 »

Yankey[81] Doodle[82] came to town,
How do you think they serv'd him?
One took his bag, another his scrip,[83]
The quicker for to starve him.[84]

« 110 »

There was an old woman had nothing,
And there came thieves to rob her;

When she cried out she made no noise,
But all the country heard her.[85]

« 111 »

I'll sing you a song,
Nine verses long,
    For a pin;
Three and three are six,
And three are nine;
You are a fool,
    And the pin is mine.[86]

« 112 »

Little Bo-peep has lost her sheep,
    And can't tell where to find them:
Let them alone, and they'll come home,
    And bring their tails behind them.

Little Bo-peep fell fast asleep,
    And dreamt she heard them bleating:
But when she awoke, she found it a joke,
    For they were still all fleeting.

Then up she took her little crook,
    Determin'd for to find them;
She found them indeed, but it made her heart bleed,
    For they'd left all their tails behind 'em.

It happen'd one day, as Bo-peep did stray,
    Into a meadow hard by;
That she espy'd their tails side by side,
    All hung on a tree to dry.

She heav'd a sigh, and wip'd her eye,
    And over the hills went stump-o,
And tried what she cou'd, as a shepherdess shou'd,
    To tack each again to its rump-o.[87]

« 113 »

I love sixpence, a jolly, jolly sixpence,[88]
    I love sixpence as my life;
I spent a penny of it, I spent a penny of it,
    I took a penny home to my wife.

76. Stokenchurch is a village on the Oxfordshire-Buckinghamshire border.

77. In the later versions, "Little Blue Betty," "Nancy Pansy," "Mary Carey," "Cicely Parsley."

78. In later versions, "in a den," "under a pan," "in a well." We prefer the earlier "at the Golden Can," perhaps because we are fascinated by the names the English give their inns and public houses.

Clark B. Firestone, in *The Coasts of Illusion*, uses public-house signs to show how names can be corrupted: "The Bag O'Nails should be the Bacchanals; the Bully Russian should be the ship *Bellerophon*; the Cat and Wheel should be St. Catherine's Wheel; the Goat and Compass should be God Encompasses Us; the Iron Devil should be *Hirondelle* (the swallow), and the Queer Door should be the *Coeur Doré* (the golden heart). The effigies of bags of nails, cats, goats and doors under these uncouth names are pictorial fables based upon bad etymology."

79. In other words, Little Brown Betty was an "ale-wife," not to be confused with the "alewife," a North American shadlike fish.

80. "Hopped."

81. The early spelling of "Yankee."

The word is of doubtful origin, said by some to be the same as the Scotch "yankie," by others to be a form of "Yenghees," a corruption by the Canadian Indians of the French *anglais*. Another explanation comes from an officer in General Burgoyne's army, who wrote, "It is derived from a Cherokee word, 'eankke,' which signifies coward and slave. This epithet, 'Yankee,' was bestowed upon the residents of New England by Virginians for not assisting them in a war with the Cherokees."

According to William Gordon's *Independence of United States*, published by the author in 1788, Yankee "was a . . . favorite word with farmer Jonathan Hastings, of Cambridge, about 1713 . . . . The inventor [sic] used it to express excellency. A *Yankee* good horse, or *Yankee* cider and the like . . . . The students at Harvard used to hire horses of him; their intercourse with him, and his use of the term on all occasions, led them to adopt it."

82. Perhaps a "doodle" is simply a dim-witted fellow. But to doodle (or deedle) is also a way of singing or humming a tune.

Frank Kidson, writing in the *Musical Quarterly* in 1917, thought the phrase "Yankee Doodle" might perhaps have come from a sprightly dance melody called "The Yankee Tootle" or "The Yankee Doodle."

83. As used here, the word "scrip" means the wallet or pouch in which Yankey Doodle carried his money. It corresponds to the "poke" pinched by the lady known as Lou.

84. We give here the nursery rhyme version of "Yankee Doodle" as it first appeared in print in the 1810 edition of *Gammer Gurton's Garland*. To Americans, however, the classic version will always be:

> *Father and I went down to camp,*
> *Along with Captain Goodin,*
> *And there we saw the men and boys*
> *As thick as hasty puddin'.*
>
> *Yankee Doodle keep it up,*
> *Yankee Doodle dandy,*
> *Mind the music and the step,*
> *And with the girls be handy.*
>
> *And there was Captain Washington*
> *Upon a slapping stallion,*

> *And all the men and boys around,*
> *I guess there was a million.*
> *Yankee Doodle went to town,*
> *Riding on a pony.*
> *Stuck a feather in his hat,*
> *And called it macaroni.*

Macaroni here refers, not to the Italian pasta, but to something that might be worn by a fop, a *macaroni*. Purists will therefore prefer the reading: "And called him macaroni."

The "Riding on a pony" version of "Yankee Doodle" is of such doubtful origin that Dr. O. G. Sonneck was asked to make a report on it for the Library of Congress in 1909; he was unable to establish the origin of either the words or the tune. The statement is made in Duyckink's *Cyclopaedia of American Literature*, and also by Mary Mapes Dodge, in her *Hans Brinker*, that the refrain was taken from an old Dutch harvest song:

> *Yankee didee doodle down*
> *Didee dudel lawnter;*
> *Yankee viver, voover, vown,*
> *Botermeik and Tawnter.*

On the other hand, Edward Everett Hale attributed it to Edward Bangs, who graduated from Harvard in 1777. Bangs was also supposed to have composed the music of the chorus, "Yankee Doodle keep it up . . . ."

I love four pence, a jolly, jolly, four pence,
   I love four pence as my life;
I spent two pence of it, I spent two pence of it,
   I took two pence home to my wife.

I love nothing, a jolly, jolly nothing,
   I love nothing as my life,
I spent nothing of it, I spent nothing of it,
   I took nothing home to my wife.**89**

« 114 »

John Cook had a little grey mare; he, haw, hum:
Her back stood up and her bones were bare; he, haw,
   hum.
John Cook was riding up Shuter's bank; he, haw,
   hum:
And there his nag did kick and prank; he, haw, hum.
John Cook was riding up Shuter's hill; he, haw,
   hum:
His nag fell down and she made her will; he, haw,
   hum.
The bridle and saddle were laid on the shelf; he,
   haw, hum:
If you want any more you may sing it yourself; he,
   haw, hum.**90**

The most popular theory, however, assigns the authorship to Dr. Richard Shuckburgh, an English surgeon and wit, who is said to have written the verse in 1775 to deride the fantastically uniformed Colonial troops. As for the tune, it probably originated in England. It occurs in *Two to One*, an opera by Samuel Arnold, performed in London in 1784.

85. There are several other nursery rhymes which seem to have stemmed from this verse.

> *There was a man and he had nought,*
>   *And robbers came to rob him;*
> *He crept up to the chimney top,*
>   *And then they thought they had him.*
> *But he got down on the other side,*
>   *And then they could not find him;*
> *He ran fourteen miles in fifteen days,*
>   *And never looked behind him.*

And the later, more sophisticated:

> *There was an old woman*
>   *And nothing she had,*
> *And so this old woman*
>   *Was said to be mad.*
> *She'd nothing to eat,*
>   *She'd nothing to wear,*
> *She'd nothing to lose,*
>   *She'd nothing to fear,*
> *She'd nothing to ask,*
>   *And nothing to give,*
> *And when she did die*
>   *She'd nothing to leave.*

86. At one time, a pin was a thing worth winning. Pins were once so valuable that when a woman married she was given "pin money." In France the people were taxed to provide the queen with pins for her boudoir. Pins as they are now known were first made in France about the fourteenth century. In 1775 the Continental Congress in the American colonies offered a prize for the first twenty-five dozen pins equal in quality to those imported from England. The one-time value of the pin is the most likely explanation of the old superstition:

> *See a pin and pick it up,*
>   *All the day you'll have good luck;*
> *See a pin and let it lay,*
>   *Bad luck you'll have all the day!*

87. It is rather surprising that this, one of the most popular of all "Mother Goose" rhymes, does not have a longer history. Try as scholars will, they cannot to this day find an earlier printed version of "Little Bo-peep" than that in *Gammer Gurton's Garland*, edition of 1810. There is a game, mentioned as early as 1364—or, more properly, an amusement—called "Bo-peep" and defined by Dr. Sam Johnson in 1755 as "The act of looking out and then drawing back as if frightened, or with the purpose to fright some other."

James O. Halliwell called "Bo-peep" a game in which two or more children hide from each other. "But," he added, "in even more ancient times the amusement appears to have been even simpler: a nurse would conceal the head of the infant for an instant and then remove the covering quickly, crying, 'Bo-peep!'" He gave this rhyme for the hide-and-seek version:

> *Bo-peep, Bo-peep:*
> *Now's the time for hide and seek.*

A ballad of the time of Queen Elizabeth I alludes to the earlier form of the amusement in these lines:

> *Halfe England ys nowght but shepe,*
> *In everye corner they playe boe-pepe . . . .*

88. Titled, in the *Garland*, "The Jolly Tester." A "tester" was a silver coin of the Tudor period, originally worth eighteen pence, later worth sixpence.

89. The above version omits the wonderful chorus, which first appeared in print in Frank Kidson's *Traditional Tunes* (1891):

> *A pint nor a quart won't grieve me,*
> *Nor false young girl deceive me;*
> *Here's to my wife, who will kiss me,*
> *When I come rolling home.*

Long a favorite with college men and servicemen, this song in World War II was usually sung with the additional refrain:

> *Rolling home, rolling home,*
> *Rolling home, rolling home,*
> *By the light of the silvery moo-oo-oon,*
> *Oh! happy is the day when the soldier*
> *[sailor] gets his pay*
> *And he goes rolling, rolling home.*

90. Titled, in the *Garland*, "The Last Will and Testament of the Grey Mare," and

« 115 »

My father he died, but I can't tell you how,
He left me six horses to drive in my plough:
    With my wing wang waddle oh,
    Jack sing saddle oh,
    Blowsey boys bubble oh,
    Under the broom.

I sold my six horses and I bought me a cow,
I'd fain made a fortune, but did not know how:
    With my wing wang waddle oh,
    Jack sing saddle oh,
    Blowsey boys bubble oh,
    Under the broom.

I sold my cow, and I bought me a calf;
I'd fain made a fortune, but lost the best half:
    With my wing wang waddle oh,
    Jack sing saddle oh,
    Blowsey boys bubble oh,
    Under the broom.

I sold my calf, and I bought me a cat;
A pretty thing she was, in my chimney corner sat:
    With my wing wang waddle oh,
    Jack sing saddle oh,
    Blowsey boys bubble oh,
    Under the broom.

I sold my cat, and I bought me a mouse;
He carried fire in his tail, and burnt down my house:
    With my wing wang waddle oh,
    Jack sing saddle oh,
    Blowsey boys bubble oh,
    Under the broom.[91]

« 116 »

Old Mother Widdle Waddle[92] jumpt out of bed,
And out at the casement she popt her head:
Crying the house is on fire, the grey goose is dead,
And the fox is come to the town, oh!

« 117 »

In love be I, fifth button high,
  On velvet runs my courting,
Sheer buckram twist, best broadcloth list,
  I leave for other sporting.
From needle, thread, my fingers fled,
  My heart is set a throbbing;
And no one by, I cross-legg'd sigh,
  For charming Betsey Bobbin.
    Betsey Bobbin, Betsey Bobbin,
    For charming Betsey Bobbin,

Her lips so sweet, are velveret,
  Her eyes do well their duty;
Her skin's to me, like dimity,
  The pattern gay of beauty.
Her hand squeez'd oft, is satin soft,
  And set my heart a throbbing,
Her cheeks, O dear, red cassimere,
  Lord! what a Betsey Bobbin!
    Betsey Bobbin, Betsey Bobbin,
    Lord! what a Betsey Bobbin!

thought by some to be a forefather of the American, "The Old Gray Mare (oh, she ain't what she used to be)."

"This excellent song, now rarely heard beyond the four walls of the nursery, appears to have been already old when Queen Elizabeth came to the throne," add the editors of *The Oxford Dictionary of Nursery Rhymes.*

91. Titled, in the *Garland*, "The Search After Fortune," this is known in America today as that popular folk ballad, "The Swapping Song." The refrain, at least, of this jolly old song may well go back to the time of Richard II.

92. "Old Mother Widdle Waddle" appears in similar verses as "Hipple-hopple," "Chittle Chattle," "Snipper Snapper," "Flipper Flapper" and "Wig Wag." But "Old Mother Widdle Waddle" was originally "Old Mother Slipper Slopper," for this "nursery rhyme" is really only one verse of a fine old song that begins:

A fox jumped up one winter's night,
And begged the moon to give him light,
For he'd many miles to trot that night
Before he reached his den O!

R. CALDECOTT

Her roguish smile can well beguile,
  Her every look bewitches;
Yet never stir, when tach'd to her,
  For Tim will wear the breeches;
I've face and mien, am spruce and keen,
  And though my heart keeps throbbing,
There's not, in fine, one man in nine,
  So fit for Betsey Bobbin,
    Betsey Bobbin, Betsey Bobbin,
    So fit for Betsey Bobbin.**93**

« 118 »

If I'd as much money as I could spend,
I never would cry old chairs to mend:
Old chairs to mend, old chairs to mend,
I never would cry old chairs to mend.

If I'd as much money as I could tell,
I never would cry old clothes to sell,
Old clothes to sell, old clothes to sell,
I never would cry old clothes to sell.**94**

« 119 »

There was a little boy and a little girl
  Liv'd in an alley:
Says the little boy to the little girl,
  Shall I, oh, shall I?

Says the little girl to the little boy,
  What shall we do?
Says the little boy to the little girl,
  I will kiss you.

« 120 »

There was an old man, and he liv'd in a wood;
  And his lazy son Jack would snooze till noon:
Nor followed his trade although it was good,
  With a bill**95** and a stump**96** for making brooms,
    green brooms;**97**
  With a bill**95** and a stump**96** for making of
    brooms,

Den O! Den O!
For he'd many miles to trot that night
Before he reached his den O!

93. Titled, in the *Garland,* "The Taylor's Courtship." In *Tik-Tok of Oz,* by the late Lyman Frank Baum, Betsy Bobbin is a little girl from Oklahoma, just about the same age as the Princess Dorothy. She was shipwrecked and, with her faithful friend Hank the Mule, had many adventures which finally ended happily in the Emerald City. Ozma invited Betsy to make her home in the Royal Palace, so that Dorothy might have a companion of her own age. Viz. *Who's Who in Oz,* by the late Jack Snow (Chicago: The Reilly & Lee Co., 1954).

94. Titled, in the *Garland,* "Old Chairs and Old Clothes." This nursery song derives from a street cry, perhaps first devised by a famous vendor named William Liston:

Get ready your money and come to me,
I sell a young lamb for one penny.
Young lambs to sell! Young lambs to sell!
I never would cry young lambs to sell,
If I'd as much money as I could tell,
I never would cry young lambs to sell.

The "Lambs" were toys.

R. CALDECOTT

95. A billhook—a curved cutting tool with which the twigs that made up the brooms were trimmed.

96. The chopping block on which the twigs were trimmed with the billhook.

97. Much might be said about "brooms, green brooms." These brooms were green because they were newly made from twigs gathered in the wood—usually, in England, from the tree called the broom, giving us the name. The early British housewife used for her cleaning a besom—which was simply a handful of twigs, often with the leaves attached. With the aid of this she did her dusting and sweeping, gathering a new besom from the wood whenever the old one wore out. Later came the broom-maker—in this case, "lazy Jack"— to provide her with a household device that attached the besom to a handle and therefore lasted somewhat longer than the simple fistful of twigs with the leaves still attached. A witch's broom, supposedly, carried her through the air to the Sabbath when properly anointed with ointments. But a broom, placed across a door or window, was also a protection against the witch: she had to count every straw or twig in the broom before she could enter the house.

98. Or Dandiprat—an old name for a small boy.

One morn in a passion, and sore with vexation,
  He swore he would fire the room,
If he did not get up and go to his work,
  And fall to the cutting of brooms, green brooms,
  And fall to the cutting of brooms.

Then Jack he arose and slip't on his clothes,
  And away to the woods very soon,
Where he made up his pack, and put it on his back,
  Crying, Maids, do you want any brooms? green
    brooms?
  Crying, Maids, do you want any brooms?

« 121 »

Little Jack Dandy-prat98 was my first suitor;
He had a dish and a spoon, and he'd some pewter;
He'd linen and woolen, and woolen and linen,
A little pig on a string cost him his first shilling.

Every pretty moral Tale,

Should o'er the infant Mind prevail.

TOMMY THUMB'S SONG BOOK FOR ALL LITTLE

MASTERS AND MISSES, C. 1788

CHAPTER VI

Tom Tit – The Piper's Son – and Some Christmas Boxes

Isaiah Thomas of Worcester, Mass.—he who had married a granddaughter of "Old Mother Goose"— has been called "The American John Newbery."

It was Thomas, we will remember, who had published Newbery's *Mother Goose's Melody* in America, and two years later he brought out *Tommy Thumb's Song Book for All Little Masters and Misses*, "To be sung to them by their Nurses, until they can sing themselves." It was supposedly written "By Nurse Lovechild, to which is added A Letter from a Lady in Nursing."[1]

Many of its "songs" had appeared previously in the second volume of Mary Cooper's *Tommy Thumb's Pretty Song Book* (c. 1744), and the suspicion arises that those which did not may have come from the *first* volume, no copy of which is known to exist today.

Thomas's little book opens with an "Artificial Memory for Infants Whereby They May Acquire the Knowledge of Animals, and Some of Their Sounds, before They Can Go or Speak."

The "Artificial Memory" is nothing more than a collection of crude woodcuts of common animals, each with its "Sound" printed beneath it. Thus an eighteenth-century infant could learn that the dog says "Bow, Wow, Wow" and the cat says "Mew, Mew, Mew." The "songs"—beginning with "Brow Bender" (Rhyme 575)—follow this "Artificial Memory."

A year or so later, c. 1790, in London, C. D. Piguenit published *The Tom Tit's Song Book,* "being a Collection of Old Songs, with which most Young Wits have been delighted."

"Tom, Tom, the Piper's Son" was introduced around 1795 in a chapbook published by J. Evans.

Then came the "Christmas Boxes"—forerunners of the Christmas annuals which, in later years, every British schoolboy hoped to find under his Christmas tree.[2]

A *Christmas Box* was published by A. Bland and Weller, with tunes by James Hook, in 1797, and a second and third volume a year later.

The Newest Christmas Box, published by Longman and Broderip, with tunes by Reginald Spofforth, provided them with competition.

And these books, too, all added something to the "Mother Goose" rhymes.

1. The only known copy is in the library of the American Antiquarian Society in Worcester. From it Frederick G. Melcher of New York produced a facsimile reproduction in 1946.

2. These "Christmas Annuals" were usually a year's issues of *The Boy's Own Paper,* or a similar publication, bound as a book between hard covers.

« 122 »
Fee, Faw, Fum,
I smell the Blood
Of an Earthly Man.

Let him be alive or dead,
Off Goes his Head.**3**

« 123 »

The Lion and the Unicorn
    Fighting for the Crown,**4**
The Lion beat the Unicorn,
    All about the Town.

Some gave them white bread,
    And some gave them brown;
Some gave them plum cake
    And drummed them out of town.**5**

« 124 »

There was a jolly miller once,
    Lived on the river Dee;
He worked and sang from morn till night,
    No lark more blithe than he.
And this the burden of his song
    Forever used to be,
I care for nobody, no! not I,
    If nobody cares for me.**6**

« 125 »

Peter White**7** will ne'er go right;
    Would you know the reason why?
He follows his nose wherever he goes,
    And that stands all awry.

3. An American version of the Giant's slogan in the famous old story of "Jack and the Bean-stalk." The lines, as used by Shakespeare in *King Lear* (Act III, Scene 4, lines 179-80) are:

> . . . *Fie, foh, and fum,*
> *I smell the blood of a British man.*

But "Englishman" is the correct ballad form: there were no Englishmen in Lear's time, and when Shakespeare was writing the play there was a movement to call all inhabitants of the island "British" in recognition of the union with Scotland. (James VI of Scotland had been proclaimed James I of England on October 24, 1604.)

In the folktales of all nations, giants are usually pictured as male, fond of eating human flesh ("I'll grind his bones to make my bread"), and capable of searching out their victims by the smell of their blood.

4. As noted in the previous rhyme, James VI of Scotland was crowned James I of England on October 24, 1604. Two unicorns supported the old Royal Arms of Scotland. One of them, with a lion on the other side, became a supporter of the new English shield. This rhyme is popularly supposed to tell the story of this union of Arms. Actually, it was stated in the earliest English natural history books that the lion and the unicorn were mortal enemies, and the legend is probably much more ancient than that. Some folklorists hold that the lion represents summer and the unicorn represents spring. The lion must always conquer the unicorn because summer invariably follows—overcomes—spring.

In *Through the Looking-Glass*, Lewis Carroll refers to "the words of the old song," and an old song this probably is, with many verses now lost to us. Martin Gardner in *The Annotated Alice* notes (p. 288) that "It was widely believed in England that Tenniel's lion and unicorn, in the illustration of this scene, were intended as caricatures of Gladstone and Disraeli respectively. There is no proof of this; but they do resemble Tenniel's *Punch* cartoons of the two political figures who often sparred with each other."

5. Only the first verse appears in *Tommy Thumb's Song Book*. The second verse first appeared in print in 1805 in *Songs for the Nursery*.

6. This old song was a favorite of Sir Walter Scott's. It became generally popular after it was incorporated into a highly successful opera, Bickerstaffe's *Love in a Village*, first performed at Covent Garden in 1762.

Actually, the miller of the nursery rhyme may have been a real person—the proprietor of the old Dee mill at Chester. It stood on a bridge where there had been a mill since the eleventh century, until it burned down in May 1895. The last descendant of the jolly miller died the year before the mill was destroyed.

7. *Mary* White in the earliest printed version of this rhyme, but *Peter* White in almost all later printings. This was originally a catch for three voices, published as early as 1701.

8. Later versions sometimes begin: "Tom Thumb, the piper's son . . . ." The chapbook in which "Tom, Tom, the Piper's Son" first appeared also contained "Tom, He Was a Piper's Son" (see next rhyme), and the two rhymes are often confused—as by Pigling Bland in Beatrix Potter's, who went to market singing:

Tom, Tom, the piper's son, stole a pig and away he ran!
But all the tune that he could play, was, "Over the hills and far away!"

"Tom" has evidently been a familiar name for a piper for a long, long time. Spenser in 1579 wrote:

Tom Piper makes us better melodie . . . .

9. Not a real pig, but a pastry pig. See "A Long Tail'd Pig, or a Short Tail'd Pig" (Rhyme 55) .

10. The refrain "Over the hills and far away" has been used by English poets and song makers for centuries. It appears in print as early as 1670 in the black-letter broadside, *The Wind hath blown my Plaid away, or, A Discourse betwixt a young Woman and the Elphin Knight*:

My plaid awa, my plaid awa,
And ore the hill and far awa,
And far awa to Norrowa,
My plaid shall not be blown awa . . . .

11. This song is apparently a version of an old metrical tale, "The Friar and the Boy," probably the nearest British approach to the German legend of the Pied Piper of Hamelin.

12. Later "Curly locks, Curly locks . . . " A Scotch version begins "Bonny lass, canny lass . . . ."

« 126 »

Tom, Tom, the piper's son.[8]
Stole a pig[9] and away did run;
The pig was eat, and Tom was beat,
Till he run crying down the street.

« 127 »

Tom, he was a piper's son,
He learnt to play when he was young,
And all the tune that he could play,
Was, "Over the hills and far away";[10]
Over the hills and a great way off,
The wind shall blow my top-knot off.
Tom with his pipe made such a noise,
That he pleased both the girls and boys,
And they stopped to hear him play,
"Over the hills and far away."

Tom with his pipe did play with such skill
That those who heard him could never keep still;
As soon as he played they began to dance,
Even pigs on their hind legs would prance.

As dolly was milking her cow one day,
Tom took his pipe and began for to play,
So Doll and the cow danced "The Cheshire Round,"
Till the pail was broken and the milk ran on the
    ground.

He met old Dame Trot with a basket of eggs,
He used his pipe and she used her legs;
She danced about till the eggs were all broke,
She began for to fret, but he laughed at the joke.

Tom saw a cross fellow was beating an ass,
Heavy laden with pots, pans, dishes, and glass;
He took out his pipe and he played them a tune,
And the poor donkey's load was lightened full
    soon.[11]

« 128 »

Pussy cat, pussy cat,[12] wilt thou be mine,
Thou shalt neither wash dishes nor feed the
    swine:[13]

13. Later, "Thou shalt not wash dishes nor yet feed the swine," which improves the meter by modern standards.

14. "Diddle, diddle, dumpling" was the street cry of the hot-dumpling sellers.

15. It might be surmised that John went to bed fuddled, and not from eating dumplings. This rhyme was a great favorite of Charles Lamb's.

16. Much—perhaps much too much—has been read into these lines. It has been said, for example (by James O. Halliwell), that "The King of Spain's daughter" was the mad Juana or Joanna of Castile, who visited the court of Henry VII in 1506. Katherine Elwes Thomas, on the other hand, held that Charles I was the proud possessor of the "little nut tree," and because of its "silver nutmeg" and "golden pear"—the silver and gold of England—he was "diligently sought in marriage by Spain for the youthful Infanta."

17. In later versions two additional lines are sometimes given:

I skipped over water, I danced over sea,
All the birds of the air couldn't catch me.

18. This rhyme was perhaps devised to teach children the names of the days of the week. Charles Lamb liked it so much he would send copies of it—in Latin—in letters to his friends. There are many versions, one of which goes:

Tom, Tom, of Islington,
Married a wife on Sunday,
Brought her home on Monday,
Bought a stick on Tuesday,
Beat her well on Wednesday,
Sick she was on Thursday,
Dead she was on Friday,
Glad was Tom on Saturday night
To bury his wife on Sunday.

A very similar song is that of "Solomon Grundy":

Solomon Grundy,
Born on a Monday,
Christened on Tuesday,
Married on Wednesday,
Took ill on Thursday,
Worse on Friday,
Died on Saturday,
Buried on Sunday,

This is the end
Of Solomon Grundy.

19. Perhaps the soldiers ordered by Parliament to escort Charles I to his execution, but more likely those sent to Charles II with the offer of the crown. The version included in the 1810 edition of *Gammer Gurton's Garland* —and titled there "The Parliament Soldiers" —reads:

High ding a ding, and ho ding a ding,
The parliament soldiers are gone to the king;
Some with new beavers, some with new bands,
The parliament soldiers are all to be hang'd.

20. This line is sometimes given as "And who do you think they be?" The last line is then given as: "Turn 'em out, knaves all three!" Given here is the "Three Men in a Tub" rhyme as we know it best today, but the earliest printed version gives a rather different picture of the three tradesmen:

Hey! rub-a-dub, ho! rub-a-dub, three maids
*   in a tub,*
And who do you think were there?
The butcher, the baker, the candlestick-
*   maker,*
And all of them gone to the fair.

"Apparently," say the editors of *The Oxford Dictionary of Nursery Rhymes,* "they have been found in a place where no respectable townfolk should be, watching a dubious sideshow at the local fair."

But sit on a cushion and sew a silk seam,
And eat fine strawberries, sugar and cream.

« 129 »

Diddle, diddle, dumpling,[14] my son John,
Went to bed with his trousers on;
One shoe off, and one shoe on,
Diddle, diddle, dumpling, my son John.[15]

« 130 »

I had a little nut tree,
    Nothing would it bear
But a silver nutmeg
    And a golden pear;
The King of Spain's daughter[16]
    Came to visit me,
And all for the sake
    Of my little nut tree.[17]

« 131 »

I married a wife on Sunday,
She began to scold on Monday,
Bad was she on Tuesday,
Middling was she on Wednesday,
Worse she was on Thursday,
Dead was she on Friday;
Glad was I on Saturday night,
To bury my wife on Sunday.[18]

« 132 »

High ding a ding, I heard a bird sing,
The parliament soldiers are gone to the king![19]
Some they did laugh, and some they did cry,
To see the parliament soldiers go by.

« 133 »

Rub-a-dub-dub,
Three men in a tub,
And how do you think they got there?[20]
    The butcher, the baker,
    The candlestick-maker,
    They all jumped out of a rotten potato,
'Twas enough to make a man stare.

Sing, sing, what shall I sing?
The cat's run away with the pudding string!

SONGS FOR THE NURSERY, 1805

CHAPTER VII

Old Mother Hubbard and Other "Songs for the Nursery"

Once upon a time—in the year 1804, actually—there lived a vivacious lady named Sarah Catherine Martin, the daughter of Sir Henry Martin, and an early love of Prince William Henry, afterwards William IV.

The story goes that when she was thirty-six (she was born in 1768 and died in 1826), she was visiting her future brother-in-law, John Pollexfen Bastard, M.P., of Kitley, Devon. One day she was chattering away in her usual fashion while her host was trying to write a letter. Annoyed, he told her to run away and write something herself—"one of your stupid little rhymes," was the way he put it.

Run away and write she did, and the result was "Old Mother Hubbard."[1]

The Comic Adventures of Old Mother Hubbard and Her Dog was first published in the following year—on June 1, 1805—by John Harris, "Suceser to E.[2] Newbery, Corner of St. Pauls Church Yard."

"The success of the publication was instantaneous," says *The Oxford Dictionary of Nursery*

Rhymes. "Harris said that 'upwards of ten thousand copies' were distributed in a few months. He reprinted it the following year, and also brought out a continuation and a sequel. . . . Pirated editions by the chapbook publishers were to be found everywhere, and it rapidly established itself as one of their stock productions. . . . There has probably been a new edition of Mother Hubbard published somewhere every year since 1805."

In that same year, 1805, a little book, handsomely illustrated with handcolored plates, was published by Benjamin Tabart and Company. This was *Songs for the Nursery Collected from the Works of the Most Renowned Poets.*

Songs for the Nursery is an important book. It brought readers the first printed versions of many of the rhymes that are among the best-known today: "Little Miss Muffet," "Bobby Shafto," and "One, Two, Buckle My Shoe," for example. It was to form a cornerstone for the American *Mother Goose's Quarto: or Melodies Complete,* published in Boston

by Munroe and Francis c. 1825. And James O. Halliwell was to use it extensively in putting together his great collection of *The Nursery Rhymes of England,* first published in 1842.

The original *Songs for the Nursery* was reissued in 1818 by William Darton, and it later went into many other editions "with copious additions."

"Considerable pains have been taken to make this collection as complete as possible," one of the later editors of *Songs for the Nursery* wrote, "and it is hoped that the addition of a few choice compositions, similar in character of modern date, will not be unacceptable."

Unfortunately, some of these "copious additions" of "choice compositions" are far from acceptable by modern standards. Some are not properly "Mother Goose" or "nursery rhymes" at all, but selections from the works of Spenser, Southey, Wordsworth, and other poets. Others, by anonymous hacks, are ill-written, tediously repetitive, and overly sentimental. Since none of these latter rhymes ever achieved any popularity whatsoever, they failed to survive—a remarkable tribute to the good taste of nineteenth-century readers. We have consequently omitted them here.

« 134 »

Old Mother Hubbard
Went to the cupboard,
To fetch her poor dog a bone;
But when she came there
The cupboard was bare
And so the poor dog had none.

She went to the baker's
To buy him some bread;
But when she came back
The poor dog was dead.

She went to the undertaker's
To buy him a coffin;
But when she came back
The poor dog was laughing.**3**

1. "Old Mother Hubbard," like Tommy Thumb, Nancy Cock, Nurse Lovechild and the rest, was a stock nursery-tale character, but there seems to be good reason to believe that Miss Martin did compose the verses as we know them today, with a little inspiration from nursery rhymes then in existence.

2. Elizabeth.

3. An archaic bit of rhyming; *loffe* is an old English word used by Shakespeare.

4. Many parodies of "Old Mother Hubbard" exist. A recent one, contributed to this book by the editors' son, goes:

> *Old Mother Hubbard*
> *Went to the cupboard,*
> *To fetch her poor daughter a dress,*
> *But when she got there,*
> *The cupboard was bare,*
> *And so was her daughter, I guess.*

5. The American "Jemmy Jed" would seem to be an offshoot of the above rhyme:

> *Jemmy Jed went into a shed,*
> *And made of a ted of straw his bed;*
> *An owl came out, and flew about*
> *And Jemmy up stakes and fled:*
> *Wasn't Jemmy Jed a staring fool,*
> *Born in the woods to be scar'd by an owl?*

6. "Little King Bobbin" and "Little King Pippin" in other versions. How King Pippin (Pepin) became a nursery-rhyme character is not quite clear. That he was, however—and before 1786—is evidenced by the fact that Elizabeth Newbery in that year titled a nursery tale *The History of Little King Pippin.*

W. CRANE

She took a clean dish
  To get him some tripe;
But when she came back
  He was smoking a pipe.

She went to the alehouse
  To get him some beer;
But when she came back
The dog sat in a chair.

She went to the tavern
  For white wine and red;
But when she came back
  The dog stood on his head.

She went to the fruiterer's
  To buy him some fruit;
But when she came back
  He was playing the flute.

She went to the tailor's
  To buy him a coat;
But when she came back
  He was riding a goat.

She went to the hatter's
  To buy him a hat;
But when she came back
  He was feeding the cat.

She went to the barber's
  To buy him a wig;
But when she came back
  He was dancing a jig.

She went to the cobbler's
  To buy him some shoes;
But when she came back
  He was reading the news.

She went to the seamstress
  To buy him some linen;
But when she came back
  The dog was a-spinning.

She went to the hosier's
  To buy him some hose;

But when she came back
   He was dressed in his clothes.

The dame made a curtsey,
   The dog made a bow;
The dame said, Your servant,
   The dog said, Bow-wow.[4]

« 135 »

There was a little boy went into a barn,
   And lay down on some hay;
An owl flew out and flew about,
   And the little boy ran away.[5]

« 136 »

Little King Boggen[6] he built a fine hall,
Pie-crust, and pastry-crust, that was the wall;
The windows were made of black puddings and
   white,

« 137 »

Lavender blue and rosemary green,
When I am king you shall be queen;
Call up my maids at four o'clock,
Some to the wheel and some to the rock;
Some to make hay and some to shear corn,
And you and I will keep the bed warm.[7]

W. CRANE

113

7. This *Songs for the Nursery* version of "Lavender Blue" is an abbreviated form of an old ballad titled "Diddle Diddle, Or, The Kind Country Lovers," first printed sometime between 1672 and 1685. In 1948 a dance version, "Lavender Blue," with words by Larry Morey and music by Eliot Daniel, was introduced in Walt Disney's motion picture, *So Dear To My Heart*. Recorded for Columbia by Dinah Shore, it swept both America and Britain.

8. It seems that almost anything can turn up in a book of "nursery" rhymes. This is one of the "Mirth" songs first printed in *Deuteromelia* in 1609. In that same year Beaumont and Fletcher introduced it into *The Knight of the Burning Pestle*, where it was sung by a character named Merrythought. A very humorous effect was said to have been achieved by drawing out the first syllable of *ginger*—gin-in-in-in-ger. The implication is of course that *liquor* had nothing whatever to do with giving the singer his "jolly red nose"—it was all the fault of the spices used in concocting the punch.

9. This "nursery rhyme" is the first of fifteen stanzas of an old ballad called "The Wiltshire Wedding," first published c. 1680. The wedding was between "Daniel Do-well" and "Doll the Dairy-Maid"—with the consent of her old "Father Leather-Coat" and her "dear and tender Mother Plodwell."

10. To Katherine Elwes Thomas, "Little Miss Muffet" was Mary Queen of Scots, and the "big spider" was John Knox. "Denouncing the frivolous 'Little Miss Muffet' from the pulpit of St. Giles until the ecclesiastical atmosphere was blue and sulphurous, the 'big spider' with angry brow and darkling mien strode down the Cannongate. Turning sharply to the right, he quickened his pace to enter Holyrood and, sitting beside her, demanded her recantation . . . ."

Another persistent tradition is that Little Miss Muffet was a Patience Muffet (or Moffett or Moufet)—mostly, it seems, because her father, Dr. Thomas Muffet, who died in 1604, was an entomologist who vastly admired spiders, and who wrote—in verse—a volume called *The Silkewormes and their flies*.

« 138 »

Nose, nose, jolly red nose,
And what gave thee that jolly red nose?
Nutmeg and ginger, cinnamon and cloves,
That's what gave me this jolly red nose.**8**

« 139 »

As I was going to sell my eggs,
I met a man with bandy legs,
Bandy legs and crooked toes,
I tript up his heels, and he fell on his nose.

« 140 »

One misty, moisty morning,
When cloudy was the weather,
There I met an old man
Clothed all in leather;
Clothed all in leather,
With cap under his chin.
How do you do, and how do you do,
And how do you do again?**9**

« 141 »

Little Miss Muffet**10**
Sat on a tuffet,**11**
Eating her curds and whey;
There came a big spider,
Who sat down beside her
And frightened Miss Muffet away.**12**

« 142 »

The man in the wilderness asked me,
How many strawberries grew in the sea?
I answered him, as I thought good,
As many as red herrings grew in the wood.**13**

« 143 »

Willy boy, Willy boy, where are you going?
I will go with you, if that I may.
I'm going to the meadow to see them a-mowing,
I'm going to help them make hay.

« 144 »

Over the water and over the lea,
   And over the water to Charley.[14]
Charley loves good ale and wine,
   And Charley loves good brandy,[15]
And Charley loves a pretty girl
   As sweet as sugar candy.[16]

Over the water and over the lea,
   And over the water to Charley.
I'll have none of your nasty beef,
   Nor I'll have none of your barley;
But I'll have some of your very best flour
   To make a white cake for my Charley.[17]

« 145 »

Hey ding a ding, what shall I sing?
How many holes in a skimmer?
Four-and-twenty—my stomach is empty;
Pray, mamma, give me some dinner.[18]

« 146 »

How many miles to Babylon?[19]
Three score miles and ten.
Can I get there by candle-light?
Yes, and back again.
If your heels are nimble and light,
You can get there by candle-light.[20]

« 147 »

What's the news of the day,
   Good neighbour, I pray?
They say the balloon
   Is gone up to the moon![21]

« 148 »

The girl in the lane, that couldn't speak plain,
   Cried, Gobble, gobble, gobble:
The man on the hill, that couldn't stand still,
   Went hobble, hobble, hobble.

11. No such word. Many illustrators show Miss Muffet seated on a three-legged stool, but as many others prefer to picture her perched on a grassy hillock.

James O. Halliwell gave as the opening lines of this rhyme:

Little Mary Ester
Sat on a tester . . . .

and Boyd Smith gave as an "older version"— but did not name his source—

Little Miss Mopsey,
Sat in the shopsey . . . .

12. The editors of *The Oxford Dictionary of Nursery Rhymes* noted, in 1951, that "An analysis of the children's books published in 1945-6 showed that of all the nursery rhymes, 'Miss Muffet' figures the most frequently, perhaps because the subject lends itself to illustration. Millais painted the picture 'Little Miss Muffet' in 1884."

13. James O. Halliwell wrote in 1843 that he had traced this rhyme to a manuscript of the seventeenth century.

14. This line sometimes appears as "And over the water to Charley and me."

15. According to Andrew Lang, this rhyme is a parody of a Jacobite ditty of 1748. "*Over the water* refers genially to that love of ale and wine which Prince Charles displayed as early as he showed military courage, at the age of fourteen, when he distinguished himself at the siege of Gaeta."

16. Only the third to sixth lines are given in *Songs for the Nursery*. A variant, given in *The Only True Mother Goose Melodies*, c. 1843, goes:

Charley loves to kiss the girls,
When they are clean and handy.

17. Burns used a refrain similar to "Over the water and over the lea" in his poem, "Come Boat Me O'er."

18. We'll recall that Little Tom Tucker had to sing for his supper—that is, he had to do something to earn it. But the traveling entertainers who for many years performed at English taverns sang for their suppers quite literally. Having rendered a selection, the performer would appeal to his audience in a few lines of doggerel that added up to, "What shall I sing next?" This and many other "nursery rhymes" reflect such requests:

Sing, sing, what shall I sing?
The cat's run away with the pudding string!
Do, do, what shall I do?
The cat has bitten it quite in two!

19. Some writers have suggested that "Babylon" is here a corruption of "Babyland."

20. Stevenson and Kipling both refer to this rhyme, and Lewis Carroll mentions it in *Sylvie and Bruno.*

James O. Halliwell, in 1849, gave "How Many Miles to Babylon?" as a rhyme for "Barley-bridge," a game much like "London Bridge."

21. There can be little question that this rhyme reflects the public's interest in the ballooning experiments being made in the late eighteenth century. The brothers Joseph and Etienne Montgolfier got the first balloon more than a half mile into the air from the market place at Annonay, France, on June 5, 1783. In August of the following year, the *Charlière* (levitated by hydrogen produced by Professor J. A. C. Charles, who gave the balloon its name) went up from the Champ de Mars in Paris and came down some fifteen miles away. Joseph Montgolfier sent a sheep, a rooster, and a duck aloft in September 1783 in a forerunner of Russian and U.S. space experiments; the animals came down unharmed.

On November 21, 1783, young Jean Francois Pilatre de Rozier and his friend the Marquis d'Arlandes made an exciting 23-minute trip across Paris in the gaily colored *Montgolfière*—the first human flight in history. In December of the same year, Professor Charles stayed in the air for one and three-quarter hours, and covered 27 miles. Blanchard introduced ballooning to England, and he and an American, Dr. John Jeffries, succeeded in making the first aerial crossing of the English Channel on January 7, 1785.

22. In later, possibly "improved" versions of this rhyme, this line reads: "So pretty and so fair."

23. The queen in this rhyme is widely sup-

« 149 »

Pussy sits beside the fire,
    How can she be fair?[22]
In comes the little Dog,
    Pussy, are you there?
So, so, Mistress Pussy,
    Pray how do you do?
Thank you, thank you, little dog,
    I'm very well just now.

« 150 »

Pussy cat, pussy cat, where have you been?
I've been to London to look at the queen.
Pussy cat, pussy cat, what did you there?
I frightened a little mouse under her chair.[23]

« 151 »

I had a little hen,[24] the prettiest ever seen,
She washed me the dishes and kept the house clean;
She went to the mill to fetch me some flour,
She brought it home in less than an hour,
She baked my bread, she brewed my ale,
She sat by the fire and told many a fine tale.

« 152 »

Dingty diddledy,
My mammy's maid,
She stole oranges,
I am afraid;
Some in her pocket,
Some in her sleeve,
She stole oranges,
I do believe.

« 153 »

Bobby Shafto's[25] gone to sea,
Silver buckles on his knee;
He'll come back and marry me,
Bonny Bobby Shafto!

Bobby Shafto's fat and fair,
Combing down his yellow hair;

He's my love forevermore,
Bonny Bobby Shafto!

Bobby Shafto's looking out,
All his ribbons flew about,
All the ladies gave a shout,
Hey for Bobby Shafto![26]

« 154 »

Pretty John Watts,
We are troubled with rats,
Will you drive them out of the house?
We have mice too in plenty,
That feast in the pantry;
But let them stay,
And nibble away,
What harm is a little brown mouse?

« 155 »

A cow and a calf,
An ox and a half,
Forty good shillings and three;
Is that not enough tocher[27]
For a shoemaker's daughter,
A bonny lass with a black e'e?[28]

« 156 »

There was a piper had a cow,
And he had nought to give her.
He pulled out his pipes and played her a tune,
And bade the cow consider.

The cow considered very well
And gave the piper a penny,
And bade him play the other tune,
"Corn rigs are bonny."[29]

« 157 »

I had a little hobby horse
And it was dapple gray,
Its head was made of pea-straw,
Its tail was made of hay.

posed to have been Elizabeth I, and the tale of the pussy cat and the mouse to relate to an actual incident that took place during her reign. As with so many of the older rhymes, there are many variations, among them:

Little girl, little girl, where have you been?
Gathering roses to take to the queen.
Little girl, little girl, what gave she you?
She gave me a diamond as big as my shoe.
Pussycat, pussycat, where have you been?
I've been to see grandmother over the green!
What did she give you? Milk in a can.
What did you say for it? Thank you, Grandam!

24. "Hen" would here seem to be used in its "humorous" seventeenth- and eighteenth-century sense of "woman" or "dear creature." In Mother Goose's Quarto, c. 1825, the rhyme begins: "I had a little doll . . . ," and in Traditional Nursery Songs, 1843, it begins: "I had a little wife . . . ."

25. Bobby Shafto is known in other versions as "Willy Foster," "Bobby Shaft," and "Billy Button." The original Bobby Shafto is said to have lived at Hollybrook, County Wicklow, and died in 1737. (Sir Walter Scott, in Redgauntlet, called this rhyme "an old Northumbrian ditty.")

26. The third verse does not appear in Songs for the Nursery. It was composed by the supporters of another Bobby Shafto—Robert Shafto of Whitworth, a candidate for Parliament in the election of 1761. He was said to have been exceedingly handsome.

27. "Tocher"—an old Scottish word meaning the dowry of a bride.

28. This is a nursery-rhyme version of a verse from "Jumpin' John," another of the old songs collected and dressed up by Burns for The Scot's Musical Museum.

29. Actually a very popular song in the late seventeenth century. Burns refers to it, and quotes the chorus:

O corn rigs and rye rigs,
O corn rigs is bonnie.

30. A first cousin of this rhyme, if not a variant of it, is:

I had a little pony,
  His name was Dapple Gray;
I lent him to a lady
  To ride a mile away.
She whipped him, she lashed him,
  She rode him through the mire
I would not lend my pony now,
  For all the lady's hire.

This "little pony" version first appeared in print in a volume called *Poetical Alphabet*, published by Henry Mozley and Sons, c. 1825. Still another version, and one that may have inspired both of the above verses, was found by James O. Halliwell in a manuscript of about 1630:

  I had a little bonny nagg
    His name was Dapple Gray;
  And he would bring me to an ale-house
    A mile out of my way.

31. This is a nursery rhyme version of the popular old song that begins:

  O dear, what can the matter be?
  Dear, dear, what can the matter be?
  O dear, what can the matter be?
  Johnny's so long at the fair.

Whether the nursery rhyme grew out of the song—or the song grew out of the nursery rhyme, as did "Lavender Blue"—is uncertain today, but it is likely that the song came first. In any case, there are many "Mother Goose" versions of the song, one being:

  Dear, dear, what can the matter be?
  Three old women got up in an apple tree,
  One stayed up, and one came down,
  And the third got stung by a bumblebee!

The song has been much parodied, and there is a raucous college version that goes, in part:

  Oh, dear, what can the matter be?
  Three old maids went into the lavat'ry,
  Didn't come out from Monday to Saturd'y,
  What can the matter be?

32. There are many versions of the central rhyme, including:

    Pussy come down
    Or I'll crack your crown . . . .
    Give her a plum,
    And down she'll come . . . .
    Send a hack
    To fetch her back . . . .

I sold him to an old woman
For a copper groat,
And I'll not sing my song again
Without a new coat.**30**

« 158 »

Johnny shall have a new bonnet,
  And Johnny shall go to the fair,
And Johnny shall have a fair ribbon
  To tie up his bonny brown hair.
And why may not I love Johnny?
  And why may not Johnny love me?
And why may not I love Johnny
  As well as another body?

And here's a leg for a stocking,
  And here's a leg for a shoe,
And he has a kiss for his daddy,
  And two for his mammy, I trow.

And why may not I love Johnny?
  And why may not Johnny love me?
And why may not I love Johnny
  As well as another body?**31**

« 159 »

Diddlety, diddlety, dumpty,
  The cat ran up the plum tree;
    Half a crown
      To fetch her down,**32**
Diddlety, diddlety, dumpty.

« 160 »

Mary had a pretty bird,
  Feathers bright and yellow,
Slender legs, upon my word,
  He was a pretty fellow.

The sweetest notes he always sung,
  Which much delighted Mary;
And near the cage she'd ever sit,
  To hear her own canary.**33**

« 161 »

On Saturday night shall be my care
To powder my locks and curl my hair;
On Sunday morning my love will come in,
When he will marry me with a gold ring.**34**

33. Later "Mother Goose" books usually give only the first verse, and sometimes change the second line to read: "Feathers red and yellow" —with an illustration showing a *parrot*!

Katherine Elwes Thomas gives an elaborate "explanation" of this rhyme in which "Mary" is Mary Queen of Scots and the "pretty bird" her Italian secretary, David Rizzio, who sang impassioned songs to her to the accompaniment of mandolin and guitar. Rizzio came to a sad end: Darnley and Lord Ruthven slit his throat, stabbed him forty times, and buried him at the foot of the stairway leading from the queen's private apartments.

34. "These lines," say the editors of *The Oxford Dictionary of Nursery Rhymes*, "have evidently become displaced from a folk-song."

Diddlty, diddlty, dumpty,
The cat ran up the plum tree,
Give her a plum, and down she'll come,
Diddlty, diddlty. dumpty

K. GREENAWAY

119

She could sing nothing but, Fiddle cum fee,
The mouse has married the humble-bee. . . .
NURSERY SONGS and LONDON JINGLES, C. 1840

CHAPTER VIII

More Catches and Ditties and Jingles and Chimes

Between 1805 and 1842, at least a score of books appeared which made one or more important contributions to the "Mother Goose" rhymes.

It was probably in 1805 that John Harris followed the success of "Old Mother Hubbard" with his *Original Ditties for the Nursery*. Probably most, if not all, of Harris's ditties *were* original, but their authors are unknown to us today.

One year later, in 1806, appeared *Rhymes for the Nursery*. Here the authors are known. *Rhymes for the Nursery* is chiefly the work of Jane Taylor (1783-1824) in collaboration with her sister Ann. The volume, published by Darton and Harvey, met with great success—so much so that it went into a 27th edition in 1835. It contains one of the best-known poems in the English language—"Twinkle, Twinkle, Little Star."

To this period also belongs the rhyme that E. V. Lucas has called "the best-known four-line verses in the English language"—"Mary Had a Little Lamb." They were written by Mrs. Sara Josepha Hale (1788-1879) of Boston, early in the year 1830, and were first published, over her initials, in a periodical she edited called *Juvenile Miscellany,* issue of September-October 1830. Later in the year they appeared in a volume of Mrs. Hale's work titled *Poems for Our Children,* but their great popularity can probably be attributed to their anonymous appearance, in 1857, in McGuffey's *Second Reader,* which was for fifty years a standard textbook in America's public schools.

The authorship of the verses has been attributed to others, notably to Mary Sawyer Tyler of Sudbury, Massachusetts, who believed herself to have been the original "Mary." According to *The Oxford Dictionary of Nursery Rhymes,* "two hundred documents" were collected to prove her claim, but it was refuted by Mrs. Hale in a letter written shortly before her death, and also by her son, Horatio Hale, in the Boston *Transcript,* April 10, 1889.

Mrs. Hale stated that the incident related in "Mary Had a Little Lamb" was "partly true," but

R. CALDECOTT

she herself pointed out that a lamb following a child to school was something that had probably happened more than once.

« 162 »

A farmer went trotting upon his grey mare,
　Bumpety, bumpety, bump!
With his daughter behind him so rosy and fair,
　Lumpety, lumpety, lump!

A raven cried, Croak! and they all tumbled down,
　Bumpety, bumpety, bump!
The mare broke her knees and the farmer his crown,
Lumpety, lumpety, lump!

This mischievous raven flew laughing away,
　Bumpety, bumpety, bump!
And vowed he would serve them the same the next
　day,
　Lumpety, lumpety, lump![1]

1. This rhyme achieved its greatest popularity after 1884, when it appeared with illustrations by Randolph Caldecott.

R. CALDECOTT

« 163 »

In a cottage in Fife
Lived a man and his wife,
Who, believe me, were comical folk;
For, to people's surprise,
They both saw with their eyes,
And their tongues moved whenever they spoke!
When quite fast asleep,
I've been told that to keep
Their eyes open they could not contrive;
They walked on their feet,
And 'twas thought what they eat
Helped, with drinking, to keep them alive!
What's amazing to tell!
I have heard that their smell
Chiefly lay in a thing call'd their nose!
And though strange are such tales,
On their fingers they'd nails,
As well as on each of their toes!**2**

R. CALDECOTT

« 164 »

Old Mother Shuttle**3**
Lived in a coal-scuttle
Along with her dog and her cat;
What they ate I can't tell,
But 'tis known very well
That not one of the party was fat.

Old Mother Shuttle
Scoured out her coal-scuttle,
And washed both her dog and her cat;
The cat scratched her nose,
So they came to hard blows,
And who was the gainer by that?

« 165 »

In an oak there liv'd an owl,
Frisky, whisky, wheedle!
She thought herself a clever fowl,
Fiddle, faddle, feedle!

Her face alone her wisdom shew,
Frisky, whisky, wheedle!

For all she said was. Whit to whoo!
  Fiddle, faddle, feedle!

Her silly note a gunner heard,
  Frisky, whisky, wheedle!
Says he, I'll shoot you, stupid bird!
  Fiddle, faddle, feedle!

Now if he had not heard her hoot, .
  Frisky, whisky, wheedle!
He had not found her out to shoot,
  Fiddle, faddle, feedle!

« 166 »

Little Jenny Flinders[4]
Sat among the cinders,
Warming her pretty little toes;
Her mother came and caught her,
And whipped her little daughter
For dirtying her clothes.[5]

« 167 »

Tweedledum and Tweedledee
  Agreed to fight a battle,
For Tweedledum said Tweedledee
  Had spoiled his nice new rattle.
Just then flew by a monstrous crow,
  As black as a tar-barrel,
Which frightened both the heroes so,
  They quite forgot their quarrel.[6]

« 168 »

Twinkle, twinkle, little star,
How I wonder what you are!
Up above the world so high,
Like a diamond in the sky.

When the blazing sun is gone,
When he nothing shines upon,
Then you show your little light,
Twinkle, twinkle, all the night.
When the traveller in the dark,
Thanks you for your tiny spark,

2. There is no evidence that Lewis Carroll knew these verses, but we think that if he had, he might have relished them.

3. "Old Mother Shuttle" is better known in America as "Old Mistress McShuttle" or "M'Shuttle."

4. "Little Polly Flinders" in most later versions.

5. Later, "For spoiling her nice new clothes."
It has been suggested, not very convincingly, that this jingle is a masked telling of the story of Amy Robsart, the wife of Lord Robert Dudley, Earl of Leicester, who was found dead at the foot of the staircase in Cumnor Palace in the year 1560. Both Queen Elizabeth I and the Earl of Leicester have been accused of the crime: Leicester had represented himself to the Queen as a widower, free to sue for her royal hand.

6. "In the 1720's," as Martin Gardner notes in *The Annotated Alice*, "there was a bitter rivalry between George Frederick Handel, the German-English composer, and Giovanni Battista Bononcini, an Italian composer. John Byrom, an eighteenth-century hymn writer and teacher of shorthand, described the controversy as follows:

> *"Some say, compared to Bononcini*
> *That Mynheer Handel's but a ninny;*
> *Others aver that he to Handel*
> *Is scarcely fit to hold a candle;*
> *Strange all this difference should be*
> *Twixt tweedle-dum and tweedle-dee.*

"No one knows whether the nursery rhyme about the Tweedle brothers originally had reference to this famous musical battle, or whether it was an older rhyme from which Byrom borrowed in the last line of his doggerel...."
The final couplet, however, has also been attributed to both Swift and Pope. Alice, in *Through the Looking-Glass*, recalled the words of this song when she met the twins marked "DUM" and "DEE."

R. CALDECOTT

He could not see which way to go,
If you did not twinkle so.

In the dark blue sky you keep,
And often through my curtains peep,
For you never shut your eye,
'Till the sun is in the sky.

As your bright and tiny spark,
Lights the traveller in the dark,—
Though I know not what you are,
Twinkle, twinkle, little star.**7**

« 169 »

Blow, wind, blow! and go, mill, go!
That the miller may grind his corn;
   That the baker may take it,
   And into bread make it,
And send us some hot in the morn.

« 170 »

Little General Monk**8**
Sat upon a trunk,
Eating a crust of bread;
There fell a hot coal
And burnt in his clothes a hole,
Now little General Monk is dead.
Keep always from the fire:
If it catch your attire,
You, too, like Monk, will be dead.**9**

7. "The Star" has often been parodied. The best-known example is the Mad Hatter's

> *Twinkle, twinkle, little bat!*
> *How I wonder what you're at!*
> *Up above the world you fly,*
> *Like a tea-tray in the sky.*

Writes Martin Gardner in *The Annotated Alice*: "Carroll's burlesque may contain what professional comics call an 'inside joke.' Bartholomew Price, a distinguished professor of mathematics at Oxford and a good friend of Carroll's, was known among his students by the nickname 'The Bat.' His lectures no doubt had a way of soaring high above the heads of his listeners."

8. This verse is thought to be "a contemporary squib on the great Cromwellian soldier who died in 1669." The reference is to George Monck, Duke of Albemarle, born in 1608.

9. The last four lines were added by James O. Halliwell in 1842.

« 171 »

Peter, Peter, pumpkin eater,[10]
Had a wife and couldn't keep her;
He put her in a pumpkin shell
And there he kept her very well.

Peter, Peter, pumpkin eater,
Had another, and didn't love her;
Peter learned to read and spell,
And then he loved her very well.

« 172 »

A carrion crow sat on an oak,
Watching a tailor shape his cloak;
Wife, cried he, bring me my bow,
That I may shoot yon carrion crow.

The tailor shot and missed his mark,
And shot his own sow through the heart;
Wife, bring brandy in a spoon,
For our poor sow is in a swoon.[11]

« 173 »

Cheese and bread for gentlemen,[12]
Hay and corn for horses,
A cup of ale for good old wives,
And kisses for young lasses.

« 174 »

Mary had a little lamb,[13]
    Its fleece was white as snow;
And everywhere that Mary went
    The lamb was sure to go.

It followed her to school one day,
    That was against the rule;
It made the children laugh and play,
    To see a lamb in school.

And so the teacher turned it out,
    But still it lingered near,
And waited patiently about
    Till Mary did appear.

10. The pumpkin is perhaps the vegetable most beloved by the creators of juvenile literature. We all remember the pumpkin coach in "Cinderella." Jack Pumpkinhead is one of the outstanding citizens of the wonderful land of Oz. And Charles Schulz, in his comic-strip "Peanuts," has recently introduced Linus's "The Great Pumpkin"—a creation that many agree should take its place beside Santa Claus and the Easter Bunny.

There is much of mystery in this, but it would seem that some of the affection for the pumpkin must have come from the custom of making a jack-o'-lantern that would frighten away the evil creatures that stalked the darkness on Hallowe'en. The jack-o'-lantern is supposed to be Irish in origin, but no pumpkins grow on the Old Sod. However, another gourd-like vegetable may have been used there.

11. In its earliest form, this old song goes back to the time of Charles I. As early as 1796 it was published as a ballad with the refrain:

With a heigh ho! the carrion crow!
Sing tol de rol, de riddle row!

The crow, like the fox, is almost always pictured as a rogue in folk tales and juvenile literature. He appears at his best as the Big Black Crow in Albert Bigelow Paine's still read and widely enjoyed *Hollow Tree* and *Deep Woods* books.

12. Sometimes "Wine and cakes for gentlemen . . . ." This is thought to be a fragment of a harvest song.

13. The modern teen-ager follows this line with: "And was the doctor ever surprised!"

14. For his *American Mother Goose,* 1938, Ray Wood collected:

> Mary had a little lamb,
>   Its fleece was white as cotton,
> And everywhere that Mary went,
>   The lamb it went a-trottin'.

15. The editors of *The Oxford Dictionary of Nursery Rhymes* suggest that this "possibly refers to the famous freebooter of the Border country, John Armstrong, who was captured by James V and hanged in 1528." The story of Johnny, or Johnie, Armstrong is told in full in a ballad that begins:

> There dwelt a man in faire Westmerland,
>   Johnie Armstrong men did call him,
> He had neither lands nor rent coming in,
>   Yet he kept eight score men in his hall . . .

16. This seventeenth-century expression—which may have been inspired by the song of "The Carrion Crow" (Rhyme 172)—is still in use (Winston Churchill, November 17, 1949). An expanded version of the rhyme that appears in later "Mother Goose" books goes:

> Robin-a-bobbin
> He bent his bow,
> Shot at a pigeon
> And killed a crow;
> Shot at another
> And killed his own brother,
> Did Robin-a-bobbin
> Who bent his bow.

There is also:

> Little Dick he was so quick
> He tumbled over the timber;
> He bent his bow to shoot a crow
> And shot a cat in a winder.

17. This is a modernized version of a rhyme of about 1830 that begins:

> Little wee laddie,
> Wha's your daddie? . . . .

In America we sing:

> Obadiah
> Jumped in the fire,
> Fire was hot,
> He jumped in the pot,
> The pot was so little
> He jumped in the kettle,
> The kettle was so black

Why does the lamb love Mary so?
  The eager children cry;
Why, Mary loves the lamb, you know,
  The teacher did reply.[14]

« 175 »

As I went to Bonner,
  I met a pig
  Without a wig,
Upon my word of honor.

« 176 »

Johnny Armstrong[15] killed a calf,
Peter Henderson got half,
Willy Wilkinson got the head,
Ring the bell, the calf is dead.

« 177 »

All of a row,
Bend the bow,
Shot at a pigeon
And killed a crow.[16]

« 178 »

There was a man, he went mad,
He jumped into a paper bag;
The paper bag was too narrow,
He jumped into a wheelbarrow;
The wheelbarrow took on fire,
He jumped into a cow byre;
The cow byre was too nasty,
He jumped into an apple pasty;
The apple pasty was too sweet,
He jumped into Chester-le-Street;
Chester-le-Street was full of stones,
He fell down and broke his bones.[17]

« 179 »

A cat came fiddling out of a barn,
With a pair of bag-pipes under her arm;
She could sing nothing but, Fiddle cum fee,

Little Tom Tucker,
He sang for his supper.
What did he sing for?
Why, white bread and butter.
How can I cut it without a knife?
How can I marry without a wife?

K. GREENAWAY

The mouse has married the humble-bee.
Pipe, cat; dance, mouse;
We'll have a wedding at our good house.**18**

« 180 »

Now I lay me down to sleep,
I pray the Lord my soul to keep;
And if I die before I wake,
I pray the Lord my soul to take.**19**

« 181 »

Little Tommy Tacket
Sits upon his cracket;**20**
Half a yard of cloth
Will make him coat and jacket;

He jumped in the crack,
The crack was so high
He jumped in the sky,
The sky was so blue
He jumped in the canoe,
The canoe was so deep
He jumped in the creek,
The creek was so shallow
He jumped in the tallow,
The tallow was so hard
He jumped in the lard,
The lard was so soft
He jumped in the loft,
The loft was so rotten
He fell in the cotton,
The cotton was so white
He took off his shoes
And stayed all night.

And Boyd Smith, in his 1919 *Mother Goose*, gave the somewhat similar rhyme which he called a jingle "said to have pleased the children of Edward III":

Anna Elise, she jumped with surprise;
The surprise was so quick, it played her a trick;
The trick was so rare, she jumped in a chair;
The chair was so frail, she jumped in a pail;
The pail was so wet, she jumped in a net;
The net was so small, she jumped on a ball;
The ball was so round, she jumped on the ground;
And ever since then she's been turning around.

18. This rhyme, found in a variety for forms, was earliest recorded in a Wiltshire manuscript dated 1740. It first appeared in print in J. G. Rusher's *Nursery Songs* or *London Jingles*, both to be dated around the year 1840.

19. If Thomas Fleet of Boston did not publish the very first "Mother Goose" book, he did indeed publish many editions of his *New-England Primer* (the first in 1737) in which this famous children's prayer is first to be found in print. Its earliest appearance in a book of "nursery rhymes," however, was probably around 1840, in J. G. Rusher's *London Jingles*, where it read:

I lay me down to rest me,
I pray to God to bless me:
If I should sleep and never wake,
I pray the Lord my soul to take.

129

Like most of the best-known rhymes, "Now I Lay Me" has often been parodied:

Now I lay me down to sleep,
A bag of peanuts at my feet.
If I should die before I wake,
Give them to my sister Kate.

20. James O. Halliwell in 1842 defined a *cracket* as "A little three-legged stool seen by the ingle of every cottage in the north of England."

21. The earlier versions usually end here. The last six lines first appeared as late as 1924 (in L. Edna Walter's *Mother Goose's Nursery Rhymes*).

Make him coat and jacket,
Breeches to the knee,
And if you will not have him,
You may let him be.

« 182 »

A little cock sparrow sat on a green tree,
And he chirruped, he chirruped, so merry was he.
A naughty boy came with his wee bow and arrow,
Says he, I will shoot this little cock sparrow;
His body will make me a nice little stew,
And his giblets will make me a little pie too.
Oh, no, said the sparrow, I won't make a stew,
So he clapped his wings and away he flew.

« 183 »

Six little mice sat down to spin;
Pussy passed by and she peeped in.
What are you doing, my little men?

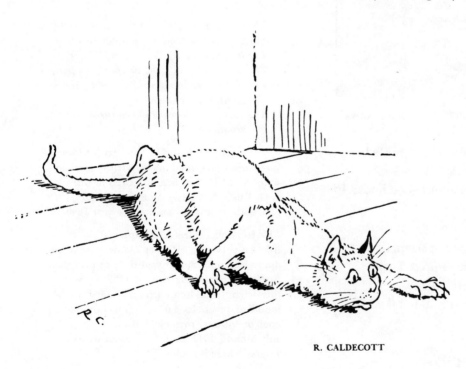

R. CALDECOTT

Weaving coats for gentlemen.
Shall I come in and cut off your threads?
No, no, Mistress Pussy, you'd bite off our heads.
Oh, no, I'll not; I'll help you to spin.
That may be so, but you can't come in.[21]
Says Puss: You look so wondrous wise,
I like your whiskers and bright black eyes;
Your house is the nicest house I see,
I think there is room for you and for me.
The mice were so pleased that they opened the door,
And Pussy soon had them all dead on the floor.

« 184 »

I had a little dog and they called him Buff,
I sent him to a shop to buy me snuff,
But he lost the bag and spilt the stuff;
I sent him no more but gave him a cuff,
For coming from the mart without any snuff.[22]

22. James O. Halliwell later gave a shortened version of this rhyme, as well as the similar:

I had a little dog, and his name was Blue Bell,
I gave him some work to do, and he did it very
well;
I sent him upstairs to pick up a pin,
He stepped in the coal-scuttle up to his chin;
I sent him to the garden to pick some sage;
He tumbled down and fell in a rage;
I sent him to the cellar to draw a pot of beer,
He came up again, and said there was none
there.

R. CALDECOTT

Needles and ribbons and packets of pins,

Prints and chintz and odd bob-a-kins. . . .

CHAPTER IX

Some That Came Later
That Might Have Come Before

Scattered through "Mother Goose" books of our own century are rhymes, printed there for perhaps the first time, which have the true spirit, the authentic flavor of the rhymes of an earlier day—rhymes of the seventeenth, the eighteenth, and the early years of the nineteenth century.

Indeed, it is known that some at least of these rhymes *were* composed and sung a hundred years or more before they first saw print in a nursery rhyme book. They seem to us to deserve, here, a chapter to themselves.

« 185 »

Huff the talbot[1] and our cat Tib
They took up sword and shield,
Tib for the red rose, Huff for the white,[2]
To fight upon Bosworth field.

Oh it was dreary that night to bury
These doughty warriors dead;
Under a white rose brave dog Huff,
And a fierce Tib under a red.

1. A hound of the variety formerly known as St. Hubert's breed, supposed to be related to the bloodhound; perhaps deriving its name from the dog borne on the arms of the Talbot family.

2. The Wars of the Roses, between the Lancastrians under Henry Tudor, Earl of Richmond, afterwards Henry VII, and the Yorkists under Richard III, ended, as the next line of this rhyme indicates, in the battle of Bosworth Field, fought August 22, 1485.

3. James O. Halliwell, in the middle of the nineteenth century, collected "as a rhyme for a game of ball":

Queen Anne, Queen Anne, you sit in the sun,
As fair as a lily, as white as a wand.
I send you three letters, and pray read one,
You must read one, if you can't read all,
So pray, Miss or Master, throw up the ball.

Historically, it has been said that "Lady Queen Anne," last Stuart ruler of England, did delight to sit in the gardens of Kensington Palace, surrounded by her royal Maids of Honor, reading light books of verse, "as fair as a lily, as brown as a bun."

Low lay Huff and long may he lie!
But our Tib took little harm:
He was up and away at dawn of day
With the rose-bush under his arm.

« 186 »

Who are you? A dirty old man
I've always been since the day I began,
Mother and Father were dirty before me,
Hot or cold water has never come o'er me.

« 187 »

I am Queen Anne, of whom 'tis said
I'm chiefly famed for being dead.
Queen Anne, Queen Anne, she sits in the sun,
As fair as a lily, as brown as a bun.[3]

« 188 »

What did I dream? I do not know;
The fragments fly like chaff.

Yet strange my mind was tickled so
I cannot help but laugh.

« 189 »

Mirror, mirror, tell me,
Am I pretty or plain?
Or am I downright ugly
And ugly to remain?

Shall I marry a gentleman?
Shall I marry a clown?
Or shall I marry old Knives-and-Scissors
Shouting through the town?**4**

« 190 »

Open the door and let me through!
Not without your buff and blue.**5**
Here's my buff and there's my blue.
Open the door and let me through!

« 191 »

There are men in the village of Erith
Whom nobody seeth or heareth,
    And there looms, on the marge
    Of the river, a barge
That nobody roweth or steereth.

« 192 »

Far from home across the sea
    To foreign parts I go;
When I am gone, O think of me
    And I'll remember you.
Remember me when far away,
    Whether asleep or awake,
Remember me on your wedding day
    And send me a piece of your cake.

4. The scissors-grinder.

5. The colors adopted by the Scottish Covenanters, the defenders of Presbyterianism against Catholicism in the sixteenth and seventeenth centuries. Their power was broken by Cromwell's conquest of Scotland in 1650. From their use of buff and blue came the expression "true blue."

« 193 »

Henry was a worthy king,
Mary was his queen,
He gave to her a lily
Upon a stalk of green.

6. A detachment of men, under the command of an officer, empowered to force men into the naval (sometimes the military) service.

7. The splinter-deck of a ship is an extra deck added below what is usually the lowest deck: the protective deck. "My love" was evidently working deep in the hull during an emergency to lose his leg by a splinter-board.

Then all for his kindness,
And all for his care,
She gave him a new-laid egg
In the garden there.

Love, can you sing?
   I cannot sing.
A story tell?
   Not one I know.
Then let us play at queen and king
As down the garden walks we go.

« 194 »

God made the bees
   And the bees make honey.
The miller's man does all the work,
   But the miller makes the money.

« 195 »

Needles and ribbons and packets of pins,
Prints and chintz and odd bod-a-kins—
   They'd never mind whether
   You laid them together
Or one from the other in packets and tins.

But packets of pins and ribbons and needles
And odd bod-a-kins and chintz and prints,

R. CALDECOTT

Being birds of a feather
Would huddle together
Like minnows on billows or pennies in mints.

« 196 »

Oh! cruel was the press-gang[6]
  That took my love from me;
Oh! cruel was the little ship
  That took him out to sea;
And cruel was the splinter-board[7]
  That took away his leg;
Now he is forced to fiddle-scrape,
  And I am forced to beg.

« 197 »

"Fire, fire!" cried the town crier;
"Where? Where?" said Goody[8] Blair;
"Down the town," said Goody Brown;
"I'll go see't," said Goody Fleet;
"So will I," said Goody Fry.[9]

« 198 »

There were two wrens upon a tree,
Whistle and I'll come to thee;
Another came, and there were three,
Whistle and I'll come to thee;
Another came and there were four.
You needn't whistle any more,
For being frightened, off they flew,
And there are none to show to you.

« 199 »

The Queen of Love went out to walk,
And saw an archer shoot a hawk;
And when she saw the poor hawk die,
The Queen of Love was heard to sigh.

« 200 »

I do not like thee, Doctor Fell,[10]
The reason why I cannot tell;
But this I know, and know full well,
I do not like thee, Doctor Fell.[11]

8. In Puritan Boston, you were called "Mister" only if you had the franchise—that is, owned property which had a value of forty pounds sterling. A person without such property, and therefore without the right to vote, was called "Goodman" and his wife "Goodwife" or "Goody."

9. This has become one of the most popular forms of the modern nursery rhyme, as witnessed by these two examples:

> Mrs. Mason bought a basin,
> Mrs. Tyson said, What a nice 'un,
> What did it cost? said Mrs. Frost,
> Half a crown, said Mrs. Brown,
> Did it indeed, said Mrs. Reed,
> It did for certain, said Mrs. Burton.
> Then Mrs. Nix up to her tricks
> Threw the basin on the bricks.
>
> What's in the cupboard?
> Says Mr. Hubbard.
> A knuckle of veal,
> Says Mr. Beal.
> Is that all?
> Says Mr. Ball.
> And enough too,
> Says Mr. Glue;
> And away they all flew.

10. Doctor Gideon Fell is the Chestertonian investigator of locked-room mysteries in a long series of detective novels and short stories created by John Dickson Carr. But the "Doctor Fell" referred to here (1625-86) was the Dean of Christ Church, Oxford.

11. The rhyme is from the works of Thomas Brown (1760), but it does not seem to have appeared in a "Mother Goose" book until 1926, when Robert Graves included it in *Less Familiar Nursery Rhymes.*

Brown from Oxford unless he could translate, extempore, the lines of Martial:

Non amo te, Sabidi, nec possum dicere quare;
Hoc tantum possum dicere, Non amo te.

Brown's immediate "translation" is said to have been the rhyme above.

12. The Duke was Frederick Augustus, Duke of York, second son of George III of England (1763-1827); the hill is said to have been Mount Cassel in Belgium, during the cam-

paign in which the Duke commanded the un-
successful English forces in Flanders; but
there is no event in the Duke's military career
that "remotely resembles the operation described in the jingle," according to the Duke's
biographer, Colonel Burne.

13. Always an ecclesiastical center; Ely cathedral, begun in 1083, is still one of the
largest in England.

14. Canute (c. 995-1035) was king of England,
Norway, and Denmark. He invaded England
with his father in 1013, again in 1015, and was
accepted as sole king after the death of Edmund in 1016.

R. CALDECOTT

« 201 »

Oh, the brave old Duke of York,
    He had ten thousand men;
He marched them up to the top of the hill,
    And he marched them down again.
  And when they were up, they were up,
    And when they were down, they were down
And when they were only half-way up,
    They were neither up nor down.[12]

« 202 »

At Islington a fair they hold,
Where cakes and ale are to be sold,
At High gate and at Holloway
The like is kept from day to day;
At Totnam and at Kentish Town,
And all those places up and down.

« 203 »

Merrily sang the monks of Ely,[13]
As King Canute[14] came rowing by.
"Row to the shore, knights," said the king,
"And let us hear these churchmen sing."

« 204 »

Terence McDiddler,
    The three-stringed fiddler,
Can charm, if you please,
    The fish from the seas.

« 205 »

Whose little pigs are these, these, these?
    Whose little pigs are these?
They are Roger the Cook's, I know by their looks;
    I found them among my peas.
Go pound them, go pound them.
    I dare not on my life,
For though I love not Roger the Cook,
    I dearly love his wife.

R. CALDECOTT

I'll sing you a song,

Though not very long, Yet I think it as pretty as any. . . .

CHAPTER X

Young Father Goose

His name was James Orchard Halliwell-Phillips, although he preferred to shorten it, as a by-line, to James O. Halliwell.

He was born in 1820, and so precocious an antiquary did he soon prove himself to be that he was made a Fellow of the Royal Society at the age of eighteen years.

At the tender age of twenty-two, Halliwell produced perhaps his greatest book. *The Nursery Rhymes of England* was published in 1842; it was revised and enlarged five times—in 1843, 1844, 1846, 1853, and c. 1860. And Halliwell in 1849 was also to produce a substantial "sequel" which he called *Popular Rhymes and Nursery Tales.*

In these volumes, Halliwell collected much that had gone before, but he also added much that was new to print. He writes that his rhymes were gathered "principally from oral tradition," but it is apparent that he also did much research in libraries; again and again he states triumphantly that he was able to trace one rhyme or another to a fifteenth-to-eighteenth-century manuscript.

More than any other man, James O. Halliwell

1. "Old King Cole" would seen to have appeared in print for the first time around 1708, in a volume called *Useful Transactions in Philosophy*, by Dr. William King.

Lewis, in his *History of Great Britain* (1729), mentions no less than three kings of England of this name. But the King Cole of the jingle is evidently that King Cole who reigned in Britain, according to the ancient chroniclers, in the third century. He was supposed to have been a brave and a popular man who ascended to the throne on the death of Asclepiod. There is a large earthwork, supposed to have been a Roman amphitheater, at Colchester, which is popularly known as "King Cole's kitchen."

2. King Cole may not have been entirely dependent for his entertainment on his fiddlers three. According to Geoffrey of Monmouth, the king's daughter was herself well skilled in music.

3. "King Stephen" in other versions.

4. Other versions are not so kind to Arthur (or Stephen):

> *When auld Prince Arthur ruled this land,*
> *He was a thievish king . . . .*
>
> *When as King Arthur ruled this land,*
> *He ruled it like a swine,*
> *He stole three pecks of barley-meal . . . .*

deserved to be called—if he chose to claim the title—"Father Goose."

For Halliwell's *Nursery Rhymes* and its sequel were to provide a wealth of material for hundreds of books to come. His collection, say the editors of *The Oxford Dictionary of Nursery Rhymes*, was "the first work to draw attention to the antiquity of the rhymes with any conviction, and the first collection which attempted to be comprehensive. [It] is the basis . . . of almost every nursery rhyme anthology, and . . . the principal English source . . . of every essay and paragraph on the origin of nursery rhymes published since."

Halliwell chose to divide his material into eighteen chapters, or "sections" as he preferred to call them: Historical, Literal, Tales, Proverbs, Scholastic, Songs, Riddles, Charms, Gaffers and Gammers,

M. PARRISH

Games, Paradoxes, Lullabies, Jingles, Love and Matrimony, Natural History, Accumulative Stories, Local, and Relics. Except for seasonal songs, lullabies and game songs, riddles and tongue twisters, nature lore, and "wise sayings"—to each of which we have devoted a later chapter—we have followed his groupings here.

Halliwell died in 1889, one of the world's most respected Spenserian and Shakespearean scholars.

In the preface to the 1853 edition of the *Nursery Rhymes,* he paid this handsome tribute to "Mother Goose":

"The nursery rhyme is the novel and light reading of the infant scholar. It occupies, with respect to the A B C, the position of a romance which relieves the mind from the cares of a riper age. . . . The infants and children of the nineteenth century have not deserted the rhymes chanted so many ages since by the mothers of the north. This is a great nursery rhyme fact—a proof that there is contained in some of these traditional nonsense rhymes a meaning and a romance, possibly intelligible only to very young minds, that exercises an influence on the minds of children. It is obvious that there must exist something of this kind, for no modern competitors are found to supply altogether the place of [this] ancient doggerel. . . ."

« 206 »

Old King Cole[1]
Was a merry old soul,
And a merry old soul was he;
He called for his pipe,
And he called for his bowl,
And he called for fiddlers three.[2]

Every fiddler, he had a fiddle,
And a very fine fiddle had he;
Twee tweedle dee, tweedle dee, went the fiddlers.
Oh there's none so rare
As can compare
With King Cole and his fiddlers three.

5. This rhyme patently derives from a very old song or ballad. Halliwell thought it had first been introduced as part of an old play. "In the sixteenth, seventeenth, and eighteenth centuries comedies were enlivened with songs introduced, as in the present day, on the mildest pretext," says *The Oxford Dictionary of Nursery Rhymes.*

6. Best known of all robber heroes, Robin Hood was a favorite figure in the ballads of England in the fourteenth and fifteenth centuries, and this is most probably a snatch from one of them. Robin Hood was supposed to have lived in the twelfth century, and there is a dubious record of him in a Latin history of 1521. This is not to say that a Robin Hood did not exist; he may have been one of the last Saxons to hold out against the Normans.

7. Scotch—"large, great."

8. Little John was Robin Hood's right-hand man from the beginning of the saga, but Friar Tuck, Maid Marian and others did not figure in the tales and ballads until the fifteenth century.

9. Halliwell took this from a tract called *Pigges Corantoe, or Newes from the North* (1642), where it was called "Old Tarleton's Song," a reference to Tarleton the jester. He noted that "It is perhaps a parody on the popular epigram of 'Jack and Jill.' I do not know the period of the battle to which it appears to allude, but Tarleton died in the year 1588, so that the rhyme must be earlier."

On the other hand, later versions of the verse give as the second line, "With forty thousand men," and it has been suggested that "the king of France" in this verse was Henry IV, who "levied a huge army of 40,000 men" in the year 1610. His purpose in so doing is not known to this day, but the enterprise, whatever it was, came to nothing when Henry was assassinated.

10. Later, "At the battle of the Nile . . . ." During the Seven Years War, Belle Isle, strategically located off the west coast of France, was under siege by the British from April to June 1761.

11. And so on and so on and so on—a device used to fob off a child who wants to be told a story.

12. Queen Elizabeth I was also known to her people as Harry's Daughter, Gloriana, and the Virgin Queen. "I have desired to have the obedience of my subjects by love and not by compulsion," she said to Parliament, and indeed, everything about their amazing, fascinating, magnificent ruler seemed to delight her subjects.

13. Elizabeth's greatest problem was to find her own successor. At her death at the age of seventy, rheumatic and toothless, she reluctantly nodded agreement to Mary, Queen of Scots' son, James V. He and his supporters were of course very unpopular with the English.

14. Halliwell noted: "The word *tory* has changed greatly in its meaning, as it originated in the reign of Elizabeth, and represented a class of 'bog-trotters,' who were a compound of the knave and the highwayman. For many interesting particulars see Croften Croker's *Researches in the South of Ireland.*"

15. Katherine Elwes Thomas noted of this rhyme: "The Duke of Monmouth, the king's favorite of all his illegitimate children, was the son of Charles II by Lucy Waters. Samuel Pepys states that there was a report, current in England at that time, that the king had been privately married to the beautiful Lucy Waters. This, of course, was vigorously denied. Many times, however, it was common talk that Charles intended to have the 'pretty boy' legitimatized and declared his successor, a report which naturally proved the subject of frequent bitter quarrels between the king and his brother.

"The Duke of Richmond . . . was another natural son of Charles II by Frances Theresa Stewart, Duchess of Richmond. The young Duke of Grafton . . . was one of the monarch's several sons by Barbara, Duchess of Cleveland, Lady Castlemain.

"In this jingle it is plain that the inference 'To please a pious brother,' the future James II, is that it had been rather more than obscurely hinted to the merrie monarch that the troublesome Monmouth should be expeditiously put out of the way. But for all his perfidies, Charles appears to have been genuinely fond of his illegitimate children, and, of them all, he adored Monmouth who was, in truth, 'a

« 207 »

When good King Arthur[3] ruled this land,
  He was a goodly king;
He bought three pecks of barley-meal[4]
  To make a bag-pudding.

A bag-pudding the king did make,
  And stuffed it well with plums;
And in it put great lumps of fat,
  As big as my two thumbs.

The king and queen did eat thereof,
  And noblemen beside;
And what they could not eat that night,
  The queen next morning fried.[5]

« 208 »

Robin Hood,[6] Robin Hood
  Is in the mickle[7] wood;
Little John,[8] Little John,
  He to the town is gone.

Robin Hood, Robin Hood,
  Is telling his beads,
All in the green wood,
  Among the green weeds.

Little John, Little John,
  If he comes no more,
Robin Hood, Robin Hood,
  He will fret sore.

« 209 »

The king of France went up the hill,
  With twenty thousand men;[9]
The king of France came down the hill,
  And ne'er went up again.

« 210 »

At the siege of Belle Isle[10]
I was there all the while—
  All the while,
  All the while,

Young Father Goose

At the siege of Belle Isle
I was there all the while....[11]

« 211 »

Good Queen Bess was a glorious dame,[12]
When bonny King Jemmy from Scotland came;[13]
We'll pepper their bodies,
Their peaceable noddies,
And give them a crack of the crown.

« 212 »

Ho! Master Teague, what is your story?
I went to the wood and killed a tory,[14]
I went to the wood and killed another;
Was it the same or was it his brother?
I hunted him in, and I hunted him out,
Three times through the bog, about and about;
When out of a bush I saw his head,
So I fired my gun, and I shot him dead.

« 213 »

See saw, sack a day;
Monmouth is a prettie boy,
    Richmond is another,
Grafton is my only joy,
And why should I these three destroy,
    To please a pious brother![15]

« 214 »

As I was going by Charing Cross,[16]
I saw a black man[17] upon a black horse;
They told me it was King Charles the First—
Oh, dear, my heart was ready to burst!

« 215 »

Hector Protector[18] was dressed all in green;
Hector Protector was sent to the Queen.
    The Queen did not like him,[19]
    No more did the King;[20]
So Hector Protector was sent back again.

pretty boy,' as pretty a boy as any of those whose royal portraits now hang beside his own in the National Portrait Gallery in London."

16. This is a Puritan rhyme satirizing the Royalists who upheld Charles I. There is indeed a statue of Charles at Charing Cross, at the top of Whitehall, moved there in 1675 from its original erection in King Street.

17. "Black" here refers to the darkness of Charles's hair.

18. Identified by Katherine Elwes Thomas as the Earl of Hertford. Her story is that Henry VIII, furious at the refusal of the queen regent of Scotland to entertain his project for a marriage between the youthful Edward VI and the little princess, Mary, Queen of Scots, determined to lash Scotland with the whip of fire. To this end Hertford was dispatched upon an invasion characterized as "too much for a wooing and too little for a conquest." Hertford sacked Leith, then set fire to everything between Arthur's Seat at Edinburgh and the Border. Hertford later invaded Scotland for a second time, burning seven monasteries, 243 villages, sixteen castles, five market towns, thirteen mills and three hospitals. He also destroyed the abbeys of Melrose, Dryburgh, and Holyrood. He then returned to England in hot haste upon receipt of the news that rivals were plotting against him in London.

19. "The Queen"—the queen regent of Scotland—of course "did not like" Hector Protector for what he had done to the land of the heather.

20. "The King"—Henry VIII—was equally furious with Hertford because his invasion had fallen short of the intended conquest.

21. Daniel Defoe (1660?-1731) is best known today for his book *Robinson Crusoe*, published in 1719. It was based on the experiences of Alexander Selkirk, a Scottish sailor. Selkirk, shipwrecked, landed on an uninhabited island off the coast of Chile. Defoe's realistic account of Selkirk's life on the island caught the public fancy and changed Defoe from a hack writer to one of established reputation.

22. The verse above first appeared in print in 1797 as "A favourite Comic Chaunt written and sung by Mr. [Jack] Cussans at the Royal

Circus and Sadler's Wells with universal applause."

23. A riddle which contains its own answer. Halliwell included it in his "Historical" rather than his "Riddles" section because, he wrote, it was "written on the occasion of the marriage of Mary, the daughter of James Duke of York, afterwards James II, with the young Prince of Orange."

« 216 »

Poor old Robinson Crusoe! 21
Poor old Robinson Crusoe!
   They made him a coat,
   Of an old nanny goat,
I wonder how they could do so!
   With a ring a ting tang,
   And a ring a ting tang,
     Poor old Robinson Crusoe!22

« 217 »

What is the rhyme for porringer?
What is the rhyme for porringer?
The king he had a daughter fair
And gave the Prince of Orange her.23

« 218 »

William and Mary, George and Anne,
Four such children had never a man!
They put their father to flight and shame,
And called their brother a shocking bad name.**24**

« 219 »

As I **25** walked by myself
And talked by myself,
    Myself said unto me,
Look to thyself,
Take care of thyself,
    For nobody cares for thee.

I answered myself,
And said to myself
    In the self-same repartee,
Look to thyself,
Or not to thyself,
    The self-same thing will be.

« 220 »

There was a monkey climbed a tree,
When he fell down, then down fell he.

There was a crow sat on a stone,
When he was gone, then there was none.

There was an old wife did eat an apple,
When she ate two, she ate a couple.

There was a horse going to the mill,
When he went on, he stood not still.

There was a butcher cut his thumb,
When it did bleed, then blood did come.

There was a lackey ran a race,
When he ran fast, he ran apace.

There was a cobbler clouting shoon,
When they were mended, they were done.

There was a chandler making candle,
When he them stripped, he did them handle.

There was a navy went to Spain,
When it returned, it came back again.**26**

24. A disrespectful rhyme about the daughters and sons-in-law of James II, and their brother, James Francis Edward Stuart, the "Old Pretender."

25. The speaker is supposed to have been William III.

26. A long list of "self-evident propositions." The last couplet, generally supposed to refer to the failure of the expedition against Cadiz in 1625, was perhaps added around that time to the previously existing couplets.

27. This little rhyme seems to have been used by adults at one time in dealing out, say, candies to children, to show their generosity.

28. The English puppet play, Punch and Judy, which probably originated in the sixteenth-century *commedia dell' arte*, has delighted (and terrified) thousands of children over the years. Punch is cruel and boastful, and his wife Judy is unfaithful and obstreperous.

In *Parlor Amusements and Evening Party Entertainments* (London: George Routledge and Sons, n.d.), the conjuror "Professor Hoffmann," best remembered today for his books on parlor magic, wrote: "It is a curious illustration of the depravity of human nature, that this eccentric drama, in which vice is throughout triumphant, and law and order go to the wall, has maintained its popularity for so many generations . . . . The hunch-backed hero still flings his offspring out of the window; still playfully murders his lawful spouse; and admiring audiences not only pardon, but applaud the merry old rascal for his many iniquities . . . ."

29. Katherine Elwes Thomas, as usual, was able to read a political significance into the simple lines above: "With England masquerading as Punch, and France as Judy, the pie over which they fought was Italy . . ."

30. Robert Graves, in his *Less Familiar Nursery Rhymes* (1926) gives this ending:
> *...He brought it crooked back,*
> *To his crooked wife Joan,*
> *And cut a crooked snippet*
> *From the crooked ham-bone.*

Who was this little crooked man with the keen eyes? He may have been General Sir Alexander Leslie of Scotland, one of the chief Covenanters. In this case, the "crooked sixpence" would be Charles I, and the "crooked stile" the border between England and Scotland. The two old antagonists at last reached an understanding and "lived in a little crooked house," but Sir Alexander was wily enough to keep the best of his officers on half pay, a measure he did not regret in 1640 when Charles reassembled his army. Sir Alexander and his forces then crossed the border "like a whirlwind" and seized Newcastle.

31. This famous limerick, one of many which have found their way into "Mother Goose" books, appeared originally in *Anecdotes and Adventures of Fifteen Gentlemen,*" published by John Marshall about 1822, perhaps written by R. S. Sharpe. While no one is sure quite how the limerick got its name, it is improbable that its place of origin was Limerick, Ireland —a theory based on little except an Irish song, each verse of which ends, "We'll all come up, come up to Limerick."

"If the origin of the word remained in obscurity, the form did not," Louis Untermeyer writes in *Lots of Limericks* (Garden City, N.Y.: Doubleday & Company, Inc., 1961). "It became the favorite of people everywhere, from serious poets to naughty schoolboys, from housewives trying to supply the fifth line in a contest which would win them an automatic dish-washer to their husbands rowdily regaling their companions at a stag party...."

32. Some authorities think that the tale of "The Babes in the Wood" was based upon an actual abandonment, and the subsequent death of two children, which took place at the hamlet of Wayland, near Watton in the midlands of Norfolk.

33. The first verse of this nursery rhyme has appeared in many "Mother Goose" books since Halliwell first recorded it in 1844. The

« 221 »

One's none;
Two's some;
Three's many;
Four's a penny;
Five's a little hundred.[27]

« 222 »

Miss One, Two, and Three
    Could never agree
While they gossipped around
    A tea-caddy.

« 223 »

Punch and Judy,[28]
Fought for a pie,
Punch gave Judy
A sad blow in the eye.

Says Punch to Judy,
Will you have more?
Says Judy to Punch,
My eye is sore.[29]

« 224 »

There was a crooked man, and he walked a crooked
    mile,
He found a crooked sixpence against a crooked stile;
He bought a crooked cat, which caught a crooked
    mouse,
And they all lived together in a little crooked
    house.[30]

« 225 »

As a little fat man of Bombay
Was smoking one very hot day,
    A bird called a snipe
    Flew away with his pipe,
Which vexed the fat man of Bombay.[31]

« 226 »

My dear, do you know,
How a long time ago,

Two little children,
Whose names I don't know,
Were stolen away on a fine summer's day,
And left in a wood, as I've heard people say.

And when it was night,
So sad was their plight,
The sun it went down,
And the moon gave no light!
They sobb'd and they sigh'd, and they bitterly cried,
And the poor little things, they lay down and died.

And when they were dead,
The robin so red
Brought strawberry leaves
And over them spread;
And all the day long,
They sang them this song,
"Poor babes in the wood! poor babes in the wood!
And don't you remember the babes in the wood?"**32**

« 227 »

Little Tommy Tittlemouse
Lived in a little house;
He caught fishes
In other men's ditches.

Little Tom (my) Tittlemouse,
Lived in a bell-house;
The bell-house broke,
And Tom Tittlemouse awoke.**33**

lesser-known second verse Halliwell did not
record until his edition of 1853. Katherine
Elwes Thomas identified "Little Tommy Tittlemouse" as Henry VIII and described his
living "in a little house" as "a merry bit of
persiflage over the king's vast possessions."

34. This is a somewhat better-known version
of the rhyme than that given by Halliwell.
"Tom Bolin" is known by many names: Tom
a Lin and Tommy Lin and Tommy o'Lin and
Tom o' the Lin and even Bryan o'Lin and
Harry Trewin and Bryan O'Flynn. One and
all, they, or he, is the hero of a Scots ballad of
which one verse goes:

*Tommy o'Lin, and his wife, and his wife's
mother,*
They all went over a bridge together:
*The bridge broke down, and they all
tumbled in,*
*What a precious concern, quoth Tommy
o'Lin.*

35. "Pothered"—worried, perplexed, bothered.

36. This nursery rhyme is a relic, says *The
Oxford Dictionary of Nursery Rhymes*, of a
folk-play "performed at Camborne, near Red-
ruth in Cornwall."

37. It is not generally known that there are
three more stanzas to this "nursery rhyme,"
which first appeared as a poem in *The European Magazine*, issue of April 1782:

The King of Spades
He kissed the maids,
Which made the Queen full sore;
The Queen of Spades

W. CRANE

She beat those maids,
And turned them out of door;
The Knave of Spades
Grieved for those jades,
And did for them implore;
The Queen so gent
She did relent
And vow'd she'd ne'er strike more.

The King of Clubs
He often drubs
His loving Queen and wife;
The Queen of Clubs
Returns his snubs,
And all is noise and strife;
The Knave of Clubs
Gives winks and rubs,
And swears he'll take her part;
For when our kings
Will do such things,
They should be made to smart.

The Diamond King
I fain would sing,
And likewise his fair Queen;
But that the Knave,
A haughty slave,
Must needs step in between;
Good Diamond King,
With hempen string,
The haughty Knave destroy!
Then may your Queen
With mind serene,
Your royal bed enjoy.

Halliwell included the first stanza of Rhyme 235 in his third (1844) edition, and then, curiously, dropped it in subsequent editions. Its present fame can probably be attributed to its use by Lewis Carroll in *Alice in Wonderland*. As Martin Gardner writes in *The Annotated Alice*: "This familiar nursery rhyme fits so neatly into Carroll's fantasy of living playing cards that he reprints it without alteration."

Actually, Carroll did alter the original very slightly. His version goes:

The Queen of Hearts, she made some tarts,
All on a summer day;
The Knave of Hearts, he stole those tarts
And took them quite away!

« 228 »

The two grey kits,
And the grey kits' mother,
All went over
The bridge together.
The bridge broke down,
They all fell in,
May the rats go with you,
Says Tom Bolin.[34]

« 229 »

My lady Wind, my lady Wind,
Went round about the house to find
A chink to get her foot in:
She tried the key-hole in the door,
She tried the crevice in the floor,
And drove the chimney soot in.

And then one night when it was dark,
She blew up such a tiny spark,
That all the house was pothered:[35]
From it she raised up such a flame,
As flamed away to Belting Lane,
And White Cross folks were smothered.

And thus when once, my little dears,
A whisper reaches itching ears,
The same will come, you'll find:
Take my advice, restrain the tongue,
Remember what old nurse has sung
Of busy lady Wind!

« 230 »

Old Abram Brown is dead and gone,
You'll never see him more;
He used to wear a long brown coat
That buttoned down before.[36]

« 231 »

Tommy kept a chandler's shop,
Richard went to buy a mop;
Tommy gave him such a whop,
That sent him out of the chandler's shop.

« 232 »

When I was a little girl,
  About seven years old,
I hadn't got a petticoat,
  To keep me from the cold.

So I went into Darlington,
  That pretty little town,
And there I bought a petticoat,
  A cloak, and a gown.

I went into the woods
  And built me a kirk,
And all the birds of the air,
  They helped me to work.

The hawk, with his long claws,
  Pulled down the stone,
The dove, with her rough bill,
  Brought me them home.

The parrot was the clergyman,
  The peacock was the clerk,
The bullfinch played the organ,
  And we made merry work.

« 233 »

Pemmy was a pretty girl,
  But Fanny was a better;
Pemmy looked like any churl,
  When little Tommy let her.

Pemmy had a pretty nose,
  But Fanny had a better;
Pemmy oft would come to blows,
  But Tommy would not let her.

Pemmy had a pretty doll,
  But Fanny had a better;
Pemmy chattered like a poll,
  When little Tommy let her.

Pemmy had a pretty song,
  But Fanny had a better;
Pemmy would sing all day long,
  But Tommy would not let her.

Bonny lass, pretty lass, wilt thou be mine?
Thou shalt not wash dishes,
Nor yet serve the swine;
Thou shalt sit on a cushion, and sew a
  fine seam,
And thou shalt eat strawberries, sugar,
  and cream!

K. GREENAWAY

151

Pemmy lov'd a pretty lad,
 And Fanny lov'd a better;
And Pemmy wanted for to wed,
 But Tommy would not let her.

« 234 »

Moss was a little man, and a little mare did buy,
For kicking and for spanking none her could come
 nigh;
She could trot, she could amble, and could canter
 here and there,
But one night she strayed away—so Moss lost his
 mare.

Moss got up next morning to catch her fast asleep,
And round about the frosty fields so nimbly did
 creep.
Dead in a ditch he found her, and glad to find her
 there,
So I'll tell you by and bye, how Moss caught his
 mare.

Rise! stupid, rise! he thus to her did say;
Arise, you beast, you drowsy beast, get up without
 delay,
For I must ride you to the town, so don't lie sleeping
 there;
He put the halter round her neck—so Moss caught
 his mare.

« 235 »

The Queen of Hearts
She made some tarts,
All on a summer's day;
The Knave of Hearts
He stole the tarts,
And took them clean away.
The King of Hearts
Called for the tarts,
And beat the Knave full sore;
The Knave of Hearts
Brought back the tarts,
And vow'd he'd steal no more.**37**

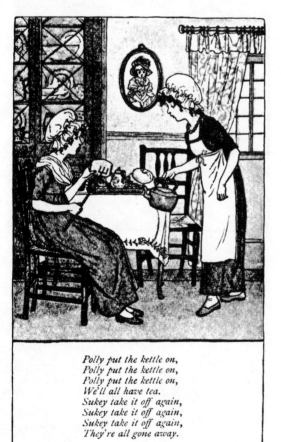

Polly put the kettle on,
Polly put the kettle on,
Polly put the kettle on,
We'll all have tea.
Sukey take it off again,
Sukey take it off again,
Sukey take it off again,
They're all gone away.

K. GREENAWAY

« 236 »

St. Dunstan,[38] as the story goes,
Once pulled the devil by the nose,
With red hot tongs, which made him roar,
That could be heard ten miles or more.

« 237 »

Polly[39] put the kettle on,
Polly put the kettle on,
Polly put the kettle on,
   We'll all have tea.

Sukey[40] take it off again,
Sukey take it off again,
Sukey take it off again,
   They've all gone away.

Blow the fire and make the toast,
Put the muffins down to roast,
Blow the fire and make the toast,
   We'll all have tea.[41]

« 238 »

Up at Piccadilly oh!
   The coachman takes his stand,
And when he meets a pretty girl,
   He takes her by the hand;
     Whip away for ever oh!
   Drive away so clever oh!
     All the way to Bristol oh!
   He drives her four-in-hand.

« 239 »

Will you lend me your mare to ride a mile?
No, she is lame leaping over a stile.
Alack! and I must go to the fair,
I'll give you good money for lending your mare.
Oh, oh! say you so?
Money will make the mare to go.[42]

« 240 »

About the bush, Willy,
   About the bee-hive,

38. St. Dunstan (924-88) was an English Benedictine monk and statesman, abbot of Glastonbury, and chief minister to King Edred. The legend has it that St. Dunstan set up in business as a brewer, and bartered his soul to the devil in return for an annual spring frost severe enough to blast the apple crop and so put a stop to the production of cider—the rival drink to beer. It was agreed, or so the story goes, that the arch-enemy should keep his part of the bargain, in perpetuity, during the three days ending on St. Dunstan's Day, May 19th.

39. In the mid-nineteenth century, "Polly" was often used as a pet-name for "Mary."

40. And "Sukey" for "Susan."

41. "Polly Put the Kettle On" was originally a popular country dance and song. Like Joe Penner's much later "You wanna buy a duck?", "Polly put the kettle on and we'll all have tea" became a much-repeated catch phrase around 1870 (Dickens has Grip, the raven, croak it in *Barnaby Rudge*). The third stanza as given in Rhyme 237, did not appear in print until 1858—in Charles H. Bennett's *Old Nurse's Book of Rhymes, Jingles, and Ditties.*

42. This nursery rhyme may have been the origin of this proverb, one of the best-known in the English language.

R. CALDECOTT

43. This rhyme reflects the low opinion held of traveling players by townspeople, who regarded the mummers as being little more than companies of beggars.

44. The editors of *The Oxford Dictionary of Nursery Rhymes* note that Moorfields was an appropriate setting for this nonsense. It was the site of the Old Bethlehem Hospital for the insane, which was moved to Moorfields from Bishops Gate Without in the year 1675.

45. "St. Paul's steeple" in the ballad "Tom Tell-truth," from which this nursery rhyme stems.

46. Another rhyme recited by the old nurses to put an end to the evening's storytelling, taken, said Halliwell, "from W. Wagner's play called *The longer thou livest, the more fecle thou art.*"

47. The last line is more usually given today as: "Lazy Elsie Marley!" This is the first stanza of a song of ten quatrains written in the middle of the eighteenth century and first printed c. 1756.

Elsie—or Ailcie or Alice—Marley was a real person. Born Alice Harrison about 1715, she married Ralph Marley of Picktree and became the attractive proprietress of a public house there called The Swan. She was famous for her gay badinage, and there were certain rumors

About the bush, Willy,
  I'll meet thee alive.

Then to my ten shillings,
  Add you but a groat,
I'll go to Newcastle,
  And buy a new coat.

Five and five shillings,
  Five and a crown;
Five and five shillings,
  Will buy a new gown.

Five and five shillings,
  Five and a groat,
Five and five shillings,
  Will buy a new coat.

« 241 »

A pretty little girl in a round-eared cap
I met in the street t'other day;
  She gave me such a thump,
That my heart it went bump;
I thought I should have fainted away!

« 242 »

Jeanie come tie my,
Jeanie come tie my,
Jeanie come tie my bonnie cravat;
I've tied it behind,
I've tied it before,
And I've tied it so often, I'll tie it no more.

« 243 »

Some up and some down,
  There's players in the town,
You wot well who they be;
  The sun doth arise,
  To three companies,
One, two, three, four make we!

Besides that we travel,
  With pumps full of gravel,
Made all of such running leather:

That once in a week,
New masters we seek,
And never can hold together.[43]

« 244 »

As I was walking o'er little Moorfields,[44]
I saw St. Paul's[45] a-running on wheels,
    With a fee, fo, fum.
Then for further frolics I'll go to France,
While Jack shall sing and his wife shall dance,
    With a fee, fo, fum.

« 245 »

The white dove sat on the castle wall,
I bend my bow and shoot her I shall;
I put her in my glove both feathers and all;
I laid my bridle upon the shelf;
If you will any more, sing it yourself.[46]

« 246 »

Elsie Marley has grown so fine,
She won't get up to serve the swine,
But lies in bed till eight or nine,
And surely she does take her time.[47]

« 247 »

Old Father of the Pye,
I cannot sing, my lips are dry;
But when my lips are very well wet,
Then I can sing with the Heigh Go Bet![48]

« 248 »

Of all the gay birds that e'er I did see,
The owl is the fairest by far to me,
For all day long she sits in a tree,
And when the night comes away flies she.[49]

« 249 »

Merry are the bells, and merry would they ring,
Merry was myself, and merry would I sing;
With a merry ding-dong, happy, gay, and free,
And a merry sing-song, happy let us be!

then current about the lengths to which she would sometimes go to show hospitality to her favorite customers. In 1768, suffering from a fever, she fell into an old coal pit full of water and was drowned. She was buried on August 7th.

A somewhat earlier version of this rhyme was recorded by Halliwell in 1842 with the name of the ale-wife being given as Nancy Dawson, who was also a real person—a dancer at Sadler's Wells and the toast of the town in the middle of the eighteenth century.

48. This appears to be an old hunting song. "Go Bet" is a very ancient sporting phrase, equivalent to "Go along." It occurs in Chaucer.

49. Like a sizable number of other nursery rhymes—including "Three Bind Mice" (Rhyme 253)—this verse comes from Ravencroft's *Deuteromelia or The Seconde part of Musicks melodie,* published in 1609. The refrain that follows these lines has given us still another "nursery rhyme." It is "Nose, Nose, Jolly Red Nose" (Rhyme 138).

50. "This popular little rhyme," say the editors of *The Oxford Dictionary of Nursery Rhymes,* "comes from *The Happy Husbandman: Or, Country Innocence,* a black-letter broadside . . . . It . . . must have been printed between August 1685 and December 1688."

R. CALDECOTT

51. The note appended to this rhyme by the editors of *The Oxford Dictionary of Nursery Rhymes* reads: "This is probably the best-known round in the world. A version of it ... was included among the 'Pleasant Roundelaies' in *Deuteromelia or The Seconde part of Musicks melodie* (1609). The editor and probable part author of this collection was Thomas Ravenscroft, a young man still in his teens, lately a chorister at St. Paul's. 'Three Blind Mice' has survived as a round through three and a half centuries ... but it is probably James O. Halliwell who is responsible for the secure position it holds in the nursery today. As far as has been ascertained the words made no appearance in children's literature prior to 1842, and [Halliwell], at first, knew only three lines of it."

Some attempts, few of them convincing, have been made to read significance into "Three Blind Mice." Thus "the farmer's wife" becomes Queen Mary I of England, so called because she was a woman of large landed properties, and the "three blind mice" become Ridley, Latimer, and Cranmer, all of whom were burned at the stake.

52. For a note on the "man in the moon," see Chapter V, Note 23.

53. Mystery veils "Aiken Drum." According to a Scottish ballad, he may have been a fighter in the battle of Sheriffmuir (1715); according to a poem in *The Dumfries Magazine* (October 1825) he may have been a strange little brownie.

Waddle goes your gait, and hollow are your hose,
Noddle goes your pate, and purple is your nose;
Merry is your sing-song, happy, gay, and free,
With a merry ding-dong, happy let us be!

Merry have we met, and merry have we been,
Merry let us part, and merry meet again;
With our merry sing-song, happy, gay, and free,
And a merry ding-dong, happy let us be!

« 250 »

My maid Mary
She minds the dairy,
While I go a-hoeing and mowing each morn;
Merrily runs the reel,
And the little spinning-wheel,
Whilst I am singing and mowing my corn.[50]

« 251 »

As I was going up the hill,
 I met with Jack the piper;
And all the tune that he could play
 Was "Tie up your petticoats tighter."

I tied them once, I tied them twice,
 I tied them three times over;
And all the song that he could sing
 Was, "Carry me safe to Dover."

« 252 »

As I was going along, long, long,
A-singing a comical song, song, song,
The lane that I went was so long, long, long,
And the song that I sung was so long, long, long,
And so I went singing along.

« 253 »

Three blind mice, see how they run!
They all ran after the farmer's wife,
Who cut off their tails with a carving knife,
Did you ever see such a sight in your life,
 As three blind mice?[51]

R. CALDECOTT

« 254 »

There was a man lived in the moon,**52** lived in the
    moon, lived in the moon,
There was a man lived in the moon,
And his name was Aiken Drum;**53**
  And he played upon a ladle, a ladle, a ladle,
  And he played upon a ladle,
  And his name was Aiken Drum,

And his hat was made of good cream cheese, good
    cream cheese, good cream cheese,
And his hat was made of good cream cheese,
And his name was Aiken Drum.

And his coat was made of good roast beef, good roast
    beef, good roast beef,
And his coat was made of good roast beef,
And his name was Aiken Drum.

And his buttons were made of penny loaves, penny
    loaves, penny loaves,
And his buttons were made of penny loaves,
And his name was Aiken Drum.

R. CALDECOTT

His waistcoat was made of crust of pies, crust of pies,
    crust of pies,
His waistcoat was made of crust of pies,
And his name was Aiken Drum.

His breeches were made of haggis bags,[54] haggis
    bags, haggis bags,
His breeches were made of haggis bags,
And his name was Aiken Drum.

There was a man in another town, another town,
    another town,
There was a man in another town,
And his name was Willy Wood;
    And he played upon a razor, a razor, a razor,
    And he played upon a razor,
    And his name was Willy Wood.

And he ate up all the good cream cheese, good cream
    cheese, good cream cheese,
And he ate up all the good cream cheese,
And his name was Willy Wood.

And he ate up all the good roast beef, good roast
    beef, good roast beef,
And he ate up all the good roast beef,
And his name was Willy Wood.

And he ate up all the penny loaves, penny loaves,
    penny loaves,
And he ate up all the penny loaves,
And his name was Willy Wood.

And he ate up all the good pie crust, good pie crust,
    good pie crust,
And he ate up all the good pie crust,
And his name was Willy Wood.

But he choked upon the haggis bags, haggis bags,
    haggis bags,
But he choked upon the haggis bags,
And that ended Willy Wood.[55]

54. The haggis—the closest thing to the national dish of Scotland—is made of the heart, liver and lungs of a sheep or calf, minced with onions and suet, seasoned and mixed with oatmeal, and boiled in the stomach of the animal which provided the heart, liver and lungs. Anyone who has ever eaten a haggis (your present editors have) can understand why the greedy Willy Wood choked to death on this stomach—the haggis bag.

55. Halliwell would seem to have collected a corrupted version of this song. The version he presented in 1842 began:

> *There was a man in our toone, in our*
>   *toone, in our toone,*
> *There was a man in our toone,*
> *And his name was Billy Pod . . . .*

« 255 »

Whistle, daughter, whistle,
    And you shall have a sheep.

Mother, I cannot whistle,
    Neither can I sleep.

Whistle, daughter, whistle,
    And you shall have a cow.
Mother, I cannot whistle,
    Neither know I how.

Whistle, daughter, whistle,
    And you shall have a man.
Mother, I cannot whistle,
    But I'll do the best I can.

« 256 »

I'll sing you a song,
Though not very long,
    Yet I think it as pretty as any,
Put your hand in your purse,
You'll never be worse,
    And give the poor singer a penny.

« 257 »

There was an old woman, as I've heard tell,
She went to the market her eggs for to sell;
She went to the market all on a market-day,
And she fell asleep on the king's highway.**56**

There came by a pedlar whose name was Stout,
He cut her petticoats all round about;
He cut her petticoats up to the knees,
Which made the old woman to shiver and freeze.

When this little woman first did wake,
She began to shiver and she began to shake,
She began to wonder and she began to cry,
"Oh! deary, deary me, this is none of I!"

"But if it be I, as I do hope it be,
I've a little dog at home, and he'll know me;
If it be I, he'll wag his little tail,
And if it not be I, he'll loudly bark and wail."

Home went the little woman all in the dark,
Up got the little dog, and he began to bark;
He began to bark, so she began to cry,
"Oh! deary, deary me, this is none of I."

R. CALDECOTT

56. In a version of "The Little Woman and the Pedlar" in the *Scots Musical Museum* (1797), we learn *why* the little old woman went to sleep:

> *She got a little drappikie, that cost her*
>   *meikle care . . . .*
>
> *If Johnnie find me Barrel-sick, I'm sure he'll*
>   *claw my skin;*
> *But I'll lye down and take a Nap before that*
>   *I gae in . . . .*

Southey, who devoted a chapter in *The Doctor* to this "lay," gallantly defended the sobriety of the little old woman, although he did admit that she may have drunk "a peg lower in the cup than she generally allowed herself to do."

159

« 258 »

There was an old woman, her name it was Peg,
Her head was of wood, and she wore a cork leg.
The neighbours all pitch'd her into the water,
Her leg was drown'd first, and her head follow'd
    a'ter.[57]

« 259 »

There was an old man who liv'd in Middle Row,
He had five hens and a name for them, oh!
Bill and Ned and Battock,
Cut-her-foot and Pattock,
Chuck, my lady Pattock,
Go to thy nest and lay.

« 260 »

There was an old woman of Leeds,
Who spent all her time in good deeds;
    She worked for the poor
    Till her fingers were sore,
This pious old woman of Leeds.[58]

« 261 »

Little Betty Blue[59]
Lost her holiday shoe,
What can little Betty do?
Give her another
To match the other,
And then she may walk out in two.

« 262 »

There was an old woman had three sons,
    Jerry, and James, and John;
Jerry was hung, and James was drowned,
    John was lost and never found,
And there was an end of her three sons,
    Jerry, and James, and John.[60]

« 263 »

There was an old man of Tobago,
Who lived on rice, gruel, and sago;

57. Halliwell collected another rhyme about this *Peg*, or someone very like her:

> *Peg, Peg, with a wooden leg,*
> *Her father was a miller,*
> *He tossed the dumpling at her head,*
> *And said he could not kill her.*

58. This limerick comes from the earliest-known book of limericks, *The History of Sixteen Wonderful Old Women*, published by John Harris in 1821.

59. "Little Betty Blue" was known to Halliwell as "Old Betty Blue."

60. This "merry catch," or something very similar to it, was probably known to Shakespeare. The rhyme first appeared in print in 1815 as the first of fourteen verses in a toy book, *The Old Woman and Her Three Sons*, published by John Harris. Very like the above is another rhyme given by Halliwell:

> *There was an old woman had three cows,*
> *Rosy and Colin and Dun.*
> *Rosy and Colin were sold at the fair,*
> *And Dun broke her heart in a fit of despair,*
> *So there was an end of her three cows,*
> *Rosy and Colin and Dun.*

And there is this, from Robert Graves's *Less Familiar Nursery Rhymes* (1926):

> *A famous old lady had three sticks,*
> *Ivory, ebon, and gold;*
> *The ivory split, the gold took a crack,*
> *And the ebon she broke about the maid's*
>   *back,*
> *So this was the end of the three sticks,*
> *Ivory, ebon, and gold.*

W. CRANE

Till, much to his bliss,
His physician said this—
To a leg, sir, of mutton you may go.**61**

« 264 »

Father Short came down the lane,
  Oh! I'm obliged to hammer and smite
  From four in the morning till eight at night,
For a bad master, and a worse dame.

« 265 »

There was an old woman called Nothing-at-all,
Who lived in a dwelling exceedingly small;
A man stretched his mouth to its utmost extent,
And down at one gulp house and old woman
    went.**62**

« 266 »

There was an old woman of Norwich,
Who lived upon nothing but porridge;
  Parading the town,
  She turned cloak into gown,
The thrifty old woman of Norwich.**63**

« 267 »

A little old man of Derby,
How do you think he served me?
He took away my bread and cheese,
And that is how he served me.

61. As Lear himself freely admitted, this limerick—from *Anecdotes and Adventures of Fifteen Gentleman*, published by John Marshall about 1822—inspired him to try his hand at the form that was to make him the single best known writer of limericks in the world. See his introduction to *More Nonsense*.

62. This sounds like a riddle, but Halliwell gave no answer. Could "Nothing-at-all" have been the hole in a doughnut?

63. Another limerick from *The History of Sixteen Wonderful Old Women*.

64. But not in the sense of the modern mother, of whom it has been said that she carries a child for nine months and then chauffeurs it for the next sixteen years.

65. Still another limerick from *The History of Sixteen Wonderful Old Women.*

66. It is probable that this "nursery rhyme" originated as an introduction song for one of the characters in a mummers' play. And perhaps not a very savory character: "Jumping Joan" in the seventeenth century was a cant term for a lady of little virtue. The last two lines are still another example of the popular "self-evident proposition."

67. This song was probably old when it was first written down in the middle of the fifteenth century. There are many versions of the opening line, among them:

I have a true love beyond the sea ....
I had four brothers over the sea ....
I have a sister over the sea ....

« 268 »

There was an old woman of Surrey,
Who was morn, noon, and night in a hurry;
   Called her husband a fool,
   Drove her children to school,**64**
The worrying old woman of Surrey.**65**

« 269 »

   Here am I,
   Little Jumping Joan;
   When nobody's with me
   I'm all alone.**66**

« 270 »

My true love lives far from me,**67**
   Perrie, Merrie, Dixie, Dominie,
Many a rich present he send to me,
   Petrum, Partrum, Paradise, Temporie,
   Perrie, Merrie, Dixie, Dominie.

He sent me a goose, without a bone,
   Perrie, Merrie, Dixie, Dominie,
He sent me a cherry, without a stone,
   Petrum, Partrum, Paradise, Temporie,
   Perrie, Merrie, Dixie, Dominie.

He sent me a Bible, no man could read,
   Perrie, Merrie, Dixie, Dominie,
He sent me a blanket without a thread,
   Petrum, Partrum, Paradise, Temporie,
   Perrie, Merrie, Dixie, Dominie.

How could there be a goose without a bone?
   Perrie, Merrie, Dixie, Dominie,
How could there be a cherry without a stone?
   Petrum, Partrum, Paradise, Temporie,
   Perrie, Merrie, Dixie, Dominie.

How could there be a Bible no man could read?
   Perrie, Merrie, Dixie, Dominie,
How could there be a blanket without a thread?
   Petrum, Partrum, Paradise, Temporie,
   Perrie, Merrie, Dixie, Dominie.

When the goose is in the egg-shell there is no bone,
Perrie, Merrie, Dixie, Dominie,
When the cherry is in the blossom, there is no stone,
Petrum, Partrum, Paradise, Temporie,
Perrie, Merrie, Dixie, Dominie.

When ye Bible is in ye press no man it can read,
Perrie, Merrie, Dixie, Dominie,
When ye wool is on ye sheep's back, there is no
thread,
Petrum, Partrum, Paradise, Temporie,
Perrie, Merrie, Dixie, Dominie.[68]

« 271 »

I saw a ship a-sailing,
A-sailing on the sea,
And oh but it was laden,
With pretty things for thee.

There were comfits in the cabin,
And apples in the hold;
The sails were made of silk,
And the masts were all of gold.

The four-and-twenty sailors,
That stood between the decks,
Were four-and-twenty white mice
With chains about their necks.
The captain was a duck[69]
With a packet on his back,
And when the ship began to move
The captain said Quack! Quack!

« 272 »

Barney Bodkin broke his nose,
Without feet we can't have toes;
Crazy folks are always mad,
Want of money makes me sad.[70]

« 273 »

If a man who turnips cries,
Cry not when his father dies,
It is proof that he would rather
Have a turnip than his father.[71]

68. As "The Riddle Song," this has become a favorite with modern ballad singers. Sometimes:

I gave my love a ring that has no end . . . .
A ring when it's rollin' it has no end.

I gave my love a baby with no cryin' . . .
A baby when it's sleepin' is no cryin'.

69. This line, it seems, was sufficient for Katherine Elwes Thomas to identify "the captain" with Sir Francis Drake. Drake—and Sir Walter Raleigh—did introduce many new "comfits" to Elizabethan England. Drake brought potatoes which he thriftily caused to have planted in Lancashire. And Sir Walter astonished England with its first invoice of tobacco. Hops, plums, cherries, apricots, grapes, and gooseberries were among the other foodstuffs introduced to English gardens by these intrepid mariners. The "four-and-twenty white mice with chains about their necks" were slaves, according to Miss Thomas.

70. These are the opening lines of a song called "A Bundle of Truths," a collection of "self-evident propositions" of the kind so popular with our forefathers. The song continues:

A farthing rush-light's very small,
Doctors wear large bushy wigs,
One that's dumb can never bawl,
Prickled pork is made of pigs.

71. The one contribution that Dr. Samuel Johnson made to nursery rhyme literature. Commenting one day that some lines of Lope de Vega were "a mere play on words," Doctor Sam spontaneously spouted the above epigram, which he declared was no worse. "The Great Cham" is himself the subject of this "lullaby" by William Blake:

Lo! the bat with leathern wing
Winking and blinking,
Winking and blinking,
Winking and blinking,
Like Doctor Johnson.

72. The ell measured, not pudding, but cloth, and its length, in England, was 45 inches.

73. A tailor's goose is a heavy smoothing iron, called a "goose" from the shape of its handle, which resembles a goose's neck.

74. Jingles like this one infuriated the American, Samuel Griswold Goodrich (b. 1793) who declared that even a child could make one up. He then produced:

> Higglety, pigglety, pop!
> The dog has eaten the mop;
> The pig's in a hurry,
> The cat's in a flurry,
> Higglety, pigglety, pop!

His jingle has subsequently found its way into several nursery rhyme collections.

75. *The Oxford Dictionary of Nursery Rhymes* notes that "The brief story of Dicky Dilver and his wife, collected by James O. Halliwell in 1884, would always have seemed to be a straightforward, if violent, nursery rhyme, had it not been for the American poet James Russell Lowell . . . ." Shortly before his death, Lowell collected, in Maine, a ballad that begins:

« 274 »

Hyer iddle diddle dell,
A yard of pudding's not an ell;[72]
Not forgotten, tweedle-dye,
A tailor's goose will never fly.[73]

« 275 »

Hey diddle dinkety, poppety, pet,
The merchants of London they wear scarlet;
Silk in the collar and gold in the hem,
So merrily march the merchant men.[74]

« 276 »

Fiddle-de-dee, fiddle-de-dee,
The fly shall marry the humble-bee.
They went to church, and married was she:
The fly has married the humble-bee.

R. CALDECOTT

« 277 »

Pussicat, wussicat, with a white foot,
When is your wedding, and I'll come to it.
The beer's to brew, the bread's to bake,
Pussy cat, pussy cat, don't be late!

« 278 »

Little Dicky Dilver
Had a wife of silver;
He took a stick and broke her back
And sold her to the miller;
The miller wouldn't have her
So he threw her in the river.[75]

« 279 »

Lucy Locket lost her pocket,
Kitty Fisher found it,
Nothing in it, nothing in it,
But the binding round it.[76]

« 280 »

Brave news is come to town,
    Brave news is carried;
Brave news is come to town,
    Jemmy Dawson's married.

First he got a porridge-pot,
    Then he got a ladle;
Then he got a wife and child,
    And then he bought a cradle.[77]

« 281 »

Willy, Willy Wilkin,
Kissed the maids a-milking,
                Fa, la, la!
And with his merry daffing,
He set them all a laughing,
                Ha, ha, ha!

« 282 »

It's once I courted as pretty a lass,
As ever you did see;

Little Dickey Diller
Had a wife of siller;
He took a stick and broke her back
And sent her to the miller ....

The remaining stanzas of the ballad recount the adventures of a grain of wheat that would seem to personify the wife of the farmer.

76. Halliwell, the first to set down this rhyme, wrote that "Lucy Locket" and "Kitty Fisher" were "two celebrated courtesans of the time of Charles II," but *The Oxford Dictionary of Nursery Rhymes* calls his statement "purely suppositional" and adds that a celebrated beauty named Kitty Fisher, at her height about 1759, "has a right to be considered if only because she was the subject of many other verses." There is a "Lucy Lockit" in Gay's *The Beggar's Opera*, but Gay may well have been employing a traditional name.

77. After "As I was Going Up Pippen Hill" (Rhyme 104), this is the first rhyme in the section Halliwell devoted to "Love and Matrimony," but only the first verse is given there.

But now she's come to such a pass,
She never will do for me.
She invited me to her own house,
Where oft I'd been before,
And she tumbled me into the hog-tub,
And I'll never go there any more.

« 283 »

As Tommy Snooks and Bessy Brooks
Were walking out one Sunday,
Says Tommy Snooks to Bessy Brooks,
Tomorrow will be Monday.**78**

« 284 »

Little Jack Jingle
He used to live single,
But when he got tired of this kind of life,
He left off being single, and liv'd with his wife.**79**

« 285 »

Did you see my wife, did you see, did you see,
Did you see my wife looking for me?
She wears a straw bonnet, with white ribands on it,
And dimity petticoats over her knee.**80**

« 286 »

Oh, madam, I will give you the keys of Canterbury,
To set all the bells ringing when we shall be merry,
If you will but walk abroad with me,
If you will but talk with me.

Sir, I'll not accept the keys of Canterbury,
To set all the bells ringing when we shall be merry;
Neither will I walk abroad with thee,
Neither will I talk with thee!

Oh, madam, I will give you a fine carved comb,
To comb out you ringlets when I am from home,
If you will but walk abroad with me,
If you will but talk with me.

Sir, I'll not accept a fine carved comb,
To comb out my ringlets when you are from home,

Neither will I walk abroad with thee,
Neither will I talk with thee!

Oh, madam, I will give you a pair of shoes of cork,[81]
One made in London, the other made in York,
If you will but walk abroad with me,
If you will but talk with me.

Sir, I'll not accept a pair of shoes of cork,
One made in London, the other made in York,
Neither will I walk abroad with thee,
Neither will I talk with thee.

Madam, I will give you a sweet silver bell,
To ring up your maidens when you are not well,[82]
If you will but walk abroad with me,
If you will but talk with me.

Sir, I'll not accept a sweet silver bell,
To ring up my maidens when I am not well,
Neither will I walk abroad with thee,
Neither will I talk with thee.

Oh, my man John, what can the matter be?
I love the lady and the lady loves not me!
Neither will she walk abroad with me,
Neither will she talk with me.

Oh, master dear, do not despair,
The lady she shall be, shall be your only dear,
And she will walk and talk with thee,
And she will walk with thee!

Oh, madam, I will give you a fine carved comb,
To comb out your ringlets when I am from home,
If you will but walk abroad with me,
If you will but talk with me.

Oh, sir, I will accept the keys of your chest,
To count your gold and silver when you have gone
    to rest,
And I will walk abroad with thee,
And I will talk with thee![83]

« 287 »

Where have you been today, Billy, my son?

78. "Tommy Snooks" was evidently not much of a conversationalist. He reminds one of the bashful wooer in the American ballad:

> But there he sat the livelong night
> And never a word did say;
> He only sat and sighed and groaned
> While I did wish for day:
> Oh, while I did wish for day!

79. This rhyme has been traced to the eighth stanza of a fifteen-stanza story of *Jacky Jingle and Sucky Shingle*, a chapbook published around 1800. The full stanza as it appears there is:

> Now what do you think
> Of little Jack Jingle?
> Before he was married
> He used to live single.
> But after he married,
> To alter his life,
> He left off being single,
> And lived with his wife.

80. This is perhaps a more modern version of the nursery rhyme that goes:

> Saw ye aught of my love coming from ye
>   market?
>
> A peck of meal upon her back,
> A babby in her basket;
> Saw ye aught of my love a coming from the
>   market?

81. Halliwell noted that this reference to shoes of cork—chopins—attested to the antiquity of these lines.

82. Halliwell noted: "Another proof of antiquity. It must probably have been written before the invention of bell-pulls."

83. This love song has its American counterpart in the ballad, "Paper of Pins."

Where have you been today, my only man?
I've been a wooing, mother, make my bed soon,
For I'm sick at heart, and fain would lay down.

What have you ate today, Billy, my son?
What have you ate today, my only man?
I've ate eel-pie, mother, make my bed soon,
For I'm sick at heart, and shall die before noon.[84]

« 288 »

I married a wife by the light of the moon,
　A tidy housewife, a tidy one;
She never gets up until it is noon,
　And I hope she'll prove a tidy one.

And when she gets up she is slovenly laced,
　A tidy housewife, a tidy one;
She takes up the poker to roll out the paste,
　And I hope she'll prove a tidy one.

She churns her butter in a boot,
　A tidy housewife, a tidy one;
And instead of a churnstaff she puts in her foot,
　And I hope she'll prove a tidy one.

She lays her cheese on the scullery shelf,
　A tidy housewife, a tidy one;
And she never turns it till it turns itself,
　And I hope she'll prove a tidy one.

« 289 »

There was a little maid, and she was afraid
That her sweetheart would come unto her;
So she went to bed, and cover'd up her head,
And fastn'd the door with a skewer.[85]

« 290 »

"Madam, I am come to court you,
　If your favour I can gain."

"Ah, ah!" said she, "you are a bold fellow,
　If I e'er see your face again!"

"Madam, I have rings and diamonds,
Madam, I have houses and land,
Madam, I have a world of treasure,
All shall be at your command."

"I care not for rings and diamonds,
I care not for houses and land,
I care not for a world of treasure,
So that I have a handsome man."

"Madam, you think much of beauty,
Beauty hasteneth to decay,
For the fairest of flowers that grow in summer
Will decay and fade away."

« 291 »

Oh, mother, I shall be married to
Mr. Punchinello,[86]
    To Mr. Punch,
      To Mr. Joe,
        To Mr. Nell,
          To Mr. Lo.
Mr. Punch, Mr. Joe,
Mr. Nell, Mr. Lo,
To Mr. Punchinello.

« 292 »

Little Johnny Jiggy Jag
He rode a penny nag,
    And went to Wigan[87] to woo;
When he came to a beck,[88]
He fell and broke his neck,—
    Johnny, how dost thou now?

I made him a hat,
Of my coat-lap,
    And stockings of pearly blue,
A hat and a feather,
To keep out cold weather,
    So, Johnny, how dost thou now?

« 293 »

Bessy Bell and Mary Gray
    They were two bonny lasses,
They built their house upon the lea,
    And covered it with rushes.

Bessy kept the garden gate,

84. "It is said," Halliwell wrote in 1849, "there is some kind of a fairy legend connected with these lines, Billy having probably been visited by his mermaid mother. Nothing at all satisfactory has however yet been produced." Yet this may be a short and simple version of perhaps the best-known of all English ballads —"Lord Randal."

85. This is probably the first verse of a bawdy ballad. There is a college song, a perennial favorite, that goes in part:

Oh, she jumped into bed
And she covered up her head,
And she swore I couldn't find her,
But I knew damn well that she lied like hell,
So I jumped right in behind her.

86. "Punchinello"—the Italian name from which Punch of Punch and Judy (see Rhyme 223) is a shortened form.

87. Wigan is a town on the river Douglas, county of Lancashire.

88. "Beck"—a brook.

89. This stems, as so many nursery rhymes do, from a Scottish ballad. Local tradition has it that Bessy Bell and Mary Gray were two handsome girls, intimate friends, who lived together for some time in a "house upon the lea" to escape the plague, which raged with great fury around Perth about 1645. Unhappily, both girls caught the plague from a young man who was in love with both of them; both girls died, and were buried together.

Georgie Peorgie, pudding and pie,
Kissed the girls and made them cry;
When the girls begin to play,
Georgie Peorgie runs away.

K. GREENAWAY

And Mary kept the pantry;
Bessy always had to wait,
    While Mary lived in plenty.**89**

« 294 »

Rowley Powley, pudding and pie,
Kissed the girls and made them cry;
When the girls began to cry,
Rowley Powley runs away.**90**

« 295 »

Little Poll Parrot**91**
    Sat in his garret
Eating of toast and tea;**92**
    A little brown mouse,
    Jumped into the house
And stole it all away.**93**

90. Better known today is:

Georgie Porgie, pudding and pie,
Kissed the girls and made them cry;
When the boys came out to play,
Georgie Porgie ran away.

Or:

Charley Barley, butter and eggs,
Sold his wife for three duck eggs,
When the ducks began to lay,
Charley Barley flew away.

"Rowley Powley" or "Georgie Porgie" is popularly thought to have been a historical character, but there is little agreement on his identity. Andrew Lang thought he was George I,

170

« 296 »

As I went over the water,
The water went over me,
I saw two little blackbirds sitting on a tree:
The one called me rascal,
The other called me thief;
I took my little black stick,
And knocked out all their teeth!**94**

« 297 »

Gray goose and gander,
   Waft your wings together,
And carry the good king's daughter
   Over the one-strand river.**95**

« 298 »

There was an old crow
   Sat upon a clod;
That's the end of my song,
   That's odd.**96**

« 299 »

Hickety, pickety,**97** my black hen,
She lays eggs for gentlemen;
Gentlemen come every day
To see what my black hen doth lay,
Sometimes nine and sometimes ten,
Hickety, pickety, my black hen.**98**

« 300 »

Pussy cat Mole**99** jumped over a coal
And in her best petticoat burnt a great hole.
Poor Pussy's weeping, she'll have no more milk
Until her best petticoat's mended with silk.

« 301 »

There was a little one-eyed gunner
Who kill'd all the birds that died last summer.

but other scholars suggest George Villiers, the Duke of Buckingham, or Charles II. This is one of the rhymes on which George Bernard Shaw, born in 1856, was brought up.

91. Here begins the section Halliwell devoted to "Natural History."

92. When it was first imported into England, tea was universally pronounced "tay," which it must be made to do here to rhyme with "away." This indicates that the rhyme is older than those in which "tee" is the accepted pronunciation that makes the rhyme.

93. Seafaring men brought the parrot to England many hundreds of years ago, and in the nineteenth century it was a favorite household pet, especially with spinsters.

"This gaudy and longevous bird, that seems to contain all the wisdom of Solomon and more than the craft of Cleopatra in his eyes," as Walter de la Mare calls the parrot, is the subject of several other nursery rhymes.

94. Halliwell later collected the version:

> *As I went over the water,*
>   *The water went over me,*
> *I heard an old man crying,*
>   *Will you buy me some furmity?*

"Furmity" or "furmenty" or "frumenty" is a seasoned dish of hulled wheat boiled in milk. In Washington Irving's *The Sketch Book* (1861), he wrote: "The squire was having his supper of frumenty . . . a standing-dish in old times for Christmas Eve."

95. It has been suggested that "the one-strand river" is the sea.

96. Halliwell described this as "an ancient Suffolk song," to be rendered by a singer with a poor voice when called upon to entertain the company.

97. Or "Higgledy, piggledy, my black hen . . . ."

98. A combination of two similar verses from Halliwell.

99. A corruption of "Miaw" or "Mew."

« 302 »

I had two pigeons bright and gay,
They flew from me the other day:
What was the reason they did go?
I cannot tell for I do not know.

« 303 »

Pussy cat eat the dumplings, the dumplings,
Pussy cat eat the dumplings,
   Mamma stood by,
   And cried, Oh, fie!
Why did you eat the dumplings?

« 304 »

The winds they did blow,
   The leaves they did wag;
Along came a beggar boy,
   And put me in a bag,

He took me to London,
   A lady did me buy,
Put me in a silver cage,
   And hung me up on high.

With apples by the fire,
   And nuts for to crack,
Besides a little feather bed
   To rest my little back.

« 305 »

The dove says coo, coo, what shall I do?
I can scarce maintain two.
Pooh, pooh, says the wren, I have got ten,
And keep them all like gentlemen![100]

« 306 »

Curr dhoo, curr dhoo,[101]
Love me, and I'll love you.

« 307 »

Charley Warley had a cow,
Black and white around the brow;

100. The dove usually lays two eggs at a time, the wren ten or more. This is therefore better "natural history" than the American verse that goes:

Jenny Wren last week was wed,
And built her nest in grandpa's shed;
Look in next week and you shall see
Two little eggs, and maybe three.

101. This line is supposed to mimic the coo of a pigeon; "dhoo" or "dhu" is *dark* in Gaelic; "curr" is probably a name or a term of endearment.

102. These lines mimic the crowing of the cock and the clucking of the hen.

103. This "rhyme," reminiscent of both "This Is the House That Jack Built" and the tale of "The Old Woman and Her Pig," opens the section that Halliwell devoted to "Accumulative Stories."

104. Halliwell noted that: "Traditional pieces are frequently so ancient, that possibility will not be outraged by conjecturing the John Ball of [this] piece to be the priest who took so distinguished a part in the rebellion temp. [tempore—in the time of] Richard II."

Open the gate and let her go through,
Charley Warley's old cow!

« 308 »
The Cock: Lock the dairy door,
  Lock the dairy door.
The Hen: Chickle, chackle, chee,
  I haven't got the key.**102**

« 309 »
There was a rat, for want of stairs,
  Went down a rope to say his prayers.

R. CALDECOTT

« 310 »
I sell you the key of the king's garden.
I sell you the string that ties the key of the king's
  garden.
I sell you the rat that gnawed the string that ties the
  key of the king's garden.
I sell you the cat that caught the rat that gnawed the
  string that ties the key of the king's garden.
I sell you the dog that bit the cat that caught the rat
  that gnawed the string that ties the key of the
  king's garden.**103**

« 311 »
John Ball**104** shot them all,
John Scott made the shot,
  But John Ball shot them all.

John Wyming made the priming;
And John Brammer made the rammer,
And John Scott made the shot,
  But John Ball shot them all.

John Block made the stock,
And John Brammer made the rammer,
And John Wyming made the priming,
And John Scott made the shot,
  But John Ball shot them all.

John Crowder made the powder,
And John Block made the stock,

105. A rhyme that could be—but perhaps mercifully has not been—treated in the same manner is:

> *Jimmy the Mowdy*
> *Made a great crowdy;*
> *Barney O'Neal*
> *Found all the meal;*
> *Old Jack Rutter*
> *Sent two stone of butter;*
> *The Laird of the Hot*
> *Boiled it in his pot;*
> *And Big Tom of the Hall*
> *He supped it all.*

A "crowdy," by the way, is a mixture of meal with hot water or milk.

106. With this charming little verse, we reach the section Halliwell called "Local."

107. "Galligaskins" were the loose breeches worn by men in the sixteenth century.

108. John Aubrey, writing in 1687, said of this rhyme: "The young Girls in and about Oxford have a Sport called Leap Candle, for which they set a candle in the middle of the room in a candlestick, and then draw up their coats into the form of breeches, and dance over the candle back and forth, with these words."

See also "Jack Be Nimble" (Rhyme 411).

And John Brammer made the rammer,
And John Scott made the shot,
 But John Ball shot them all.

John Puzzle made the muzzle,
And John Crowder made the powder,
And John Block made the stock,
And John Brammer made the rammer,
And John Scott made the shot,
 But John Ball shot them all.
John Clint made the flint,
And John Puzzle made the muzzle,
And John Crowder made the powder,
And John Block made the stock,
And John Brammer made the rammer,
And John Scott made the shot,
 But John Ball shot them all.

John Patch made the match,
And John Clint made the flint,
And John Puzzle made the muzzle,
And John Crowder made the powder,
And John Block made the stock,
And John Brammer made the rammer,
And John Scott made the shot,
 But John Ball shot them all.**105**

« 312 »

King's Sutton is a pretty town,**106**
 And lies all in a valley;
There is a pretty ring of bells,
 Besides a bowling-alley;
Wine and liquor in good store,
 Pretty maidens plenty;
Can a man desire more?
 There ain't such towns in twenty.

« 313 »

The little priest of Felton,
The little priest of Felton,
He killed a mouse within his house,
And nobody there to help him.

« 314 »

The tailor of Bicester
He has but one eye;
He cannot cut a pair of green galligaskins,[107]
If he were to die.[108]

« 315 »

A man went hunting at Reigate,
And wished to leap over a high gate;
Says the owner, "Go round,
With your gun and your hound,
For you never shall leap over my gate."

« 316 »

Old Boniface[109] he loved good cheer,
And took his glass of Burton,[110]
And when the nights grew sultry hot
He slept without a shirt on.

« 317 »

Higham on the hill,
  Stoke in the vale;
Wyken for buttermilk,
  Hincklyey for ale.[111]

« 318 »

There were three cooks of Colebrook,[112]
And they fell out with our cook;
And all was for a pudding he took
From the three cooks of Colebrook.[113]

« 319 »

Baby and I
Were baked in a pie,
The gravy was wonderful hot.
We had nothing to pay
To the baker that day
And so we crept out of the pot.[114]

« 320 »

What are little boys made of?

109. The word "boniface" as a name for publicans derives from the character Boniface, the jovial innkeeper in Farquhar's *Beaux' Stratagem.*

110. The reference is to the water of Burton-on-Trent, England, used in manufacturing beers and ales. In the brewing trade, to "burtonize" is to treat water with gypsum or some similar substance to imitate the natural waters of Burton.

111. There might almost be another chapter to this book, titled "Mother Goose's Baedeker." For there is also:

Sutton for good mutton,
Cheam it is for beef,
Metcham for a pretty girl,
Croydon for a thief.

And:

I went to Noke,
But nobody spoke;
I went to Thame,
It was the same;
Burford and Brill
Were silent and still,
But I went to Beckley
And they spoke directly.

112. Now Colnbrook.

113. A snatch from John Hilton's *Catch that Catch can*, 1658.

114. After several rhymes we have encountered before, this old favorite opens the section Halliwell called "Relics."

115. The third through seventh stanzas do not appear in Halliwell, but are later additions.

116. This rhyme, said to have been a favorite of Longfellow's, has long been ascribed to Robert Southey, but there is no evidence to associate him with it. There is a brief American version that goes:

> *Girls are dandy,*
> *Made of candy—*
> *That's what little girls are made of.*
> *Boys are rotten,*
> *Made of cotton—*
> *That's what little boys are made of.*

117. In the original version, from Maria Edgeworth's story, *The Mimic* (1796), this song begins: "Violante, in the pantry..." Halliwell also gave the variant:

> *Hie, hie, says Anthony,*
> *Puss in the pantry*
> *Gnawing, gnawing*
> *A mutton mutton-bone;*
> *See how she tumbles it,*
> *See how she mumbles it,*
> *See how she tosses*
> *The mutton mutton-bone.*

What are little boys made of?
  Frogs and snails
  And puppy-dogs' tails,
That's what little boys are made of.

What are little girls made of?
What are little girls made of?
  Sugar and spice
  And all that's nice,
That's what little girls are made of.

What are young men made of?[115]
What are young men made of?
  Sighs and leers
  And crocodile tears,
That's what young men are made of.

What are young women made of?
What are young women made of?
  Ribbons and laces,
  And sweet pretty faces,
That's what young women are made of.

What are old women made of?
What are old women made of?
  Bushes and thorns
  And old cow's horns,
That's what old women are made of.

What are our sailors made of?
What are our sailors made of?
  Pitch and tar,
  Pig-tail and scar,
That's what our sailors are made of.

What are our soldiers made of?
What are our soldiers made of?
  Pipeclay and drill,
  The foeman to kill,
That's what our soldiers are made of.[116]

« 321 »

Hannah Bantry,[117] in the pantry,
  Gnawing at a mutton bone,
    How she gnawed it,

How she clawed it,
When she found herself alone.

« 322 »

We are all in the dumps,
For diamonds are trumps;
The kittens are gone to St. Paul's!
The babies are bit,
The moon's in a fit,
And the houses are built without walls![118]

« 323 »

Darby and Joan were dress'd in black,
Sword and buckle behind their back;
Foot for foot, and knee for knee,
Turn about Darby's company.

« 324 »

Barber, barber, shave a pig,[119]
How many hairs to make a wig?[120]
Four and twenty, that's enough,
Give the barber a pinch of snuff.[121]

« 325 »

Parson Darby wore a black gown
And every button cost half-a-crown;
From port to port, and toe to toe,
Turn the ship and away we go!

« 326 »

Around the green gravel the grass grows green,
And all the pretty maids are plain to be seen;[122]
Wash them with milk, and clothe them with silk,
And write their names with a pen and ink.[123]

« 327 »

Old Sir Simon[124] the king,
And young Sir Simon the squire,
And old Mrs. Hickabout
Kicked Mrs. Kickabout
Round about our coal fire.

118. By a considerable stretch of their imaginations, some commentators have seen in this jingle a commemoration of the visit of Elizabeth I to London on November 24, 1588, to give thanks at St. Paul's for her nation's deliverance from the Spanish Armada.

119. To "shave a pig" is perhaps a colloquial way of saying "to do something not worth doing."

120. The pig-wig rhyme has been hard-worked. See "As I Went to Bonner" (Rhyme 175) . And Lear used it in two of his limericks.

121. Halliwell in his 1844 edition gave another "barber" rhyme in the lesser-known:

The barber shaved the mason,
As I suppose,
Cut off his nose,
And popped it in a basin.

122. This rhyme would seem to refer to the "promenade" of marriageable maidens still a custom in Central and South American countries. In English-speaking countries in earlier days, such a "promenade" usually took place after church on a Sunday. The "marriageable maidens" strolled while the young bloods of the town looked them over with an eye to selecting a future wife. In the Latin countries, the young ladies were accompanied by their duennas, and it was thought highly complimentary for the young men to address remarks to the duenna regarding her young lady's accomplishments that Anglo-Americans would regard as highly insulting.

123. In later versions, the last line reads: "And the first to go down shall be married."

124. "Old Sir Simon" was supposed to have been a Falstaffian gentleman who kept the Devil Tavern in Fleet Street and died in the year 1627.

Spring is showery, flowery, bowery;

Summer is hoppy, croppy, poppy;

Autumn is wheezy, sneezy, freezy;

Winter is slippy, drippy, nippy.

CHAPTER XI

Mother Goose's Almanack

Country people live by the calendar, and Sam Adams
to the contrary, the English, from whom we got most
of our nursery rhymes, are not entirely a nation of
shopkeepers.[1]

The English husbandman watched the weather at
certain seasons, and on certain Saints' Days, with
special concern, for this weather foretold what the
weather would be like in the days and the weeks to
come. And often he put his beliefs about the weather
into doggerel rhyme.

But if there was a time for work, there was also a
time for play, a time for feasting and festival, for dil-
lying and dallying and dancing on the green. Song
was natural to such an occasion, and soon the gran-
nies who minded the children had carried snatches
of these songs back to the nursery.

There are literally hundreds of these seasonal
songs and sayings, and we can bring you here only a
small sampling of them—the "nursery rhymes for
certain times" that children have most enjoyed and
longest remembered, and even today call for most
often when New Year's or Easter or Christmas is at
hand.

1. Adams is purported to have called the English this in an oration delivered at the State House in Philadelphia, August 1, 1776. Perhaps he had been reading *Tract Against Going to War for the Sake of Trade* (1763), in which Josiah Tucker, Dean of Gloucester (1712-99) wrote: "What is true of a shopkeeper is true of a shopkeeping nation."

2. "The best-known mnemonic rhyme in the language—probably through its inclusion in the canons of the nursery," say the editors of *The Oxford Dictionary of Nursery Rhymes.* "It appears in most nursery rhyme books subsequent to 1825." In English the rhyme goes back at least to an old play of 1606, *The Return from Parnassus*; it is also found in both Latin and French, but which is the older is not known. The dominical letters attached to the first days of the months of the years were to be remembered by the initial letters of the words in these mnemonics:

Astra Dabit Dominus, Gratisque Beabit
Egenos,
Gratia Christicolae Feret Aurea Dona Fideli.

At Dover Dwells George Brown Esquire,
Good Christopher Finch and David Friar.

There were historical mnemonics:

William the Conqueror, ten sixty-six,
Played on the Saxons oft-cruel tricks.

Columbus sailed the ocean blue,
In fourteen hundred and ninety-two.

The Spanish Armada met its fate
In fifteen hundred and eighty-eight.

In sixteen hundred and sixty-six,
London burnt like rotten sticks.

And this for remembering the order of the Royal Houses (Norman, Plantagenet, Lancaster, York, Tudor, Stuart, Hanover, Windsor):
No Plan Like Yours to Study History Wisely.

The signs of the zodiac might be remembered by:

The Ram, the Bull, and the Heavenly Twins,
And next the Crab, the Lion shines,
The Virgin and the Scales,
The Scorpion, Archer, and He-Goat,
The Man that carries the Watering-pot,
The Fish with the glittering tails.

3. But the country people of England used to say that

« 328 »

Thirty days hath September,
April, June, and November;
All the rest have thirty-one,
Excepting February alone,
And that has twenty-eight days clear
And twenty-nine in each leap year.[2]

JANUARY

« 329 »

January brings the snow,
Makes our feet and fingers glow.[3]

« 330 »

Wassail,[4] wassail, to our town,
The cup is white, the ale is brown:
The cup is made of the ashen tree,
And so is the ale of the good barley.

Little maid, pretty maid, turn the pin,
Open the door and let us come in:[5]
God be here, God be there,
I wish you all a Happy New Year.[6]

« 331 »

I saw three ships come sailing by,
  Come sailing by, come sailing by,
I saw three ships come sailing by,
  On New-Year's day in the morning.

W. CRANE

And what do you think was in them then,
　Was in them then, was in them then?
And what do you think was in them then?
　On New-Year's day in the morning?

Three pretty girls were in them then,
　Were in them then, were in them then,
Three pretty girls were in them then,
　On New-Year's day in the morning.

One could whistle, and one could sing,
　And one could play the violin;
Such joy there was at my wedding,
　On New Year's day in the morning.**7**

« 332 »

He who is born on New Year's morn
Will have his own way as sure as you're born.

« 333 »

Married when the year is new,
He'll be loving, kind, and true.

« 334 »

This knot I knit,
To know the thing I know not yet,
That I may see
The man that shall my husband be,
How he goes, and what he wears,
And what he does all the days.**8**

The blackest month of all the year
Is the month of Janiveer.

This was not only because the sun is at its feeblest in January but also because all sorts of otherworldly beings were supposed to roam the earth during the critical twelve days following Christmas.

4. From the Anglo-Saxon "wes hāl," be in health.

5. In many parts of England, people used to sit up all night on the last day of the old year to make sure that the right sort of person was the first to set foot over their doorstep on New Year's morning. In the North, it was said that it must be a man and a dark man. In the South, a fair- or red-headed man could "bring in the luck," but a woman was unlucky everywhere.

6. Or:

God be here, God be there,
We wish you all a happy year;
God without, God within,
Let the Old Year out and the New Year in.

This wassail song comes from Somerset. Originally the wassailers would carry with them a drinking bowl containing a spiced drink called Lamb's Wool with which to toast their neighbors. On New Year's Day, on Twelfth Night in other places, the orchards as well as the people were wassailed:

Here's to thee, old apple tree,
Whence thou may'st bud
And whence thou may'st blow,
And whence thou may'st bear apples enow;
Hats full and caps full,
Bushels full and sacks full,
And our pockets full too.

Apples and pears, with right good corn,
Come in plenty to every one;
Eat and drink good cake and hot ale,
Give earth to drink, and she'll not fail.

In Herefordshire it was also the custom, on the eve of Twelfth Day (that is, on the night of January 5th), for the tenant farmers to drink to the master's ox:

We drink to thee and thy white horn,
Pray God send master a good crop of corn,
Wheat, rye, barley, and all sorts of grain:
If alive at the next time, I'll hail thee again.

181

7. A very similar song (in many versions) is sung as a Christmas carol:

As I sat on a sunny bank
On Christmas Day in the morning,
I saw three ships come sailing by,
On Christmas Day in the morning.
And who do you think were in those ships
But Joseph and his fair lady;
He did whistle and she did sing,
And all the bells on earth did ring,
For joy our Saviour he was born
On Christmas Day in the morning.

8. St. Agnes's Eve, the night of January 20th, was one of the most important dates in the year for maidens eager to know whom they would marry. To make use of the divination in the rhyme, the girl had to leave her home and go to a strange locality. When she retired to sleep that night she was to take her right-leg stocking and knit the left garter around it, saying the words in the rhyme. At the conclusion she was to lie down on her back with her hands under her head, and her future husband would surely appear in a dream and salute her with a kiss. The charm was rendered more certain if the girl went supperless to bed.

9. January 25th. The old almanac-makers counted it a very unlucky day.

10. James O. Halliwell also gave the variant:

As the days lengthen,
So the storms strengthen.

11. The feast celebrated on February 2nd, commemorating the Purication of the Virgin Mary and the Presentation of Christ in the Temple (Luke ii, 22-29) —so called because candles for the altar or other sacred purposes are blessed on that day.

12. In the United States, February 2nd is Groundhog or Woodchuck Day, alluding to the tradition that on that day the animal comes out of his hole, and if he casts a shadow, he runs back, in which case a return of wintry weather is to be expected.

13. Titled, in *Gammer Gurton's Garland*, where this rhyme first appeared, "The Valentine."

14. The custom of choosing a sweetheart or "valentine" on February 14th goes back to the

« 335 »

If St. Paul's Day[9] be fair and clear,
It does betide a happy year;
But if it chance to snow or rain,
Then will be dear all kind of grain;
If clouds or mist do dark the sky,
Great store of birds and beasts shall die;
And if the winds do fly aloft,
Then war will vex the kingdom oft.

FEBRUARY

« 336 »

February brings the rain,
Thaws the frozen lake again.

« 337 »

As the days grow longer,
The storms grow stronger.[10]

« 338 »

If Candlemas Day[11] be fair and bright,
Winter will have another flight;
But if it be dark with clouds and rain,
Winter is gone, and will not come again.[12]

« 339 »

When February birds do mate,
You wed nor dread your fate.

« 340 »

The rose is red, the violet's blue,[13]
The honey's sweet, and so are you,
Thou art my love and I am thine;
I drew thee to my Valentine:[14]
The lot was cast and then I drew,
And fortune said it shou'd be you.[15]

MARCH

« 341 »

March brings breezes, loud and shrill,
To stir the dancing daffodill.

« 342 »

Daffy-down-dilly is new come to town,
With a yellow petticoat, and a green gown.[16]

« 343 »

If you wed when March winds blow,
Joy and sorrow you'll both know.[17]

« 344 »

March winds and April showers
Bring forth May flowers.

« 345 »

March winds and May sun
Make clothes white and maids dun.

« 346 »

March will search, April will try,
May will tell ye if ye'll live or die.

« 347 »

In beginning or in end
March its gifts will send.

« 348 »

There were three jovial Welshmen,
  As I have heard men say,
And they would go a-hunting
  Upon St. David's Day.[18]

All the day they hunted
  And nothing could they find,
But a ship a-sailing,
  A-sailing with the wind.

One said it was a ship,
  The other he said, Nay;
The third said it was a house,
  With the chimney blown away.

And all the night they hunted
  And nothing could they find,
But the moon a-gliding,
  A-gliding with the wind.

Daffy-down-dilly has come up to town,
In a yellow petticoat and a green gown.

K. GREENAWAY

old belief, prevalent even before the time of Chaucer, that birds begin mating on St. Valentine's Day, so called in honor of Valentine, who was beheaded by the Romans on that day. It was thought that the first woman seen by a man, or man seen by a woman, on St. Valentine's Day, was destined to become a lover:

> *To-morrow is S. Valentine's day,*
> *All in the morning betime,*
> *And I a Maid at your Window*
> *To be your Valentine!*

15. *The Oxford Dictionary of Nursery Rhymes* gives a version of this rhyme which ends:

> *These are the words you bade me say*
> *For a pair of new gloves on Easter day.*

The editors note: "Gloves, which have always possessed a strong social significance, were a customary compliment or 'forfeit' gift between lovers. Claudio sent Hero a pair of perfumed gloves in *Much Ado About Nothing*. Gay, in *The Shepherd's Week*, and Scott, in *The Fair Maid of Perth*, tell how the maiden who ventures to kiss a sleeping man wins from him a pair of gloves."

16. "Daffy-down-dilly" is of course the daffodil in this little song of welcome to one of the first flowers of spring.

A later version of the rhyme goes:

> *. . . with a petticoat green, and a bright*
> *yellow gown,*
> *And her white blossoms are peeping around.*

17. And:

> *If you marry in Lent*
> *You will live to repent.*

18. See Chapter II, Note 35.

19. Only the first five verses appear in *The Top Book of All* (c. 1760), where this song was first published.

20. This song stems from a black-letter broadside ballad, *Choice of Inventions, Or Seuerall sorts of the figure of three* entered in the Stationer's register on January 2, 1632.

21. The Monday before the beginning of Lent on Ash Wednesday. So called because

One said it was the moon,
  The other he said, Nay;
The third said it was a cheese,
  And half of it cut away.[19]

And all the day they hunted
  And nothing could they find,
But a hedgehog in a bramble bush,
  And that they left behind.

The first said it was a hedgehog,
  The second he said, Nay;
The third said it was a pincushion,
  And the pins stuck in wrong way.

And all the night they hunted
  And nothing could they find,
But a hare in a turnip field,
  And that they left behind.

The first said it was a hare,
  The second he said, Nay;
The third said it was a calf,
  And the cow had run away.

And all the day they hunted
  And nothing could they find,
But an owl in a holly tree,
  And that they left behind.

One said it was an owl,
  The other he said, Nay;
The third said 'twas an old man,
  And his beard growing grey.[20]

« 349 »

Collop Monday,[21]
Pancake Tuesday,[22]
Ash Wednesday,
Dark Thursday,
Friday's lang but will be done,
And hey for Saturday afternoon.

« 350 »

It is the day of all the year,
Of all the year the one day,

And here come I, my Mother dear,
To bring you cheer,
A-mothering on Sunday.**23**

« 351 »

Hot cross buns!
Hot cross buns!
One a penny, two a penny,
Hot cross buns!
If your daughters do not like them
Give them to your sons;
But if you haven't any of these pretty little elves
You cannot do better than eat them yourselves.**24**

« 352 »

He who is born on Easter morn
Will never know want or care or harm.

« 353 »

Here's two or three jolly boys all of one mind,
We've come a pace-egging and hope you'll be kind.
I hope you'll be kind with your eggs and your beer,
And we'll come no more pace-egging until the next
    year.**25**

APRIL

« 354 »

April brings the primrose sweet,
Scatters daisies at our feet.

« 355 »

April weather:
Rain and sunshine, both together.

« 356 »

Cuckoo, cuckoo,
What do you do?
In April
I open my bill;
In May
I sing night and day;

collops—small pieces of meat, especially slices of bacon—were indulged in on that day, a relic of the traditional feasting before fast.

22. Shrove Tuesday, the day before Lent begins. In ancient times people went to church to confess and be shriven on this day. Pancakes were the traditional fare. The best-known pancake celebration in England today is the Westminster School Greeze, where pancakes are tossed over a bar by the cook and struggled for by a small mob of selected boys. The boy who gets the largest piece is presented with a guinea by the Dean. There is also the housewives' race in the Buckinghamshire village of Olney, a revival of an event that is said to date from 1445. The church bell is rung for the competitors to gather at the market square, two previous bells having warned them to mix and cook their pancakes. Then the Pancake Bell is sounded and the women set off from the church porch, tossing their pancakes three times as they run. Each woman must wear an apron and a hat or scarf over her head. The verger is entitled to kiss the winner, and the prize of a prayerbook is given by the Vicar.

23. Mothering Sunday, in the British Isles, is the fourth Sunday in Lent, and it is the pleasant custom on that day to visit one's mother. Mother should be given a present of some sort —tea or flowers or a cake. The day corresponds with Mother's Day in this country.

24. A street cry, chanted on Good Friday morning, when hot cross buns were—and are —traditionally eaten for breakfast.

25. In the Northwest of England it is still the custom for boys to go about "pace-egging"— begging for eggs—on Easter Sunday, while the older boys present the Pasch, Pascal, or Pace play—a mummers' play.

R. CALDECOTT

R. CALDECOTT

In June
I change my tune;
In July,
Away I fly;
In August
Away I must.

« 357 »

Marry in April when you can,
Joy for maiden and for man.

« 358 »

Fool, fool, April fool,
You learn nought by going to school![26]

MAY

« 359 »

May brings flocks of pretty lambs,
Skipping by their fleecy dams.

« 360 »

Trust not a day
Ere birth of May.

« 361 »

He that goes to see his wheat in May,
Comes weeping away.

« 362 »

A swarm of bees in May
Is worth a load of hay;
A swarm of bees in June
Is worth a silver spoon;
A swarm of bees in July
Is not worth a fly.**27**

« 363 »

Plant pumpkin seeds in May,
And they will run away.
Plant pumpkin seeds in June,
And they will come soon.

« 364 »

Cut thistles in May,
They grow in a day;
Cut them in June,
That is too soon;
Cut them in July,
Then they will die.

« 365 »

He that would live for aye,
He must eat sage in May.

« 366 »

Marry in the month of May,
And you'll surely rue the day.**28**

« 367 »

Trip and go, heave and hoe,
Up and down, to and fro,
From the town to the grove
Two and two, let us rove;
A-maying, a-playing;
Love hath no gainsaying;

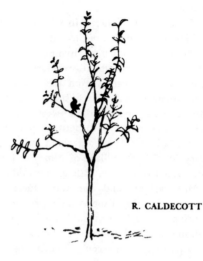

R. CALDECOTT

26. In the old days, it was proper to fool people only until noon on April 1st. One that trespassed on this rule could be told that:

April-fool time's past and gone,
You're the fool, and I am none.

27. James O. Halliwell wrote that he found this quoted "as early as 1687."

28. But:

Who first beholds the light of day
In Spring's sweet flowery month of May
And wears an emerald all her life
Shall be a loved and happy wife.

29. There are May carols as well as Christmas carols, and this is one of them—a song to be sung on May Day, May 1st, a day on which there were feasts and ceremonies throughout England to mark the passing of winter and spring and the coming of summer. This ushering-in began with the young people of the village going out overnight into the woods and fields to look for fresh green boughs and flowers, and (some said) to indulge in too free love-making.

May dawn was ushered in with horn-blowing. Hopeful girls ran out to bathe their faces in the dew (see our next rhyme). Cream and cakes were the traditional breakfast fare. The young men, returning from the woods with branches of birch and larch, stuck them in the ground at the doors of their sweethearts "till the street became a path between pale green trees." As late as 1901 "a garland hung above every door" in the village of Abney in Derbyshire. Later in the day, little girls would make a May garland, and the May Queen—and sometimes a May King—would preside over dancing and a feast around the Maypole, a tall, slim tree with its branches lopped off, but perhaps a bunch of green left at the top.

> *To the Maypole haste away,*
> *For it is a holiday . . . .*

30. The hawthorn tree, as its name implies, is a holy tree, once thought to be a trysting place for the earth spirits. It was often planted at crossroads, since such spirits were thought to gather there. To cut the blossoms of this "miniature monarch of the forest," or to damage it in any way would bring misfortune, but to tie a rag to its branch as an offering was to invite good luck. Funerals, passing a hawthorn tree, would stop to place a stone there, thus forming cairns which must on no account be disturbed.

Washing in the morning dew is a very old rule for beauty, as the following rhyme attests:

> *Beauty come,*
> *Freckles go,*
> *Dewdrops make me*
> *White as snow.*

31. Or Royal Oak Day, or Restoration Day, a festival which still survives locally in England. It is a double commemoration of the

So merrily trip and go,
So merrily trip and go.**29**

« 368 »

The fair maid who, the first of May,
Goes to the fields at break of day,
And walks in dew from the hawthorn tree
Will ever after handsome be.**30**

« 369 »

The 29th of May is Oakapple Day,**31**
Ring-a-ting-ting! God save the King!

« 370 »

Stand fast, root; bear well, top;
God send us a yowling sop!**32**
Every twig, apple big,
Every bough, apple enow,
Hats full, caps full,
Fill quarter sacks full.**33**

JUNE

« 371 »

June brings tulips, lilies, roses,
Fills the children's hands with posies.

« 372 »

Calm weather in June
Sets corn in tune.

« 373 »

June, too soon,
July, stand by;
August, it must,
September, remember,
October, all over.**34**

« 374 »

Marry when June roses grow,
Over land and sea you'll go.

« 375 »

Whitsun[35] bright and clear
Will bring a fertile year.
Whitsun rain, blessings for wine,
Whitsun wet, Christmas fat.

« 376 »

Two make it,
Two bake it,
Two break it.[36]

JULY

« 377 »

Hot July brings cooling showers,
Apricots, and gillyflowers.

« 378 »

In July,
    Some reap rye;
In August,
    If one will not the other must.

« 379 »

Those who in July are wed,
Must labor for their daily bread.

« 380 »

Knee high
By the Fourth of July.[37]

« 381 »

St. Swithin's day,[38] if thou dost rain,
    For forty days it will remain;
St. Swithin's day, if thou be fair,
    For forty days 'twill rain na mair.[39]

« 382 »

If you plant turnips on the twenty-fifth of July,
You will have turnips, wet or dry.

birthday of Charles II and of his return to London after the rebellion, May 29, 1660. The allusion is to his concealment in an oak tree near Boscobel House, Shropshire, after his defeat by Cromwell at the battle of Worcester on September 3, 1651.

32. The hope was for sufficient rain to put the land in a soppy wet state. This was thought to be good land on which to sow seed—a very questionable belief reflected in the proverb:

Sow in the sop,
'Twill be heavy a-top.

33. This charm for ensuring a heavy harvest was to be sung to the fruit trees during Rogation Days—the Monday, Tuesday, and Wednesday before Ascension Thursday, celebrated on the fortieth day after Easter Sunday in honor of the ascension of the Messiah into heaven forty days after His resurrection.

34. The "rule" for the appearance of hurricanes.

35. Whitsunday, or Pentecost, occurs exactly fifty days after Easter Sunday. It commemorates the day upon which the Holy Ghost descended upon the apostles and when the three thousand were baptized.

36. On St. John's—or Midsummer—Eve, the night of the 23rd of June, it was once the custom for two girls to bake a cake without speaking to each other. This "dumb-cake" was then broken in half. Each girl would put a piece of the cake under her pillow. She was then sure to dream of her future husband.

37. American farmers apply this proverb in their cornfields to see if they have raised a good crop.

38. July 15th. Swithin (or Swithun), Bishop of Winchester and famous builder, died in 862. His body, so the story goes, was buried at his own request outside the church "in a vile and unworthy place, under the drip of the eaves, where the sweet rain of heaven might fall upon his grave." A century later it was decided to move his remains to the interior of the church on July 15th; by way of protest the saint arranged for a forty-day deluge, whereby the monks were persuaded to abandon their project.

AUGUST

« 383 »

August brings the sheaves of corn,
Then the harvest home is borne.

« 384 »

Dry August and warm
Doth harvest no harm.

« 385

None in August should over the land,
In December none over the sea.

« 386 »

Whoever wed in August be,
Many a change is sure to see.

« 387 »

The boughs do shake and the bells do ring,
So merrily comes our harvest in,
Our harvest in, our harvest in,
So merrily comes our harvest in.

We've ploughed, we've sowed,
We've reaped, we've mowed,
We've got our harvest in.

« 388 »

Here's a health unto our master,
The founder of the feast;
And I hope to God with all my heart,
His soul in heaven may rest;
That everything may prosper,
Whatever he takes in hand;
For we be all his servants,
And all at his command.

SEPTEMBER

« 389 »

Warm September brings the fruit;
Sportsmen then begin to shoot.

39. "It has long been known," Richard Inwards wrote in *Weather Lore* (London: Rider and Company, 1950), "that St. Swithin's Day gives no clue to the weather of the next six weeks. So far as London is concerned, averages suggest that the old saying would be better reversed, for when 15th July is dry seventeen of the following forty days ordinarily bring rain in some quantity, amounting in all to three and a quarter inches, whereas after a wet 15th July the corresponding figures are sixteen days with rain and a total of two and a half inches."

40. The subject here is hours of sleep.

41. Michaelmas, September 29th, is the day of the Feast of St. Michael, a holiday on which one might sleep late. Like St. Swithin's Day (see Rhyme 381), St. Michael's Day was thought to give a clue to the weather to come:

If St. Michael brings many acorns, Christmas will cover the fields with snow.

If Michaelmas Day be fair, the sun will shine much in the winter, though the wind at north-east will frequently reign long and be very sharp and nipping.

If, on the other hand, the day be dark, look for a light Christmas.

« 390 »

September blow soft
Till the fruit's in the loft.

« 391 »

Marry in September's shine,
Your living will be rich and fine.

« 392 »

Nature requires five,[40]
   Custom gives seven;
Laziness takes nine,
   And Michaelmas eleven.[41]

OCTOBER

« 393 »

Fresh October brings the pheasant;
Then to gather nuts is pleasant.

M. PARRISH

« 394 »

Good October, a good blast,
To blow the hog acorn and mast.

« 395 »

Button to chin
When October comes in;
Cast not a clout
Till May be out.

« 396 »

If in October you do marry,
Love will come, but riches tarry.

« 397 »

O good St. Faith, be kind tonight,[42]
And bring to me my heart's delight.
Let me my future husband view,
And bring visions chaste and true.

« 398 »

St. Simon and Jude, on you I intrude,
By this paring I hold to discover,
Without any delay, to tell me this day
The first letter of my true lover.[43]

W. CRANE

« 399 »

This is the night of Hallowe'en
When all the witches might be seen;
Some of them black, some of them green,
Some of them like a turkey bean.

« 400 »

If you love me, pop and fly;
If you hate me, lay and die.[44]

« 401 »

Hemp-seed I set,
Hemp-seed I sow,
The young man that I love,
Come after me and mow.

42. St. Faith's Day is October 6th.

43. Or:

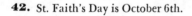

I pare this pippin round and round again,
My sweetheart's name to flourish on the plain.
I fling the unbroken paring o'er my head,
My sweetheart's letter on the ground is read.

October 28th was the day on which a young girl should try this love charm. To make it work, she had to turn around three times and throw the unbroken apple (or potato) paring over her left shoulder. It then supposedly formed itself into the telltale initial letter.

44. These lines are said to a chestnut placed in the fire—a species of divination practiced by children, especially on Hallowe'en.

I sow, I sow,
Then, my own dear,
Come hoe, come hoe,
And mow and mow.**45**

NOVEMBER

« 402 »

Dull November brings the blast;
Then the leaves are whirling fast.

« 403 »

November takes flail,
Let no more ships sail.

« 404 »

Ice in November to walk a duck,
The winter will be all rain and muck.

« 405 »

If you wed in bleak November,
Only joys will come, remember.

« 406 »

At Brill on the hill
The wind blows shrill;
The cook no meat can dress;
At Stow-in-the-Wold**46**
The wind blows cold,
I know no more than this.

« 407 »

The north wind doth blow,
And we shall have snow,**47**
And what will poor robin do then?
  Poor thing.

He'll sit in a barn,
And keep himself warm,
And hide his head under his wing,
  Poor thing.**48**

45. It was once the custom for young girls to recite these lines while sowing hemp-seed on Hallowe'en, as a charm to bring about an early marriage. Another love divination to be practiced on Hallowe'en was to take two roses and twine them together, naming one for yourself and one for your sweetheart. Then you recited this verse:

Twine, twine, and intertwine,
Let my love be wholly mine.
If his heart be kind and true,
Deeper grows his rose's hue.

46. Brill and Stow-on-the-Wold are both near Oxford, in an area rich in nursery rhyme locales.

47. A mass of weather lore has accumulated about the winds and the directions from which they blow, some of which we shall find in Chapter XII. "Wind from the north, cold and snow," is one of the best-known predictions about the north wind. "When the wind is in the north, the skillful fisher goes not forth," is another. "All bad things come out of the north. A bleak, bad wind, and a biting frost, and a scolding wife come out of the north." On the other hand, it has been said that "A northern air brings weather fair" (Fair weather cometh out of the north"—Job, xxxvii, 22) and that "The north wind makes men more cheerful, and begets a better appetite to meat."

48. There are a number of related rhymes:

Little cock robin peep'd out of his cabin,
To see the cold winter come in,
Tit, for tat, what matter for that,
He'll hide his head under his wing.

On the other hand, we are told that:

When the snow is on the ground,
  Little Robin Red-breast grieves;
For no berries can be found,
  And on the trees there are no leaves.

The air is cold, the worms are hid,
  For the poor bird what can be done?
We'll strew him here some crumbs of bread,
  And then he'll live till the snow is gone.

49. On the uneasy night of November 2nd, All Souls' Day, the spirits of the dead are abroad. Once children went from door to door singing this song, in England; and in France a table was laid and the door left ajar, waiting for the coming of the ancestors.

50. In the year 1604 certain Catholic gentlemen, oppressed by the anti-Catholic laws of England (see Chapter I), plotted to blow up the Parliament House and thus rid the country of the Protestant lords. This secret plan, known as the Gunpowder Plot, was to be carried out by Guy Fawkes (1570-1606), an ardent Catholic who had won fame fighting for the Spaniards at the capture of Calais. Fawkes and his fellow conspirators rented a house adjoining the House of Parliament, and dug their way through to a cellar beneath the House of Lords, where they planted gunpowder and set fuses. The fatal day was fixed for November 6, 1605. Someone, however, wrote a letter to a friend telling him to keep away from Parliament on that day. Search was made, and on the night of November 4th, Fawkes and his gunpowder were discovered. On January 31, 1606, he was dragged on a hurdle to the Parliament House and executed in front of it.

51. And forgot it has not been. November 5th is still celebrated in England with bonfires and fireworks, and small boys go through the streets with figures representing Guy Fawkes which they burn. From this figure comes the word "guy," as used in England to describe anyone of queer appearance.

52. The old wives' program for Thanksgiving Week.

53. For centuries, jumping over a candle has been both a sport and a way of telling fortunes in England. A candlestick with a lighted candle in it was placed on the floor. The person who could jump over it without putting out the flame was assured of having good luck for a full year. This custom was particularly associated with the festivities conducted by the lace-makers of Wendover in Buckinghamshire on November 25th, St. Catherine's Day. This day, the last popular holiday before Advent, was also, in medieval times, a day for weddings:

« 408 »

A soul-cake, a soul-cake,
Please good mistress a soul-cake;
One for Peter and one for Paul
And one for the Lord who made us all;
An apple, a pear, a plum or a cherry,
Any good thing to make us merry.**49**

« 409 »

Please to remember
The fifth of November,
  Gunpowder treason and plot;**50**
I know no reason
Why gunpowder treason
  Should ever be forgot.**51**

« 410 »

Monday—wash.
Tuesday—scour.
Wednesday—bake.
Thursday—devour.**52**

« 411 »

Jack be nimble,
Jack be quick,
Jack jump over
The candle stick.**53**

DECEMBER

« 412 »

Chill December brings the sleet,
Blazing fire, and Christmas treat.

« 413 »

When December snows fall fast,
Marry, and true love will last.

« 414 »

Cold and raw the north wind doth blow
Bleak in the morning early,
All the hills are covered with snow,
And winter's now come fairly.

« 415 »

St. Thomas Grey, St. Thomas Grey,
The longest night and the shortest day.**54**

« 416 »

St. Thomas's-day**55** is past and gone,
And Christmas is a-most a-come,
   Maidens arise
   And make your pies,
And save poor tailor Bobby one.

« 417 »

Christmas is coming, the geese are getting fat,
Please to put a penny in an old man's hat;
If you haven't a penny, a ha' penny will do,
If you haven't got a ha' penny, God bless you.

« 418 »

Bounce, buckram, velvet's dear,
Christmas comes but once a year;**56**
And when it comes, it brings good cheer,
But when it's gone it's never near.

« 419 »

On Christmas Eve I turned the spit,
I burnt my fingers, I feel it yet;
The cock sparrow flew over the table;
The pot began to play with the ladle.**57**

« 420 »

Dame, get up and bake your pies,
   Bake your pies, bake your pies;
Dame, get up and bake your pies,
   On Christmas day in the morning.

Dame, what makes your maidens lie,
   Maidens lie, maidens lie;
Dame, what makes your maidens lie,
   On Christmas day in the morning?

Dame, what makes your ducks to die;
   Ducks to die, ducks to die;

On Catherine's day
Your wedding is gay;
But Andrew's day
Takes the feasting away.

St. Andrew's Day was November 30th.

54. A rhyme for St. Thomas's Day, December 21st.

55. December 21st, the shortest day of the year.

"After sunset on the day of Saint Thomas the Apostle," writes Francis X. Weiser in *The Holyday Book* (New York: Harcourt Brace and Company, 1956), "farmers will walk through the buildings and around the farmyard, accompanied by a son or one of the farm hands. They carry incense and holy water, which they sprinkle around as they walk. Meanwhile, the rest of the family and servants are gathered in the living room reciting the rosary. This rite is to sanctify and bless the whole farm in preparation for Christmas, to keep all evil spirits away on festive days, and to obtain God's special protection for the coming year. In some parts of central Europe ancient customs of 'driving demons away' are practiced during the nights before and after Christmas (*Rauchnächte*: rough nights) with much noise, cracking of whips, ringing of hand bells, and parades of horribly masked figures."

Several weather superstitions are connected with St. Thomas's Day also:

Look at the weathercock on St. Thomas's Day at twelve o'clock, and see which way the wind is, for there it will stick for the next (lunar) quarter.

In Lancashire, they say: Frost on the shortest day indicates a severe winter.

56. A line that appears in many other pieces of doggerel, including:

Christmas comes but once a year
And when it comes it brings good cheer,
A pocketful of money, and a cellar full of
   beer,
And a good fat pig to last you all the year.

57. Like "The Sow Came in with a Saddle" (Rhyme 33), this rhyme stems from a mummers' Christmas play as performed in the middle of the nineteenth century.

Dame, what makes your ducks to die,
   On Christmas day in the morning?

Their wings are cut and they cannot fly,
   Cannot fly, cannot fly;
Their wings are cut and they cannot fly,
   On Christmas day in the morning.[58]

« 421 »

It blew
It snew
It friz
   on
Christmas
Day,
   so
merry
they say.[59]

« 422 »

Here come I,
   Little David Doubt;
If you don't give me money,
   I'll sweep you all out.
Money I want,
   And money I crave;
If you don't give me money,
   I'll sweep you all to the grave![60]

« 423 »

God bless the master of this house,
   The mistress bless also,
And all the little children
   That round the table go;
And all your kin and kinsmen,
   That dwell both far and near,
I wish you a merry Christmas,
   And a happy new year.

« 424 »

The first day of Christmas,
My true love sent to me
A partridge[61] in a pear tree.[62]

58. A song widely known in the latter half of the eighteenth century. It may have started out in life as a Christmas carol.

59. "Snow on Christmas night, good hop crop next year," some farmers still say. And: "A windy Christmas and a calm Candlemas are signs of a good year." And:

   Hours of sun on Christmas Day
   So many frosts in the month of May.

60. James O. Halliwell wrote of this: "A Christmas custom in Lancashire. The boys dress themselves up with ribands, and perform various pantomimes, after which one of them, who has a blackened face, a rough skin coat, and a broom in each hand, sings [the rhyme]."

61. The partridge is known as a bird that deserts its young. Hence in church symbolism it indicates abandonment of one's faith. Here it may imply fickleness on the part of "My true love."

62. The partridge that perches in trees—the Red Leg partridge—was not successfully introduced into England from France until about 1770. If the phrase is taken literally, it may therefore indicate a French origin of this carol of great antiquity (certainly it is well known in France). On the other hand, the "pear tree" possibly refers to a one-time Christmas custom wherein a young girl would back into a pear tree, then circle it three times. This was thought to reward her with an image of her own true love.

The second day of Christmas,
My true love sent to me
Two turtle doves, and
A partridge in a pear tree.

The third day of Christmas,
My true love sent to me
Three French hens,[63]
Two turtle doves, and
A partridge in a pear tree.

The fourth day of Christmas,
My true love sent to me
Four colly birds,[64]
Three French hens,
Two turtle doves, and
A partridge in a pear tree.

The fifth day of Christmas,
My true love sent to me
Five gold rings,[65]
Four colly birds,
Three French hens,
Two turtle doves, and
A partridge in a pear tree.

The sixth day of Christmas,
My true love sent to me,
Six geese a-laying,
Five gold rings,
Four colly birds,
Three French hens,
Two turtle doves, and
A partridge in a pear tree.

The seventh day of Christmas,
My true love sent to me
Seven swans a-swimming,
Six geese a-laying,
Five gold rings,
Four colly birds,
Three French hens,
Two turtle doves, and
A partridge in a pear tree.

63. These would be Breton hens—another indication that the carol is probably of French origin.

64. "Colly" or "colley birds" are "collied" birds, that is, coal-black birds.

65. The presents sent on the first Seven Days were *all* birds—the "Five gold rings" were not actually gold rings but refer to the five golden rings of the ringed pheasant.

The eighth day of Christmas,
My true love sent to me
Eight maids a-milking,
Seven swans a-swimming,
Six geese a-laying,
Five gold rings,
Four colly birds,
Three French hens,
Two turtle doves, and
A partridge in a pear tree.

The ninth day of Christmas,
My true love sent to me
Nine drummers drumming,
Eight maids a-milking,
Seven swans a-swimming,
Six geese a-laying,
Five gold rings,
Four colly birds,
Three French hens,
Two turtle doves, and
A partridge in a pear tree.

The tenth day of Christmas,
My true love sent to me
Ten pipers piping,
Nine drummers drumming,
Eight maids a-milking,
Seven swans a-swimming,
Six geese a-laying,
Five gold rings,
Four colly birds,
Three French hens,
Two turtle doves, and
A partridge in a pear tree.

The eleventh day of Christmas,
My true love sent to me
Eleven ladies dancing,
Ten pipers piping,
Nine drummers drumming,
Eight maids a-milking,
Seven swans a-swimming,
Six geese a-laying,

R. CALDECOTT

66. The Twelve Days are those between Christmas and Epiphany, traditionally a time of great ceremony. It is thought by some that the gifts of the song slyly refer to penances exacted for failure to observe certain fine points of ritual during this period, and this in turn may account for the fact that in the North of England to this day the song has been part of a game of forfeits in which anyone unable to carry the song a line forward and correctly repeat the lines previously added by other members of the company has to contribute something to the amusement of the assembly in the way of a song or a story or, perhaps, a kiss.

67. Young readers might find it fun to calculate how many partridges in pear trees, turtle doves, French hens, colly birds and so forth the young lady had received at the end of the Twelfth Day.

Five gold rings,
Four colly birds,
Three French hens,
Two turtle doves, and
A partridge in a pear tree.

The twelfth day of Christmas,**66**
My true love sent to me
Twelve lords a-leaping,
Eleven ladies dancing,
Ten pipers piping,
Nine drummers drumming,
Eight maids a-milking,
Seven swans a-swimming,
Six geese a-laying,
Five gold rings,
Four colly birds,
Three French hens,
Two turtle doves, and
A partridge in a pear tree.**67**

W. CRANE

Whose table shall I spread?

For whom make the bed?

Whose name shall I carry

And whom shall I marry?

Whether it's cold, or whether it's hot,

There's going to be weather, whether or not.

CHAPTER XII

Mother Goose's Charms, Auguries, and Nature Lore

While there were certain seasons and certain days of the year when divinations—particularly love divinations—were held to be especially effective, the supernatural—the sense of Outside Forces which could control man's destiny for good or ill—was with our ancestors from first of the year to last.

Omens were everywhere.

In what one saw on the road:

> White horse, white horse,
> Ding, ding, ding,
> On my way I'll find something.

In the behavior of birds and animals:

> Redbird, redbird, fly to the right,
> And I'll see my true love by Saturday night.

In a minor bodily accident:

> A scratch up and down
> Is a lover found,
> A scratch across
> Is a lover lost.

Many of the rhymes in this chapter have been taken from TOUCH BLUE compiled by Lillian Morrison and published by the Thomas Y. Crowell Company. Copyright © 1958 by Lillian Morrison. A number of the annotations were derived from material in the same book.

201

1. Reginald Scot, *The Discoverie of Witch-craft*, 1584.

2. Our distinguished predecessors, Iona and Peter Opie, add a charming note to this rhyme in *The Oxford Dictionary of Nursery Rhymes*:

"The English nursery is on friendly terms with the moon. Little children bow to it when it is new, see a man in it when it is eight days old, and cry when they can't have it. Yorkshire nurses say: 'Moon penny bright as silver, come and play with little childer.' The lads and lassies of Lancashire say: 'I see the moon, and the moon sees me; God bless the priest that christened me.' And when the moon shines into the bedrooms of trawlermen's children, then say: 'I see the moon, and the moon sees me, God bless the sailors on the sea.' . . . American children are similarly fanciful, cf. *Rocket in My Pocket*, Carl Withers, 1948, 'I see the moon, the moon sees me, The moon sees somebody I want to see.' "

This, as we have said, is charming. But *I see the moon, and the moon sees me* may have origins more sinister than charming. To sleep in the light of the moon, in ancient folk-belief, was to court *lunacy*. This rhyme may, originally, have been intended as a spell to ward off the (supposed) evil effects of exposure to moonlight, particularly to the light of a full moon. Friday's moon was thought to be particularly baleful:

Friday's moon,
Come when it wool,
It comes too soon.

Or:

Friday's moon,
Once in seven years comes too soon.

The moon's phases on Saturday and Sunday also held significance for our ancestors:

Saturday's new, and Sunday's full,
Was never fine, nor never wool.

Luna, on the other hand, was "every woman's friend" (see next rhyme).

3. This prayer to the Moon Goddess was accompanied by an elaborate ritual, part of which was to place under one's pillow a prayerbook on which rested a key, a ring, a flower, a sprig of willow, a small heart-cake, a crust of bread, and four playing cards: the

But one could also court an augury:

Whoever my true love may be,
Come and eat this apple with me.

And one could use a charm to cure a burn:

Three holy men went out walking,
They did bless the heat and the burning;
They blessed that it might not increase;
They blessed that it might quickly cease.

Most important of all, no doubt, were the rhymes designed to protect oneself, one's family, one's home and one's domestic animals from "ghoulies and ghosties, long-leggity beasties, and things that go bump in the night"—from "bull beggers, spirits, witches, urchens, elves, hags, fairies, satyrs, pans, faunes, syrens, kit with the cansticke, tritons, centaurs, dwarfes, giants, imps, calcars, conjurors, nymphes, changlings, Incubus, Robin, goodfellowe, the spoorne, the mare, the man in the oke, the hellwaine, the firedrake, the puckle, Tom thombe, hob goblin, Tom tumbler, boneles, and such other bugs, that we are afraid of our own shadows. . . ."[1]

Here is one such charm:
    Saint Francis and Saint Benedight
    Bless this house from wicked wight.
    From the night-mare and the goblin,
    That is hight Good-fellow Robin;
    Keep it all from evil spirits,
    Fairies, weezels, rats and ferrets,
    From curfew time
    To the next prime.

We start in this chapter with the signs and portents and predictions for the weather that man once found in the moon, the stars, the winds, the clouds, and the aspects of the skies.

« 425 »

I see the moon, and the moon sees me,
God bless the moon, and God bless me.[2]

« 426 »

Luna, every woman's friend,
To me thy goodness condescend,
Let this night in visions see
Emblems of my destiny.[3]

« 427 »

Pale moon doth rain,
Red moon doth blow,
White moon doth neither rain nor snow.

« 428 »

Sow peas and beans in the wane of the moon;
Who soweth them sooner, he soweth too soon.

« 429 »

If the moon shows a silver shield,
Be not afraid to reap your field.

« 430 »

Star light, star bright,
First star I see tonight,
I wish I may, I wish I might,
Have the wish I wish tonight.[4]

« 431 »

When the stars begin to huddle
The earth will soon become a puddle.

« 432 »

No weather is ill,
If the wind be still.

W. CRANE

ten of clubs, the nine of hearts, the ace of spades, and the ace of diamonds. A similar rhyme goes:

All hail to the moon! all hail to thee!
I prithee, good moon, declare to me
This night who my husband must be!

Charms of this kind worked best if the wish was made on a *new* moon, as many rhymes attest.

There was also a belief that a wish on the new moon was a cure for warts:

What I see is growing,
What I rub is going.

4. Or:

I see specks, specks see me,
I'll see somebody tomorrow
I don't expect to see.
Star light, star bright,
Very first star I see tonight,
Tell me, tell me, all I wish to know.
Does the one that I adore
Love me less or love me more?
Star light, star bright, tell me, is it so?

5. A mass of weather wisdom has accumulated respecting the wind and the direction from which it blows. Richard Inwards in his *Weather Lore* devotes twenty pages to the subject.

6. James O. Halliwell, who first collected this, would seem to have picked up a curiously corrupted version of this piece of weather lore. For "mackerel's cry" read "mackerel sky," a sky in which the clouds are of the type called cirro-cumulus, composed of white flakes or very small rounded masses, without shadows, arranged in ripples, groups or lines. Dozens of weather proverbs attest that a mackerel or curdly sky is "never long dry." Today, as a weather prophecy in rhyme, the usual reading is:

Mackerel sky,
Mackerel sky,
Never long wet
And not long dry.

There is also:

Mackerel scales and mare's tails
Make lofty ships carry low sails.

7. There is no better known bit of weather lore in the world—as witnessed by the number of rhyme forms this prophecy takes:

The ev'ning red, and the morning gray,
Are tokens of a bonny day.

When the morning sun is red,
The ewe and the lamb go wet to bed.

Evening red and morning grey,
Send the traveller on his way;
Evening grey and morning red
Bring the rain upon his head.

If the evening's red and the morning gray,
It is the sign of a bonny day;
If the evening's gray and the morning red,
The lamb and the ewe will go wet to bed.

8. "Little children," John Aubrey wrote in 1687, "have a custome when it raines to sing, or charme away the Raine; thus they all joine in a chorus and sing thus, viz.

"Raine, raine, goe away,
Come againe a Saterday.

"I have a conceit that this childish custome is of Great Antiquity yᵗ it is derived from ye Gentiles."

Aubrey's "childish custome" prevails all over the world to the present day, although the "charme" used may vary considerably with the time and the place:

Rain on the green grass,
And rain on the tree,
Rain on the house-top,
But not on me.

Rain, rain, go to Spain,
Never show your face again.

Rain, rain, go to Germany,
And remain there permanently.

Rain, rain, go away,
Don't come back till Christmas day,
Little Johnny wants to play.

Sometimes, on the other hand, rain is invited:

Rain, rain, come down and pour,
Then you'll only last an hour.

In Yorkshire, there are similar rhymes about snow. At the first snow of the year, the boys sing:

Snow, snow faster,
The cow's in the pasture.

« 433 »
The sharper the blast,
The sooner it's past.

« 434 »
When the wind is in the east,
'Tis neither good for man or beast;
When the wind is in the north,
The skilful fisher goes not forth;
When the wind is in the south,
It blows the bait in the fishes' mouth;
When the wind is in the west,
Then 'tis at the very best.[5]

« 435 »
The south wind brings wet weather,
The north wind wet and cold together;
The west wind always brings us rain,
The east wind blows it back again.

« 436 »
Comes the rain before the wind,
Then your topsail you must mind.
Comes the wind before the rain,
Haul your topsail up again.

« 437 »
The mackerel's cry,
Is never long dry.[6]

« 438 »
When the clouds are upon the hills,
They'll come down by the mills.

« 439 »
When clouds appear like rocks and towers,
The earth's refresh'd by frequent showers.

« 440 »
When the dew is on the grass,
Rain will never come to pass.

W. CRANE

« 441 »

Fog on the hill
Brings water to the mill.
Fog on the moor
Brings sun to the door.

« 442 »

A red sky at night is a shepherd's delight,
A red sky in the morning is a shepherd's warning.**7**

« 443 »

Rain, rain, go away,
Come again another day.**8**

« 444 »

A sunshiny shower,
Won't last half an hour.

But when they have had enough of snow, they sing:

> Snow, snow, give over,
> The cow's in clover!

There is also the American snow-rhyme:

> Snow, snow faster;
> Ally-ally-blaster;
> The old woman's plucking her geese,
> Selling the feathers a penny apiece.

9. James O. Halliwell in 1849 gave a similar scrap of weather lore:

> If there be a rainbow in the eve,
> It will rain and leave;
> If there be a rainbow in the morrow,
> It will neither lend nor borrow.

10. And seafarers put it this way:

Rainbow in the east,
Sailors at peace.
Rainbow in the west,
Sailors in distress.

11. But if you should have the misfortune to "gently stroke" the nettle, look for some leaves from the dockweed:

Nettle in, dock out,
Dock rub nettle out.

12. A warning against poison ivy.

13. Groundsel was an herb much used by the white witches for doctoring, especially in poultices, because of the plant's absorbent qualities.

14. A sprig of yarrow should be plucked at the time of the new moon and placed under one's pillow to make this divination work. Or a sprig of rosemary and a sprig of thyme should be sprinkled three times with water and a sprig placed in each shoe. Put a shoe on each side of the bed, and say:

St. Valentine, that's to lovers kind,
Come ease the trouble of my mind,
And send the man that loves me true
To take the sprigs out of my shoe.

15. Or:

Hate her.
Have her.
This year.
Next year.
Sometime.
Never.

Almost any group of objects may be used to determine whether "he loves me" or "he loves me not," but traditionally divination rhymes of this kind should be recited while pulling the petals one at a time from a daisy, considered a symbol of fidelity. Another rhyme for the same purpose goes:

« 445 »

Rain before seven
Fine before eleven.

« 446 »

Rainbow i' the morning,
Shipper's warning;
Rainbow at night,
Shipper's delight.[9]

« 447 »

Rainbow in the east,
Sign of a farmer's feast.
Rainbow in the west,
Sign of a farmer's rest.[10]

« 448 »

Winter's thunder
Is the world's wonder.

« 449 »

A storm of hail
Brings frost on its trail.

« 450 »

If you gently stroke a nettle,
It will sting you for your pains,
Grasp it like a man of mettle
And it soft as silk remains.[11]

« 451 »

Berries red, have no dread,
Berries white, poisonous sight.
Leaves three, quickly flee.[12]

« 452 »

Through storm and wind,
Sunshine and shower,
Still will ye find
Groundsel in flower.[13]

« 453 »

Good night, fair yarrow,
Thrice goodnight to thee;
I hope before tomorrow's dawn
My true love I shall see.**14**

« 454 »

1. He loves me.
2. He don't!
3. He'll have me.
4. He won't!
5. He would if he could.
6. But he can't.
7. So he don't.**15**

« 455 »

One leaf for fame, one leaf for wealth,
One for a faithful lover,
And one leaf to bring glorious health,
Are all in a four-leaf clover.**16**

« 456 »

If you find even ash,**17** or four-leaved clover,
You will see your love afore the day's over.

« 457 »

Burn ash-wood green,
'Tis a fire for a queen;
Burn ash-wood sere,
'Twill make a man swear.**18**

« 458 »

Bourtree,**19** bourtree, crooked rung,
Never straight and never strong,
Ever bush and never tree,
Since our Lord was nailed on thee.

« 459 »

If the oak is out before the ash,
Then we'll only have a splash;
If the ash is out before the oak,
Then we'll surely have a soak.

One I love, two I love,
  Three I love, I say,
Four I love with all my heart,
  Five I cast away;
Six he loves, seven she loves, eight both love.
  Nine he comes, ten he tarries,
Eleven he courts, twelve he marries.
Thirteen they quarrel,
Fourteen they part,
Fifteen he dies of a broken heart.

16. Which, it is said, is why a four-leaf clover is so lucky. But almost any sprig of clover can be used to bring you luck:

Find a two, put it in your shoe;
Find a three, let it be;
Find a four, put it over the door;
Find a five, let it thrive.

17. A branch of ash with an even number of leaves growing on it. This is how a girl uses it:

The even-ash leaf in my hand,
The first I meet shall be my man.
The even-ash leaf in my glove,
The first I meet shall be my love.
The even-ash leaf in my bosom,
The first I meet shall be my husband.

Or:

The even-ash I double in three,
The first I meet my true love shall be;
If he be married let him pass by,
But if he be single let him draw nigh.

The ash, even-leaved or not, may be used to cure warts:

Ash tree, ashen tree,
Pray buy this wart of me.

18. And it is said of other woods:

Oak-logs will warm you well,
That are old and dry;
Logs of pine will sweetly smell
But the sparks will fly.

Birch-logs will burn too fast,
Chestnut scarce at all;
Hawthorn-logs are good to last—
Catch them in the fall.

Holly-logs will burn like wax,
You may burn them green;
Elm-logs like to smouldering flax,
No flame to be seen.

Beech-logs for winter time,
Yew-logs as well;
Green elder-logs it is a crime
For any man to sell.

Pear-logs and apple-logs,
They will scent your room,
Cherry-logs across the dogs
Smell like flower of broom.

Ash-logs, smooth and grey,
Burn them green or old,
Buy up all that come your way—
Worth their weight in gold.

"Mother Goose" also has it that:

When a fire burns without "blowing"
You'll have company without knowing.

19. The "bourtree" is the elder.

20. Rules for shelter during a storm.

21. A farthing.

22. "So potent is the flower or berry or wood of the rowan or witchwood or quicken or whicken-tree or mountain ash against the wiles of the elf-folk, that dairymaids use it for cream-stirrers and cowherds for a switch," Walter de la Mare writes.

23. Read: "Hold the witches all in dread." We are also told that:

Vervaine and dill
Hinder witches of their will.

24. In Norfolk, England, the lady-bird is known as the "burny bee," and people there once sang:

Burnie bee, burnie bee,
Tell me when your wedding be?
If it be to-morrow day,
Take your wings and fly away.

Later versions of "Lady Bird," the first rhyme in the earliest known nursery rhyme book, often add the lines:

All except one
And that's little Ann
And she has crept under the warming pan.

Or, in Yorkshire, England, where the lady-bird was known as the "lady-cow," the added lines went:

All but one that lig under a stone,
Fly thee home, lady-cow, ere it be gone.

« 460 »

Beware of an oak,
It draws the stroke.
Avoid an ash,
It courts the flash.
Creep under the thorn,
It will save you from harm.[20]

« 461 »

When elm leaves are as big as a farden,[21]
You *may* plant your kidney beans in the garden;
When elm leaves are as big as a shilling,
It's time to plant kidney beans if you're willing;
When elm leaves are as big as a penny,
You *must* plant kidney beans—if you mean to have any!

« 462 »

Rowan-tree[22] and red thread
Gar the witches tyne their speed.[23]

« 463 »

Who sets an apple tree may live to see its end,
Who sets a pear tree may set it for a friend.

« 464 »

An apple a day
Sends the doctor away.

A. RACKHAM

Apple in the morning,
Doctor's warning.

Roast apple at night,
Starves the doctor outright.

Eat an apple going to bed,
Knock the doctor on the head.

Three each day, seven days a week,
Ruddy apple, ruddy cheek.

« 465 »

A cherry year,
A merry year;
A pear year,
A dear year;
A plum year,
A dumb year.

« 466 »

Onion's skin very thin,
Mild winter coming in.
Onion's skin thick and tough,
Coming winter cold and rough.

« 467 »

Lady Bird, Lady Bird,
Fly away home,
Your house is on fire,
Your children will burn.**24**

« 468 »

Millery, millery, dustipoll,**25**
How many sacks have you stole?
Four and twenty and a peck:
Hang the miller up by his neck.**26**

« 469 »

If bees stay at home, rain will soon come;
If they fly away, fine will be the day.

When a lady-bird—a ladybug in America—lights upon you, you are supposed to recite this rhyme to drive it away unharmed, for it is very unlucky to kill or injure the creature. If spoken to politely enough, the ladybug, it is said, will even fly to one's sweetheart:

Lady-bird, lady-bird, fly from my hand,
Tell me where my true love stands,
Up-hill or down-hill or by the sea sand,
Lady-bird, lady-bird, fly from my hand.
Fly, lady-bird, fly!
North, south, east or west;
Fly to the pretty girl
That I love best.

The little insect, for some reason buried in the veils of antiquity, is regarded with awe almost everywhere in the world, and in many places it seems to have some religious connection. This is reflected in its very name in English, which means "Our Lady's bird."

25. A very old nickname for a miller.

26. When a white moth—a "moth-miller"—flew into the nursery, an English child would address these lines to it "for luck."

27. And, for your own good health, note well the color of spiders:

Black, sad,
Brown, glad,
White, good luck attend you.

28. Francis Douce, at one time the Keeper of Manuscripts in the British Museum and a noted collector of "songs for the nursery," added a note to this rhyme which was later printed in the 1810 edition of *Gammer Gurton's Garland*:

"It was probably the custom, on repeating these lines, to hold the snail to a candle, in order to make it quit the shell. In Normandy it was the practice at Christmas for boys to run round fruit-trees, with lighted torches, singing these lines:

"Taupes et mulots,
Sortez de vos clos,
Sinon vous brûlerai et la barbe et les os."

It would seem that the snails were regarded as vermin, injurious to the fruit, and that the first four lines of this rhyme were employed as a sort of conjuration aimed at getting rid of the pests.

29. It was thought in Scotland that the following day would be "bonny" if the snail obeyed the injunction to shoot out his horns. There are other snail superstitions—one being that a snail, placed on ashes, will trace out the initials of a future lover. He also removes warts:

> *Wart, wart on the snail's black back,*
> *Go away soon and never come back.*

30. James O. Halliwell later gave two other versions of "Snail, Snail":

> *Snail, snail, shoot out your horns;*
> *Father and mother are dead;*
> *Brother and sister are in the back yard,*
> *Begging for barley bread.*
> *Sneel, snaul,*
> *Robbers are coming to pull down your wall;*
> *Sneel, snaul,*
> *Put out your horn,*
> *Robbers are coming to steal your corn,*
> *Coming at four o'clock in the morn.*

31. James O. Halliwell, who collected this, did not seem to be aware of it, but this is the song of the eleventh hag in Ben Jonson's *The Masque of Queens*, 1609, as the editors of *The Oxford Dictionary of Nursery Rhymes* point out. Jonson himself annotated the verse (for Queen Elizabeth I), saying: "These also, both by the confessions of Witches, and testemonye of writers, are of principal vse in they[r] witchcraft."

32. In most European countries, it is thought

« 470 »

If you wish to live and thrive,
Let the spider walk alive.**27**

« 471 »

Snail, Snail,
Come out of your hole,
Or Else I'll beat you,
As black as a Coal.**28**

Snail, snail,
Put out your horns,**29**
I'll give you bread
And barley corns.**30**

« 472 »

I went to the toad that lives under the wall,
I charmed him out, and he came at my call;
I scratched out the eyes of the owl before,
I tore the bat's wing: what would you have more?**31**

« 473 »

Magpie, magpie, chatter and flee,
Turn up thy tail, and good luck to me.**32**

« 474 »

Crow on the fence,
Rain will go hence.
Crow on the ground,
Rain will come down.

« 475 »

The cuckoo is a bonny bird,
She sings as she flies;
She brings us good tidings,**33**
And tells us no lies.

She sucks little birds' eggs**34**
To make her voice clear,
And never cries Cuckoo!
Till spring-time of the year.

« 476 »

When the cuckoo comes to the bare thorn,
Sell your cow and buy your corn,
But when she comes to the full bit,
Sell your corn and buy your sheep.

« 477 »

A robin redbreast in a cage
Sets all heaven in a rage.

« 478 »

The robin and the redbreast,
The robin and the wren—
If you take out of their nest,
You'll never thrive again.

The robin and the redbreast,
The martin and the swallow—
If you touch one of their eggs,
Bad luck will sure to follow.**35**

« 479 »

When the peacock loudly calls,
Then look out for rain and squalls.

« 480 »

When sea birds fly to land,
A storm is at hand.

« 481 »

If chickens roll in the sand,
Rain is at hand.

« 482 »

If a rooster crows when he goes to bed
He'll get up with rain on his head.

« 483 »

If the cock moult before the hen,
We shall have weather thick and thin,
But if the hen moult before the cock,
We shall have weather hard as a block.

to be lucky to meet *one* magpie, raven, **or** crow:

> One's lucky,
> Two's unlucky,
> Three is health,
> Four is wealth,
> Five is sickness
> And six is death.

But in Maine, people say:

> One crow sorrow,
> Two crows joy,
> Three crows a letter,
> Four crows a boy.

33. Traditionally, the cuckoo's call was first heard each year on the first of May. Superstitious farmers believed that if the call came from the north, it foretold tragedy; if from the south, it indicated a good harvest; if from the west, good luck in general; if from the east, luck in love.

According to another superstition, a young lady, upon hearing the cuckoo, should kiss her hand to the bird and say:

> Cuckoo, cuckoo,
> Tell me true,
> When shall I be married?

The number of times the cuckoo cried in answer was then supposed to indicate the number of years the young lady had to wait.

34. It is true that the Old World cuckoo refuses to build a nest of its own and has the distressing habit of devouring all the eggs in the nests of other birds. The American cuckoo does build its own nest and rear its own family, but the cowbird, or blackbird, of the grackle family, has the same parasitic habits as the European cuckoo.

35. *For sure, the robin and the wren*
Are God Almighty's cock and hen.

36. *Some* say. But we vastly prefer:

> A whistling girl and a crowing hen
> Would drive the devil out of his den.

And it is also well known that "They will come to no good en'."

37. There are several shorter versions of this "horse's prayer to its master":

> Up hill, spare me,
> Down hill, 'ware me,

211

On level ground spare me not,
And in the stable forget me not.

Up the hill take care of me;
Down the hill take care of thee;
Give me no water when I am hot;
On level ground spare me not.

38. Rules for buying a horse. Rules for selling a horse:

Four white feet, sell him right away;
Three white feet, keep him not a day;
Two white feet, sell him to a friend;
One white foot, keep him to the end.

39. A "cushy cow" is a cow without horns.

40. A silver cow-tie.

41. Milk-cows were a favorite target of the English witch's mischief-making, and this "nursery rhyme" was originally a charm used by milkmaids to induce bewitched cows to give up their milk.

42. When pixies get into the churn and prevent the cream from clotting, English farmwives repeat this charm, preferably three times, to make the butter come. The charm has also been recorded in North Carolina, where it is said that "The ugliest face peering into a cream jar will help turn the cream (clot the cream) so that churning is possible."

43. A strange line found in other charms. It may go back to St. Peter and the story told of the time when the Lord relieved him of his troubles.

R. CALDECOTT

« 484 »

A black-nosed kitten will slumber all day,
A white-nosed kitten is ever glad to play,
A yellow-nosed kitten will answer to your call,
And a gray-nosed kitten I wouldn't have at all.

« 485 »

Wherever the cat of the house is black,
Its lasses of lovers will have no lack.

« 486 »

A whistling girl and a flock of sheep
Are two good things for a farmer to keep.**36**

« 487 »

Going up hill whip me not,
Coming down hill hurry me not,
On level ground spare me not,
Loose in the stable forget me not,
Of hay and corn rob me not,
Of clean water stint me not,
With sponge and water neglect me not,
Of soft bed deprive me not,
Tired and hot wash me not,
If sick or cold chill me not,
With bit or rein oh, jerk me not,
And when you are angry strike me not.**37**

« 488 »

One white foot, buy him;
Two white feet, try him;
Three white feet, wait and see,
Four white feet, let him be.
Four white feet and a white nose,
Take off his hide and feed him to the crows.**38**

« 489 »

When a cow tries to scratch her ear,
It means a shower is very near.
When she thumps her ribs with her tail,
Look out for thunder, lightning, and hail.

« 490 »

Cushy cow,[39] bonny, let down thy milk,
And I will give thee a gown of silk;
A gown of silk and a silver tee,[40]
If thou will let down thy milk to me.[41]

« 491 »

Come, butter, come,[42]
Come, butter, come;
Peter stands at the gate[43]
Waiting for a butter cake.
Come, butter, come.

« 492 »

It is time to cock your hay and corn,
When the old donkey blows his horn.[44]

« 493 »

Laugh before it's light,
You'll cry before it's night.

« 494 »

Do not change it back all day
For that will drive your luck away.[45]

« 495 »

Hay, hay, load of hay,
Make a wish and turn away.

« 496 »

Money, money, come to me,
Before the day is less;
I spy polka dots
On the lady's dress.

« 497 »

If you see the cuckoo sitting,
The swallow a-flitting,
And a filly-foal lying still,
You all the year shall have your will.

R. CALDECOTT

44. "Brays"—as in this nursery rhyme:

Donkey, donkey, old and gray,
Ope your mouth and gently bray;
Lift your ears and blow your horn,
To wake the world this sleepy morn.

45. If you put on a piece of clothing inside
out when you dress in the morning. You
should also be very careful about mending
clothes while you are wearing them:

Just so many stitches as you take on you,
Just so many lies you'll have told about you.

And:

If you mend your clothes on your back,
You will live much money to lack.

Also, watch the wearing of your shoes:

Wear at the toe, spend as you go,
Wear at the side, be a rich bride,
Wear at the heel, spend a good deal,
Wear on the ball, live to spend all.

M. PARRISH

« 498 »

If I am to marry rich,
Let me hear a cock crow.
If I am to marry poor,
Let me hear a hammer blow.[46]

« 499 »

It's a sure sign and a true,
That at the very moment,
Your true love thinks of you.[47]

« 500 »

If you find a hairpin,
Stick it in your shoe;
The next boy you talk with
Is sure to marry you.

« 501 »

Go over, meet with clover;
Go through, meet with a shoe;
Go under, meet with a blunder.[48]

« 502 »

If you stub your toe,
You'll see your beau;
Kiss your thumb,
He'll be sure to come.

« 503 »

Step in a hole,
You'll break your mother's sugar bowl.

Step on a crack,
You'll break your mother's back.

Step in a ditch,
Your mother's nose will itch.

Step in the dirt,
You'll tear your father's shirt.

Step on a nail,
You'll put your father in jail.

« 504 »

Drop a spoon,
Company soon.**49**

Knife falls,
Gentleman calls.

Fork falls,
Lady calls.

« 505 »

Touch blue,
Your wish will come true.

« 506 »

Those dressed in blue
Have lovers true;
In green and white,
Forsaken quite.**50**

« 507 »

If you love me, love me true,
Send me a ribbon, and let it be blue;
If you hate me, let it be seen,
Send me a ribbon, a ribbon of green.**51**

« 508 »

Married in white, you have chosen just right,
Married in gray, you'll go far away,
Married in blue, your lover is true,
Married in red, you'll wish you were dead,
Married in black, better turn back,
Married in green, ashamed to be seen,
Married in yellow, jealous of your fellow,
Married in brown, you'll live out of town,
Married in pearl, you'll live in a whirl.

« 509 »

Whatever happens twice
Is sure to happen thrice.

46. Or:

If I am to marry far,
Let me hear a bird cry.
If I am to marry near,
Let me hear a cow low.
If I am to single die,
Let me hear a knocking by.

47. If your shoelace comes untied.

48. How and how not to get over a fence.

49. Or:

Spoon falls,
Baby calls.

50. Or:

Green's forsaken,
Yellow's forsworn,
Blue's the color
That shall be worn.

Or:

Blue is true,
Yellow's jealous,
Green's forsaken,
Red's brazen,
White is love
And black is death.

51. Or:

If your love for me is true,
Send me quick a bow of blue.
If you ever of me think,
Send me quick a bow of pink.
If you have another fellow,
Let me have a bow of yellow.
If your love for me is dead,
I'll know it if your bow is red.

52. Lines to be spoken when two people have said the same thing at the same time. They should link the little fingers of their right hands while reciting this formula.

53. A rhyme used to affirm that one is speaking the truth. Others:

Certain true, black and blue,
Lay me down and cut me in two.

I ring, I ring, a pinky!
If I tell a lie
I'll go to the bad place
Whenever I die.

White pan, black pan,
Burn me to death,
Take a big knife
And cut my breath,
Ten miles below the earth.

54. The gift of a knife was once thought to sever a friendship, unless the above charm was said by the donor.

55. Lines to be said by two girls breaking a wishbone.

56. James O. Halliwell's version of the familiar formula by which a small child, using counters of some sort—a counter for each line in the rhyme—determines "what he will be when he grows up." The best-known English versions are:

Tinker,
Tailor,
Soldier,
Sailor,
Gentleman,
Apothecary,
Plough-boy,
Thief.

Soldier brave, sailor true,
Skilled physician, Oxford blue,
Learned lawyer, squire so hale,
Dashing airman, curate pale.

Army, Navy,
Medicine, Law,
Church, Nobility,
Nothing at all.

In Scotland, they say:

A laird, a lord,
A cooper, a thief,
A piper, a drummer,
A stealer of beef.

« 510 »

Speak of a person, and he will appear,
Then talk of the devil, and he'll draw near.

« 511 »

A name that's spoken before eating
You'll use ere nightfall as a greeting.

« 512 »

"What comes out of a chimney?"
"Smoke."
"May your wish and my wish never be broke."[52]

« 513 »

Make a rhyme, make a rhyme,
See your beau before bedtime.

« 514 »

Cross my heart and hope to die,
Cut my throat if I tell a lie.[53]

« 515 »

If you love me as I love you,
No knife shall cut our love in two.[54]

« 516 »

Shortest to marry;
Longest to tarry.[55]

« 517 »

My belief:
A captain,
A colonel,
A cow-boy,
A thief.[56]

« 518 »

Blue eye beauty,
Grey eye greedy,
Black eye blackie,
Brown eye brownie.[57]

« 519 »

Little head, little wit,
Big head, not a bit.

« 520 »

Beware of that man be he friend or brother
Whose hair is one color and beard another.

« 521 »

Dimple in your chin,
Your living comes in;
Dimple in your cheek,
You've your living to seek.**58**

« 522 »

If you've got a mole above your chin,
You'll never be beholden to any of your kin.**59**

« 523 »

Specks on the fingers,
Fortune lingers;
Specks on the thumbs,
Fortune comes.

« 524 »

A gift, a ghost,
A friend, a foe,
A letter to come,
A journey to go.**60**

« 525 »

If your nose itches,
Your mouth is in danger;
Kiss a fool,
And meet a stranger.**61**

« 526 »

Hickup, hickup, go away!
Come again another day;
Hickup, hickup, when I bake,
I'll give to you a butter-cake.**62**

In America, we say:

Rich man,
Poor man,
Beggarman,
Thief.
Doctor,
Lawyer,
Merchant,
Chief.

Girls can say:

Rich girl, poor girl, beggar girl, crook,
Schoolgirl, phone girl, servant girl, cook.

57. This is the way this rhyme has appeared in nursery rhyme books for over a hundred years. But James O. Halliwell, who first collected it, would appear to have picked up a corrupted version of the rhyme usually given as:

Blue eye beauty,
Do your mother's duty;
Brown-eyed pickle pie,
Turn around and tell a lie;
Green-eyed greedy gut,
Eat all the world up.

There is also:

If a woman's eyes are gray,
Listen to what she's got to say.
If a woman's eyes are black,
Give her room and clear the track.
If a woman's eyes are brown,
Never let your own fall down.
If a woman's eyes are green,
Whip her with a switch that's keen.
If a woman's eyes are blue,
Take her, she's the one for you.

58. Or:

A dimple in your cheek,
You are gentle and meek.
A dimple in your chin,
You've a devil within.

Or:

A dimple in your cheek,
Many hearts you will seek;
A dimple in your chin,
Many hearts you will win.

There is a pleasant belief that a dimple is the mark left by an angel's kiss—or by an angel's finger touching the chin or cheek.

59. And "Mother Goose" also avers that:

> *A mole on your arm,*
> *Will do you no harm.*
> *A mole on the lip,*
> *You're a little too flip.*
> *A mole on the neck,*
> *Money by the peck.*
> *A mole on the back,*
> *Money by the sack.*
> *A mole on the ear,*
> *Money by the year.*

60. A fortune-telling rhyme, to be said while counting the white spots on the nails of one's hand.

61. An itch on the hand:

> *Rub it on wood*
> *And it will come good.*

And if your ears are burning, someone is talking about you:

> *Right for love and left for spite,*
> *But either side is good at night.*

To stop the itching, wet your finger, touch your ear, and say:

> *If it's good talk, itch away,*
> *If it's bad talk, skip, I say.*

62. And here is another "cure":

> *Hickup, snickup,*
> *Rise up, kick up!*
> *Three drops in the cup*
> *Are good for the hickup.*

You say this rhyme as you bend over and sip three drops from the *far* side of the cup. Each of us probably has his own special cure for this minor everyday ailment. In New England, hiccoughs during church are particularly feared, and some of the older people still go to services armed with "meetin' seeds"—fennel, dill, and caraway.

63. Sometimes:

> *And a piece of silver in the heel of her shoe.*

Or the bride may be advised to be married in:

> *Something new, something old,*
> *Something borrowed, something stoled.*

64. On the other hand:

> *First a son, and then a daughter,*
> *You've begun just as you oughter.*

« 527 »

If you sit on the table,
You'll be married before you're able.

« 528 »

Something old, something new,
Something borrowed, something blue,
And a penny in her shoe.**63**

« 529 »

Happy is the bride that the sun shines on;
Blessed are the dead that the rain falls on.

« 530 »

Wash and wipe together,
Live in peace forever.

« 531 »

Rock a cradle empty,
Babies will be plenty.

« 532 »

First a daughter, then a son,
And the world is well begun.**64**

« 533 »

Monday's child is fair of face,
Tuesday's child is full of grace,
Wednesday's child is full of woe,
Thursday's child has far to go,
Friday's child is loving and giving,
Saturday's child works hard for his living,
And the child that is born on the Sabbath day
Is bonny and blithe, and good and gay.**65**

« 534 »

Monday for health,
Tuesday for wealth,
Wednesday the best day of all,
Thursday for losses,
Friday for crosses,
Saturday no luck at all.**66**

« 535 »

Yellow stones on Sunday,
Pearls on Monday,
Rubies on Tuesday,
Sapphires on Wednesday,
Garnets or red stones on Thursday,
Emeralds or green stones on Friday,
Diamonds on Saturday.**67**

« 536 »

If you sneeze on Monday, you sneeze for danger;
Sneeze on a Tuesday, kiss a stranger;
Sneeze on a Wednesday, sneeze for a letter;
Sneeze on a Thursday, something better;
Sneeze on a Friday, sneeze for sorrow;
Sneeze on a Saturday, see your sweetheart tomorrow;
Sneeze on a Sunday, your safety seek,
Or the devil will take you for the rest of the week.**68**

« 537 »

Cut them on Monday,**69** you cut them for health;
Cut them on Tuesday, you cut them for wealth;
Cut them on Wednesday, you cut them for news;
Cut them on Thursday, a new pair of shoes;
Cut them on Friday, you cut them for sorrow;
Cut them on Saturday, see your true love tomorrow;
Cut them on Sunday, ill luck will be with you all the
    week.

« 538 »

They that wash on Monday
    Have all the week to dry;**70**
They that wash on Tuesday
    Are not so much awry;
They that wash on Wednesday
    Are not so much to blame;
They that wash on Thursday
    Wash for shame;
They that wash on Friday,
    Wash in need;
And they that wash on Saturday,
    Oh! they are sluts indeed.

65. There are numerous variations of this well-known "prophecy," but none of them is very old.

66. Rules for the day of the week on which to marry.

67. Wear these stones on these days if you wish "to have luck."

68. Man once believed that the essence of life, the spirit or soul, resided in the head in the form of the breath. The soul, then, could be accidentally expelled for a longer or a shorter time by that dangerous thing, a sneeze.

On the other hand, some primitive peoples believe that sneezing indicates an *intrusion* into the body of evil spirits. A relic of this belief is the English "God bless you!", the German "*Gesundheit*," the Italian "*Felicita*," and the French "*Que Dieu vous bénisse*" when someone sneezes. When a Greek or a Chinese sneezes, his companions bow low, and the list might be extended almost indefinitely. The rhyme given is one of the best-known "sneeze" superstitions, but there are dozens of others. To sneeze on the threshold of a friend, for example, is believed by many to be a bad omen.

The number of times that one sneezes is significant:

> *Once a wish,*
> *Twice a kiss,*
> *Three times a letter,*
> *Four times something better.*

And the time at which one sneezes is also fraught with significance:

> *Sneeze before you eat,*
> *See your sweetheart before you sleep.*
> *Sneeze between twelve and one,*
> *Sure sign somebody'll come.*
> *Sneeze between one and two,*
> *Come to see you.*
> *Sneeze between two and three,*
> *Come to see me.*
> *Sneeze between three and four,*
> *Somebody's at the door.*

69. Your fingernails, that is.

70. On Saturday, November 11, 1620—November 21 by present-day reckoning—the Pilgrim Fathers, after sixty-six days at sea aboard the *Mayflower*, first stepped ashore in the New World at Provincetown on Cape Cod, Massachusetts. Two days later the Pilgrim women went ashore for the first time and began scrubbing the grime out of their families' clothing. Thus Monday became the week's traditional washday. The program for the entire week, in those days, was:

Wash on Monday,
Iron on Tuesday,
Bake on Wednesday,
Brew on Thursday,
Churn on Friday,
Mend on Saturday,
Go to meeting on Sunday.

71. Or, every Friday night for three Fridays in a row, throw a pinch of salt on the fire and say:

It is not this salt that I wish to burn
But my lover's heart that I wish to turn,
So that he may not rest nor happy be
Until he comes to me.

72. The couplet means that if you move to a new home on a Saturday, you will not enjoy living there very long.

73. This little rhyme reflects the belief that it is good luck to remove the left shoe before the right when going to bed, bad luck to reverse the process. Of hundreds of other "going-to-bed" superstitions and divinations, there are:

Put your shoes towards the street,
Leave your garters on your feet,
Put your stockings on your head,
And you'll dream of the man you're going
*   to wed.*

When I my true love want to see,
I put my shoes in the shape of a T.

Husband mine that is to be,
Come this night and rescue me.

« 539 »

Monday alone,
Tuesday together,
Wednesday we walk
When it's fair weather.
Thursday we kiss,
Friday we cry,
Saturday's hours
Seem almost to fly.
But of all days in the week
We will call
Sunday, the rest day,
The best day of all.

« 540 »

Rain on Monday,
Sunshine next Sunday.

« 541 »

Friday's a day that will have its trick,
The fairest or foulest day of the week.

« 542 »

On Friday night I go backwards to bed,
I sleep with my petticoat under my head,
To dream of the living and not of the dead,
To dream of the man that I am to wed.**71**

« 543 »

This is silver Saturday,
The morn's the resting day;
Monday up and to it again,
And Tuesday push away.

« 544 »

Saturday's flitting
Is a sign of short sitting.**72**

« 545 »

Go day, come day,
God send us Sunday.

« 546 »

Sunday sail, never fail,
Friday sail, ill luck and gale.

« 547 »

Left and right
Bring good at night.**73**

« 548 »

Matthew, Mark, Luke and John,
Bless the bed that I lie on.
Four corners to my bed,
Four angels round my head;
One to watch and one to pray
And two to bear my soul away.**74**

« 549 »

Dreams at night are the devil's delight,
Dreams in the morning are the angels' warning.**75**

74. This was once, in the country districts of England, the best-known prayer, repeated more often than the Lord's Prayer. Originally, as the "White Paternoster," it was a night-spell; as the "Black Paternoster," a distorted version of it was used as an enchantment by witches. No one can say with any certainty just how ancient it is; it may be half Celtic magic and half Christian ritual.

This is one of the most parodied of verses:

Matthew, Mark, Luke, and John,
Stole a pig and away they run;
The pig got loose and they stole a goose,
And all got thrown in the calaboose.

Matthew, Mark, Luke, and John,
I'm off my horse and I want to get on.
Open the gate or I'll be gone.

75. Libraries could, and have, been assembled in which the only volumes are concerned with oneiromancy, the "science" of foretelling the future by dreams. All nations, at all times, have to some extent held the belief. If any reader is interested in pursuing the subject, he might well begin with Chapter VI of *The Encyclopedia of Occult Sciences* (New York: Robert M. McBride Co., Inc., 1939). Meantime, these dream rhymes from "Mother Goose":

Dream of fruit out of season,
You'll be angry without a reason.

Dream of beauty,
Wake to duty.
Dream of duty,
Wake to beauty.

Friday night's dream
    On the Saturday told,
Is sure to come true,
    Be it never so old.

And it is also advised that:

Friday night's dream mark well,
Saturday night's dream never tell.

M. PARRISH

Some friend must now, perforce,

Go forth and bid my boy

To saddle me my wooden horse,

For I mean to conquer Troy.

CHAPTER XIII

Mother Goose's Lullabies and Game Songs

"The earliest and simplest form in which the nursery rhyme appears is the lullaby, which may be defined as a gentle song used for the purpose of inducing sleep," James O. Halliwell wrote in 1849. "The etymology is to be sought for in the verb *lull*, to sing gently. . . ." One of the earliest lullabies to have descended to our day occurs in the play *Philotimus,* 1583. . . . And another is introduced into the comedy of *Patient Grisel,* printed in the year 1603:

> "Hush, hush, hush, hush!
>   And I dance my own child,
>   And I dance my own child,
>   Hush, hush, hush, hush!"

As Halliwell says, the lullaby is a simple form, yet of all the "Mother Goose" rhymes, it is lullabies, perhaps, which come the closest to being true poetry. And this is not surprising, for poets of stature have not scorned to write lullabies. One who certainly composed such a slumber song was Thomas Dekker (1572?-1632), and you will find his contribution here as Rhyme 557.

But the child grows older. At first he is delighted

1. The subtitle of *Tom Thumb's Play Book*, Boston: A. Barclay, 1771.

2. The antiquarian Joseph Ritson seems to have been the first to suggest that the English "Hush a by" may have been a corruption of *He bas, la le loup!* (*Hush, here comes the wolf*)—an expression used by French nurses to "soothe" their little charges when they were being obstreperous.

3. The opening lines of this rhyme, probably the best-known lullaby in English, tell us that once, long ago, a mother would hang her baby's cradle on the bough of a tree and let the wind do the work of rocking it. "Sometimes," Robert Chambers wrote in the second volume of his famous *Book of Days*, "in the hop grounds, we have seen a cradle with the baby asleep in it, swinging between the tall hop-bines." Indeed, there is a legend that a Pilgrim youth who sailed to America on the *Mayflower* composed this rhyme after seeing the American Indian women so rock their children in birchbark cradles (some illustrations in "Mother Goose" books reflect this tradition).

4. Sometimes, later, "When the wind ceases" or "When the tree shakes...."

5. Katherine Elwes Thomas read into these lines the "long and exciting history of James Stuart, the Pretender...." but this is not a popular theory with most students of the nursery rhyme. The editor of the *Melody* added to this rhyme both a bit of philosophy and a maxim: "This may serve as a warning to the proud and ambitious, who climb so high that they generally fall at last"—and: "Content turns all it touches into gold."

by such simple infant fare as the toe-counting rhymes, like "This Little Pig Went to Market." He does not suspect that from them he is learning to count to five.

All too soon, however, he discovers that his nurse or his parents are buttressed with a wealth of verses "To teach Children their Letters as soon as they can speak ... to allure LITTLE ONES in the first Principles of Learning."[1]

When he can escape from such sugar-coated learning, when he is free to do just as he wants to do, the child at first is likely to turn to such solitary pleasures as riding a hobby-horse, swinging, or simply marching up and down—and often each of these pursuits has a rhyme to go with it.

"English children accompanied their amusements with trivial verses from a very early period," Halliwell wrote.

Next comes a game with a companion of the child's own age—teeter-tottering, perhaps?—and here, too, there are "trivial verses" to accompany the amusement.

Then comes group play. Who, of all these children, is to be "It"? We meet with the counting-out rhyme.

And so it goes, this chapter on "Mother Goose's Lullabies and Game Songs" until, at the end, you will find rhymes once recited by people well into middle age—people who could still find a child's delight in such trials of one's wits as "I Love My Love with an A," in such tests of one's dexterity as "My Father, He Left Me...."

« 550 »

Hush a by Baby[2]
  On the Tree Top,
When the Wind blows
  The Cradle will rock;[3]
When the Bough breaks[4]
  The Cradle will fall,
Down tumbles Baby,
  Cradle and all.[5]

M. PARRISH

A. RACKHAM

« 551 »

Bee baw bunting,[6]
Daddy's gone a hunting,[7]
To get a little lamb's skin,[8]
To lap his baby bunting in.[9]

« 552 »

Rock-a-bye, baby, thy cradle is green,
Father's a nobleman, Mother's a queen;
And Betty's a lady, and wears a gold ring;
And Johnny's a drummer, and drums for the king.

« 553 »

Hush-a-bye baby,
    Daddy is near,
Mammy's a lady,
    And that's very clear.

« 554 »

Bye, baby bumpkin,
Where's Tony Lumpkin?[10]
My lady's on her death-bed,
With eating half a pumpkin.

« 555 »

Baby, baby, naughty baby,
Hush, you squalling thing, I say.
Peace this moment, peace, or maybe
Bonaparte will pass this way.

Baby, baby, he's giant,
Tall and black as Rouen steeple,
And he breakfasts, dines, rely on't,
Every day on naughty people.

Baby, baby, if he hears you,
As he gallops past the house,
Limb from limb at once he'll tear you,
Just as pussy tears a mouse.

And he'll beat you, beat you, beat you,
And he'll beat you all to pap,
And he'll eat you, eat you, eat you,
Every morsel snap, snap, snap.

6. "Bunting" is an old form of endearment, probably meaning (*Oxford English Dictionary*) "short and thick . . . as a plump child."

7. *Songs for the Nursery* (1805) inserts here the lines:

Mother's gone a milking,
Sister's gone a silking,
Brother's gone to buy a skin . . . .

8. Or, later, "a rabbit skin" or "a hare's skin" or "a bullie's skin" or "a lammie's skin" or "a sturdy lion's skin."

9. Later rhymes of a similar kind go:

Bye, bye, baby bunting,
Your Daddy's gone a-hunting,
Your Mammy's gone the other way,
To beg a jug of sour whey
For little baby bunting.

Father's gone a-flailing,
Brother's gone a-nailing,
Mother's gone a-leasing,
Granny's gone a-pleasing,
Sister's gone to Llantwit Fair,
Baby, baby, will go there.

10. In Goldsmith's *She Stoops to Conquer*, "Tony Lumpkin" is a coarse but kindly young fellow, the son of Mrs. Hardcastle by an earlier marriage. Since Goldsmith probably edited the first *Mother Goose's Melody*, it would be natural to expect to find this lullaby in it. But it was James O. Halliwell, not Goldsmith, who first collected it.

·HVSH·A·BY BABY··

W. CRANE

« 556 »

Sleep, baby, sleep,
Thy father guards the sheep;
Thy mother shakes the dreamland tree
And from it fall sweet dreams for thee,
 Sleep, baby, sleep.

Sleep, baby, sleep,
Our cottage vale is deep;
The little lamb is on the green,
With woolly fleece so soft and clean—
 Sleep, baby, sleep.

Sleep, baby, sleep,
Down where the woodbines creep;
Be always like the lamb so mild,
A kind and sweet and gentle child,
 Sleep, baby, sleep.

« 557 »

Golden slumbers kiss your eyes,
Smiles awake you when you rise,
Sleep, pretty wanton; do not cry,
And I will sing you a lullaby:
Rock them, rock them, lullaby:

Care is heavy, therefore sleep you;
You are care, and care must keep you.
Sleep, pretty wanton; do not cry,
And I will sing you a lullaby:
Rock them, rock them, lullaby.

« 558 »

Hush, little baby, don't say a word,
Papa's going to buy you a mocking bird.

If the mocking bird won't sing,
Papa's going to buy you a diamond ring.

If the diamond ring turns to brass,
Papa's going to buy you a looking-glass.

If the looking-glass gets broke,
Papa's going to buy you a billy-goat.

If the billy-goat runs away,
Papa's going to buy you another today.

« 559 »

Hush, my baby, do not cry,
Papa's coming by and by;
When he comes he'll come in a gig,
Hi cockalorum, jig, jig, jig.

« 560 »

Oh my Kitten a Kitten
And Oh my Kitten my Deary
Such a sweet pap[11] is this
There is not far nor Neary.

Here we go up up up,
Here we go down down down,
Here we go backwards & forwards,
& Here we go roundroundround.[12]

« 561 »

How many days has my baby to play?
Saturday, Sunday, Monday,
Tuesday, Wednesday, Thursday, Friday,
Saturday, Sunday, Monday.
Hop away, skip away,
My baby wants to play,
My baby wants to play every day.**13**

« 562 »

Dance, little baby, dance up high:
Never mind, baby, mother is by;
Crow and caper, caper and crow,
There, little baby, there you go;
Up to the ceiling, down to the ground,
Backwards and forwards, round and round:
Dance, little baby, and mother shall sing,
With the merry gay coral,**14** ding-a-ding, ding.

« 563 »

Dance to your daddy,
  My little babby,
Dance to your daddy, my little lamb!
  You shall have a fishy
  In a little dishy,
You shall have a fishy when the boat comes in.

Dance to your daddy,
  My little babby,
Dance to your daddy, my little lamb;
  You shall have an apple,
  You shall have a plum,
  You shall have a rattle-basket,
When your dad comes home.

« 564 »

Catch him, crow! Carry him, kite!
Take him away till the apples are ripe;
When they are ripe and ready to fall,
Here comes baby, apples and all!

11. "Pap"—pet.

12. Sometimes one wanted to play with the baby, not just to lull it to sleep. Here is our first rhyme for such an occasion. It comes, appropriately enough, from *Tommy Thumb's Pretty Song Book*, the earliest known book of nursery rhymes, and it appeared there exactly as it appears here. This rhyme was later sung by children swinging, and it may have been sung originally to a tune in 9/8 time, a jig. The words as given here would seem to have appeared in print for the first time around 1740. The rhyme has been ascribed, without much authority, to the great satirist Jonathan Swift (1667-1745). When Goldsmith included this rhyme in *Mother Goose's Melody*, he added the maxim: "Idleness hath no advocate, but many friends."

13. Another "playing with the baby" rhyme, this one from *Songs for the Nursery*, although only the first four lines appeared there; the refrain is a later addition.

14. This refers to the baby's rattle, often, in the nineteenth century, bedecked with a sprig of coral.

A. RACKHAM

« 565 »

To market, to market,
    To buy a plum bun:
Home again, home again,
    Market is done.**15**

« 566 »

This is the way the ladies ride,
Nimble, nimble, nimble, nimble;
This is the way the gentlemen ride,
A gallop, a trot, a gallop, a trot;
This is the way the farmers ride,
Jiggety jog, jiggety jog;
And when they come to a hedge—they jump over!
And when they come to a slippery space—
They scramble, scramble, scramble,
    Tumble-down Dick!**16**

« 567 »

Young Roger came tapping at Dolly's window,
    Thumpaty, thumpaty, thump.
He begged for admittance, she answered him, No,
    Glumpaty, glumpaty, glump.
My Dolly, my dear, your true love is here,
    Dumpaty, dumpaty, dump.
No, no, Roger, no, as you come you may go,
    Stumpaty, stumpaty, stump.**17**

« 568 »

Trit trot to market to buy a penny doll;
Trit trot back again, the market's sold them all.

« 569 »

Hie to the market, Jenny come trot,
Spilt all her butter milk, every drop.
Every drop and every dram,
Jenny came home with an empty can.

« 570 »

A robin and a robin's son
Once went to town to buy a bun,

To market, to market, to buy a plum cake,
Home again, home again, market is late;
To market, to market, to buy a plum bun,
Home again, home again, market is done.

K. GREENAWAY

They couldn't decide on plum or plain,
And so they went back home again.

« 571 »

Donkey, donkey, do not bray,
Mend your pace and trot away;
Indeed, the market's almost done,
My butter's melting in the sun.

« 572 »

Come up, my horse, to Budleigh Fair;
What shall we have when we get there?
Sugar and figs and elecampane;[18]
Home again, home again, master and dame.[19]

« 573 »

Dingle, dingle, doosey,
    The cat's in the well;
The dog's away to Belingen,
    To buy the bairn a bell.[20]

« 574 »

Weave the diaper[21] tick-a-tick tick,
Weave the diaper tick—
Come this way, come that
As close as a mat,
Athwart and across, up and down, round about,
And forward, and backwards, and inside and out;
Weave the diaper thick-a-thick thick,
Weave the diaper thick![22]

« 575 »

Brow Bender,[23]
Eye Peeper,[24]
Nose Dropper,[25]
Mouth Eater,[26]
Chin Chopper,[27]
Knock at the door,[28]
Ring the bell,[29]
Lift up the latch,
Walk in,[30]
Take a chair,

15. This rhyme—from *Songs for the Nursery*, 1805—is the earliest "Mother Goose" version of many "To Market" rhymes, rhymes designed to be used for "knee-trotting" a child.

In 1844 James O. Halliwell found the following verse partially quoted in Florio's *New World of Words*, 1611, and published it in *The Nursery Rhymes of England*:

To market, to market, a gallop, a trot,
    To buy some meat to put in the pot;
Three pence a quarter, a groat a side,
    If it hadn't been killed it must have died.

Best known today is the comparatively modern:

To market, to market, to buy a fat pig,
    Home again, home again, jiggety-jig;
To market, to market, to buy a fat hog,
    Home again, home again, jiggety-jog.

Another "To market" rhyme, which also bears a family resemblance to "This Is the Way the Ladies Ride" (see next rhyme) goes:

To market ride the gentlemen,
    So do we, so do we;
Then comes the country clown,
    Hobbledy gee, hobbledy gee!

16. This favorite old rhyme is to be sung while jumping a child up and down on one's crossed legs. The child faces the adult, and is held by its two hands. On the last line, the child is let slip down over one's toes to the ground.

Two similar rhymes, almost as well known, are:

Here comes my lady with her little baby,
  A nim, a nim, a nam,
Here comes my lord with his trusty sword,
  A trot, a trot, a trot,
Here comes old Jack with a broken pack,
  A gallop, a gallop, a gallop.

Here goes my lord,
  A trot, a trot, a trot, a trot;
Here goes my lady,
  A canter, a canter, a canter, a canter;
Here goes my young master,
  Jockey-hitch, jockey-hitch, jockey-hitch,
    jockey-hitch;
Here comes my young miss,
  An amble, an amble, an amble, an amble;
The footman lags behind to tipple on ale and
    wine,
And goes a gallop, a gallop, a gallop, a gallop
    to make up his time.

17. This rhyme was originally, most probably, a fragment of a love ballad. It earned its place in "Mother Goose" books as another knee-trotting rhyme.

18. A sweetmeat made from the root of a large coarse European herb.

19. Or:

Gee up, Neddy, to the fair;
What shall we buy when we get there?
A penny apple and a penny pear;
Gee up, Neddy, to the fair.

20. The editors of *Gammer Gurton's Garland* added to this rhyme the note: "This is a Scottish ditty, on whirling round a piece of lighted paper to the child. The paper is called the dingle doosey."

"A dingle doosey (or dousie)," wrote J. Mactaggart in his *Gallovidian Encyclopedia* (1824), "is a piece of wood burned red at one end as a toy for children. The mother will whirl the ignited stick very fast, when the eye, by following it, seems to see a beautiful red circle. She accompanies this pleasant show to her bairns with the following rhyme:

"Dingle-dingle-dousie,
The cat's a' lousy:

232

Sit by there,
How do you do this morning?**31**

« 576 »

Dance, Thumbkin, dance,**32**
Dance, ye merry men, every one:
But Thumbkin, he can dance alone,
Thumbkin, he can dance alone.

Dance, Foreman, dance,
Dance, ye merry men, every one:
But Foreman, he can dance alone,
Foreman, he can dance alone.

Dance, Longman, dance,
Dance, ye merry men, every one:
But Longman, he can dance alone,
Longman, he can dance alone.

Dance, Ringman, dance,
Dance, ye merry men, every one:
But Ringman, he can dance alone,
Ringman, he can dance alone.

Dance, Littleman, dance,
Dance, ye merry men, every one:
But Littleman, he can dance alone,
Littleman, he can dance alone.

« 577 »

This Pig went to Market,
That Pig staid at Home;
This Pig had roast Meat,
That Pig had none;
This Pig went to the Barn door,
And cry'd Week, Week, for more.**33**

« 578 »

See, saw, Margery Daw,**34**
The old hen flew over the malt house,
She counted her chickens one by one,
Still she missed the little white one,
And this is it, this is it, this is it.**35**

Ding-dingle-dousie,
The dog's a' fleas.
Dingle-dingle-dousie,
Be crouse ay, be crouse ay;
Dingle-dingle-dousie,
Ye'se hae a brose o' pease . . . ."

Today television seems to have taken the place of the dingle-dousie.

21. The word "diaper" here means a cloth of linen or cotton, usually white, and having a simple pattern of the same name.

22. "This," wrote Halliwell, "should be accompanied by a kind of pantomimic dance, in which the motions of the body and arms express the process of weaving; the motion of the shuttle, &c." He later gave the variant:

I can weave a diaper thick, thick, thick,
And I can weave a diaper thin,
I can weave diaper out of doors
And I can weave diaper in.

23. This infant amusement is intended to teach the baby the names of its features. On this line, you touch the baby's forehead.

24. Touch the baby's eyes.

25. Touch the baby's nose.

26. Touch the baby's mouth.

27. Touch the baby's chin. The earliest-printed version, in *Tommy Thumb's Song Book* (1788), ends here.

28. Tickle the baby's chin.

29. Pull the baby's ear or hair.

30. Here the baby's nose is raised, a finger is popped in its mouth—and the child, hopefully, crows with delight.

31. There are many variations of "Brow Bender," perhaps the best known being that collected by James O. Halliwell and first published by him in 1846:

Here sits the Lord Mayor,
Here sits his men,
Here sits the cockadoodle,
Here sits the hen,
Here sits the little chickens,
Here they run in,
Chin chopper, chin chopper,
Chin chopper, chin.

With this rhyme, the "face-tapper" touches successively the forehead, eyes, right cheek, left cheek, tip of nose, mouth, and then chucks the infant under the chin.

32. A "dance" to be performed by each of the five fingers in turn, for the amusement of little children. It is not generally remembered today that our word "thumb," for one finger of the hand, is a heritage from the days when *every* finger had a distinct name. After "thumb," there came "toucher," "longman," "lecheman" (because the leech, or doctor, invariably tasted everything by means of that finger), and "little man."

In Essex, the five fingers were called Tom Thumbkin, Bess Bumpkin, Long Linkin, Bill Wilkin, and Little Dick; in Scotland, Thumbkin, Lickpot, Langman, Berrybarn, and Pirlie Winkie; elsewhere in the British Isles:

Tommy Thumbkin
Billy Winkie
Long Duster
Jacky Molebar
Little Perky

Tommy Tomkins
Billy Wilkins
Long Larum
Betsy Bedlam
Little Bob

Bill Milker
Tom Thumper
Long Lazy
Cherry Bumper
Tippity, Tippity Townend

These and similar names appear in many other rhymes used in infant amusements:

Thumbikin, thumbikin, broke the barn,
Pinnikin, Pinnikin, stole the corn.
Long back'd Gray
Carried it away.
Old Mid-man sat and saw,
But Peesy-weesy paid for a'!

Thumb bold,
Thibity-thold.
Langman,
Lick pan,
Mamma's little man.

English nurses also gave fanciful names to the toes. Here are some of them, from the big toe to the little toe:

« 579 »

Incey wincey spider, climbed the water spout,[36]
Down came the rain and washed poor spider out.
Out came the sunshine, dried up all the rain;
Incey wincey spider, climbed the spout again.

« 580 »

Shoe the Colt,
  Shoe the Colt,
Shoe the Wild Mare,[37]
Here a nail,
There a Nail,
  Yet she goes bare.[38]

« 581 »

My mother and your mother
  Went over the way;
Said my mother to your mother,
  It's chop-a-nose day.[39]

« 582 »

My father was a Frenchman,
A Frenchman, a Frenchman,
My father was a Frenchman,
And he bought me a fiddle.
  He cut it here,
  He cut it here,
He cut it through the middle.[40]

« 583 »

A good child, a good child,
As I suppose you be,
You'll neither laugh nor smile,
At the tickling of your knee.[41]

« 584 »

When Jack's a very good boy,
  He shall have cakes and custard ;
But when he does nothing but cry
  He shall have nothing but mustard.[42]

« 585 »

Cobbler, cobbler, mend my shoe,
Yes, good master, that I'll do;
Here's my awl and wax and thread,
And now your shoe is quite mended.[43]

« 586 »

Wash, hands, wash,
  Daddy's gone to plough,
If you want your hands wash'd,
Have them wash'd now.[44]

« 587 »

Down with the lambs,
  Up with the lark,
Run to bed children
  Before it gets dark.

« 588 »

Good night, God bless you,
Go to bed and undress you.

« 589 »

Good night, sweet repose,
Half the bed and all the clothes.

« 590 »

Go to bed first,
A golden purse;
Go to bed second,
A golden pheasant;
Go to bed third,
A golden bird.

« 591 »

He that lies at the stock,
Shall have a gold rock;
He that lies at the wall,
Shall have a gold ball;
He that lies in the middle,
Shall have a gold fiddle.[45]

Harry Whistle
Tommy Thistle
Harry Whible
Tommy Thible
Little Oker-bell

Tom Barker
Long Rachel
Minnie Wilkin
Milly Larkin
Little Dick

Toe Tipe
Penny Wipe
Tommy Tistle
Billy Whistle
Tripping-go

The "Oker-bell" in the first series comes from the Scandinavian *oker*, a field; the field-bell is a flower.

33. For well over a century, this has been the best-known toe- or finger-counting rhyme in the English language. Today, most of us would quote it as:

This little pig went to market,
This little pig stayed home,
This little pig had roast beef,
This little pig had none,
And this little pig cried, Wee-wee-wee
  All the way home.

Of many variants, the two that appear most often in "Mother Goose" books are:

Let us go to the wood, says this little pig;
What to do there? says that pig;
To look for my mother, says this pig;
What to do with her? says that pig;
Kiss her to death, says this pig.
This pig went to the barn.
This eat all the corn.
This said he would tell.
This said he wasn't well.
This went week, week, week, over the door
  sill.

The editor of *Mother Goose's Melody* added the maxim to this rhyme: "If we do not govern our passions our passions will govern us."

34. See Notes 95 and 96, this chapter.

35. Another toe-counting rhyme.

36. The spider's adventures are to be enacted with the fingers.

37. This line has provided the title for at least two novels, one by the late Gene Fowler in 1931, the other by Edmund Gilligan in 1956.

James O. Halliwell later collected:

> *Pitty Patty Polt,*
> *Shoe the wild colt!*
> *Here a nail,*
> *And there a nail,*
> *Pitty Patty Polt.*

And:

> *Shoe the colt, shoe!*
> *Shoe the wild mare;*
> *Put a sack on her back*
> *See if she'll bear.*
> *If she'll bear,*
> *We'll give her some grains;*
> *If she won't bear,*
> *We'll dash out her brains!*

« 592 »

Whenever the moon begins to peep,
Little boys should be asleep;
The great big sun shines all the day,
That little boys can see to play.[46]

« 593 »

Up the wooden hill
    To Bedfordshire,
Down Sheet Lane
    To Blanket Fair.

« 594 »

Little man in coal pit
    Goes knock, knock, knock;
Up he comes, up he comes,
    Out at the top.[47]

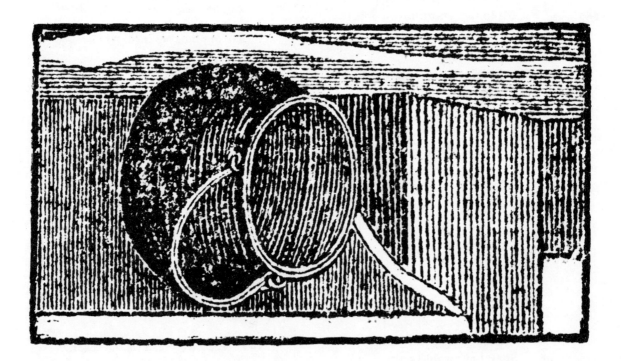

236

« 595 »

Good night,
Sleep tight,
Wake up bright
In the morning light,
To do what's right
With all your might.**48**

« 596 »

There were two Blackbirds
  Sat upon a Hill,**49**
The one nam'd Jack,
  The other nam'd Gill,**50**
Fly away Jack,**51**
  Fly away Gill,
Come again, Jack,
Come again Gill.**52**

« 597 »

Tom Brown's
Two little Indians,
Two little Indians,
One would not play,
The other would not stay,
Tom Brown's two
Little Indian Boys.**53**

« 598 »

Put your finger in foxy's hole,
  Foxy is not at home:
Foxy is at the back door,
  Picking of a bone.**54**

« 599 »

Pease Porridge**55** hot,
  Pease Porridge cold,
Pease Porridge in the Pot
  Nine Days old.
Some like it hot,
  Some like it cold,
Some like it in the pot
  Nine days old.**56**

Better-known today, however, are these variants:

Shoe a little horse,
* Shoe a little mare,*
But let the little colt go bare, bare, bare.

Shoe the horse and shoe the mare,
But let the little colt go bare.

38. This is a rhyme used to amuse infants—the words are repeated while patting the soles of the baby's feet. It may also have had something to do with a boys' game, "Shoe the Wild Mare," played in the seventeenth century, usually around Christmastime.

The editor of the *Melody* followed this rhyme with a maxim he attributed to *Vattel:* "Ay, ay, drive the nail when it will go: that's the way of the world, and is the method pursued by all our financiers, politicians, and necromancers." We do not know how the editor restrained himself from saying "other necromancers."

39. An infant amusement. On the last line the child's nose is held between finger and thumb and "chopped off" with the other hand.

40. This is one of the more strenuous "infant amusements." The nurse holds out the child's arm. At the first "cut it here," she strikes the child's wrist gently with the side of her hand; at the second, she strikes the child's shoulders; at "cut it through the middle," she strikes the elbow joint.

41. Or:

> Tickle, tickle,
> On the knee,
> If you laugh
> You don't love me.

Tickling rhymes were also used as prophecies of a sort:

> Tickle ye, tickle ye in the hand.
> If you laugh, you are a man.
> If you cry, you are a baby.
> If you dance, you are a lady.
>
> An old maid, an old maid,
> You will surely be,
> If you laugh or if you smile
> While I tickle round your knee.

A person who could keep a straight face while his or her hand was being tickled could also keep a secret:

> Can you keep a secret?
> I don't believe you can!
> You mustn't laugh,
> You mustn't cry,
> But do the best you can.

A catch—for the amusement of adults rather than of children—is this: Tickle someone in the palm of the hand. The first thing that person says "will be the first thing he (or she) will say after being married." This can be very amusing to young people if a victim can be found who is not in on the joke.

42. A rhyme used by the old nurses to induce their little charges "to be good."

43. "English nurses," James O. Halliwell wrote, "used these lines when a child's shoe was tight, and patted the foot to induce him to allow it to be tried on." As usual with the older verses, there are many variations. Here are two:

> Cobbler, cobbler, mend my shoe,
> Yes, good master, that I'll do.
> Stitch it up and stitch it down,
> And then I'll give you half a crown.
>
> Cobbler, cobbler, mend my shoe,
> Get it done by half-past two;
> Half-past two is much too late,
> Get it done by half-past eight.

44. James O. Halliwell called this "a formula for making young children submit to the operation of having their hands washed. *Mutatis mutandis*, the lines will serve as a specific for everything of the kind, as brushing hair, &c." Which he demonstrated by providing this version:

> Warm, hands, warm,
> The men are gone to plough,
> If you want to warm your hands,
> Warm your hands now.

45. The editors of *The Oxford Dictionary of Nursery Rhymes* note: "Rhyme for inducing children to settle down for the night in the days when everybody from king to kitchen-maid slept more than one to a bed. The stock is the outer rail of the bedstead. Goldsmith said that the stock was considered the place of honor."

46. A "go-to-sleep-now" rhyme.

47. A rhyme for "skinning the rabbit"—getting the child undressed.

48. And the almost inevitable parody:

> Good night,
> Sleep tight,
> Don't let
> The bedbugs ['squitoes] bite.

49. The version with which we are more familiar today begins:

> Two little dicky birds,
> Sitting on a wall . . . .

50. Nineteenth-century versions of this rhyme replaced the possibly pagan "Jack" and "Gill" with the names of two of the apostles, Peter and Paul.

51. A later (1843) version ends:

> When Jack flew away
> Around the mill,
> Then Jack did return to Mistress Jill.

52. The editor of the *Melody* added the ancient proverb: "A bird in the hand is worth two in the bush."

This verse is meant to accompany a simple slight-of-hand trick which has been amusing children for two centuries. A clear description of the trick is given in *The Oxford Dictionary of Nursery Rhymes*: "A piece of stamp paper is stuck to each index finger, one being dubbed 'Peter' [Jack] and the other 'Paul' [Gill]. The

Spell me that in four Letters?
I will, T-H-A-T.**57**

« 600 »

Patty Cake, Patty Cake,**58**
Baker's Man;
That I will Master,
As fast as I can;
Prick it and prick it,
And mark it with a T,**59**
And there will be enough
For Jackey and me.**60**

« 601 »

Clap hands, clap hands,
  Hie Tommy Randy,
Did you see my good man?
  They call him Cock-a-bandy.

Silken stockings on his legs,
  Silver buckles glancin',
A sky-blue bonnet on his head,
  And oh, but he is handsome.

two fingers are placed at the edge of a table. On the command 'fly away' the appropriate hand is whipped over the shoulder and instantly returned with the middle finger substituted for the index so that the stamp paper is concealed. On the command 'come back' the reverse operation takes place, and the stamp paper reappears."

53. James O. Halliwell called this rhyme the accompaniment to a game, but did not describe it. The editors of *The Oxford Dictionary of Nursery Rhymes* think that it is probably an infant amusement similar to "There Were Two Blackbirds" (Rhyme 596). Whether or not this rhyme inspired the writing of "Ten Little Injuns" (Rhyme 818) is an interesting speculation.

54. The speaker holds his fist in such a way that if a child puts in its finger, the finger can be secured by "Foxy at the back door," still leaving the hole at the top open.

55. A thin pudding made of pease meal.

56. This rhyme is both a riddle and a clapping game, played by children on cold days to keep their hands warm. The first four lines and the final couplet were first published c.

The Annotated Mother Goose

A. RACKHAM

1765 in Newbery's *Mother Goose's Melody*, where the editor appended this maxim to the rhyme: "The poor are seldomer sick for want of food, than the rich by the excess of it."

57. This "catch" is later given as:

Spell me that without a P,
And a clever scholar you will be.

There is also:

Round and round the rugged rock
The ragged rascal ran,
How many R's are there in that?
Now tell me if you can.

58. "Patty cakes" or "pat-a-cakes" are small cakes with currants in them, still popular at bake shops in Oxford.

59. John Bellenden Ker read "Baker's Man" as "Beker's-man," an old Saxon word for the mass man or priest. The "mark it with a T" he took to mean "to make the form of a T with the finger and thus to cross or bless in the Catholic form."

60. Like "Pease Porridge Hot," this verse often accompanies a hand-clapping game. It appeared as early as 1698 as an infants' ditty in the comedy *The Campaigners*, by Thomas d'Urfey (1653-1723). The editor of the *Melody* added the maxim: "The surest way to gain our ends is to moderate our desires."

« 602 »

Clap hands, clap hands,
Till father comes home;
For father's got money
But mother's got none.**61**

« 603 »

My Mother said that I never should
Play with the gypsies in the wood,
The wood was dark; the grass was green;
In came Sally with a tambourine.**62**

I went to the sea—no ship to get across;
I paid ten shillings for a blind white horse;
I upon his back was off in a crack,
Sally tell my Mother I shall never come back.**63**

« 604 »

May my geese fly over your barn?
Yes, if they'll do me no harm.
Fly over his barn and eat all his corn.**64**

« 605 »

Here is the church, and here is the steeple;
Open the door and here are the people.
Here is the parson going upstairs,
And here he is a-saying his prayers.**65**

« 606 »

Handy-dandy, Jack-a-dandy,
Which good hand will you have?**66**

« 607 »

Great A, little a,
Bounceing B;**67**
The Cats in ye Cupboard,
And She can't See.**68**

« 608 »

Here's A, B, and C,
D, E, F, and G,**69**
H, I,**70** K, L, M, N, O, P, Q,

R, S, T, and U,
W, X, Y, and Z,
And here's the child's Dad,
Who is sagacious and discerning,
And knows this is the Fount of Learning.**71**

« 609 »

A, B, C, and D,
Pray, playmates, agree.
E, F, and G,
Well so it shall be.
J, K, and L,
In peace we will dwell.
M, N, and O,
To play let us go.
P, Q, R, and S,
Love may we possess.**72**
W, X, and Y,
Will not quarrel or die.
Z, and amperse-and,
Go to school at command.

« 610 »

Great A was alarmed at B's behavior,
Because C, D, E, F, denied G a favor.
H had a husband with I, J, K, and L.
M married Mary, and taught her scholars how to
    spell;
A, B, C, D, E, F, G, H, I, J, K, L, M, N,
O, P, Q, R, S, T, U, V, Double U, X, Y, Z.**73**

« 611 »

A was an apple-pie,
B bit it,
C cut it,
D dealt it,
E eat it,
F fought for it,
G got it,
H had it,
I inspected it,
J jumped for it,

61. Or:

*Clap hands, Daddy comes
With his pocket full of plums,
And a cake for Baby.*

Or:

*Clap hands, Daddy's coming
Up the waggon way,
His pockets full of money
And his hands full of clay.*

62. Or:

*. . . If I did, she would say,
Naughty girl to disobey.*

63. This old rhyme, probably, like "Pease Porridge Hot," the accompaniment to a hand-warming game, does not seem to have appeared in print until the poet Walter de la Mare included it in his *Come Hither* (1923).

64. Two children sit opposite each other. The first turns his or her fingers one over the other and sings the first line given here. The other child answers with the second line, upon which the first unfolds the fingers and waves the hand over the head, chanting the third line.

65. There is perhaps no need to describe the finger-locking game which accompanies this rhyme. Not quite so well known is a similar finger game:

*Here are my lady's knives and forks,
Here is my lady's table,
Here is my lady's looking-glass,
And here is the baby's cradle.*

66. A child—or a grownup—puts a hand with nothing in it and a hand with something in it behind the back and recites this little rhyme. Or you can say:

*Handy-dandy, riddlety ro,
Which will you have, high or low?*

67. This is the first of many rhymes we shall encounter which were designed to help children learn their ABC's, but such rhymes are very old indeed. "As early as the fifteenth century," James O. Halliwell wrote in 1849, " 'Mayster Benet,' who was rector of Sandon, in Essex, in 1440, and afterwards a prebend of St. Paul's, composed or translated an alphabet rhyme."

Some scholars think that this rhyme is a corruption of one repeated in Elizabethan times by old and young when playing battledore and shuttlecock. Apparently the rhyme, as first given in *Tommy Thumb's Pretty Song Book* (c. 1744), inspired some early printers of juvenile books to display as their sign the device: *AaB*. The London printer John Marshall was one who did so, and his shop became known as "the Great A and bouncing B Toy Factory." The opening lines are frequently given as: "*A, B, C, tumble down D . . . .*"

68. The later *Mother Goose's Melody* added the admonition: "Yes she can see that you are naughty, and don't mind your book."

69. This rhyming alphabet, designed to teach a child his ABC's, was titled in the *Melody* "A Learned Song."

70. Note that "V" as well as "J" is missing, as in many of the older alphabets.

71. An American version of this rhyme, in *Mother Goose's Quarto*, c. 1825, ends:

> *And here's good Mama, who knows,*
> *This is the font whence learning flows.*

William A. Wheeler, in 1869, gave this version:

> *Here's A, B, C, D, E, F, and G,*
> *H, I, J, K, L, M, N, O, P, Q, R, S, T, U, V,*
> *W, X, Y, and Z—*
> *And O, dear me,*
> *When shall I learn*
> *My A, B, C.*

Wheeler noted that the exclamation "O, dear me" "is thought to be a corruption of the Italian *O Dio mio*," O my God.

The editor of the *Melody* added a note to the above verse which he attributed to *Mope's Geography of the Mind*: "This is the most learned ditty in the world; for indeed there is no song can be made without the aid of this, it being the gamut and ground work of them all." Which nobody can deny.

72. This is the way this alphabet rhyme most often appears in even modern books of "Mother Goose," but later editors sometimes insert here the couplet:

> *T, U, and V,*
> *Come let us agree.*

> K kept it,
> L longed for it,
> M mourned for it,
> N nodded at it,
> O opened it,
> P peeped in it,
> Q quartered it,
> R ran for it,
> S stole it,
> T took it,
> U upset it,
> V viewed it,
> W wanted it,
> X, Y, Z, and ampersand
> All wished for a piece in hand.[74]

« 612 »

A was an archer, who shot at a frog,[75]
B was a butcher, and had a great dog,[76]
C was a captain, all covered with lace,
D was a drunkard, and had a red face.
E was an esquire, with pride on his brow,
F was farmer, and followed the plough.
G was a gamester, who had but ill-luck,
H was a hunter, and hunted a duck.
I was an innkeeper, who loved to carouse,
J was a joiner, and built up a house.
K was King William, once governed this land,[77]
L was a lady, who had a white hand.
M was a miser, and hoarded up gold,
N was a nobleman, gallant and bold.
O was an oyster girl, and went about town,
P was a parson, and wore a black gown.
Q was a queen, who wore a silk slip,
R was a robber, and wanted a whip.
S was a sailor, and spent all he got,
T was a tinker, and mended a pot.
U was a usurer, a miserable elf,
V was a vintner, who drank all himself.
W was a watchman, and guarded the door,
X was expensive, and so became poor.
Y was a youth, that did not love school,
Z was a zany, a poor harmless fool.

« 613 »

A for the ape, that we saw at the fair;
B for a blockhead, who ne'er shall go there;
C for a collyflower, white as a curd;
D for a duck, a very good bird;
E for an egg, good in puddings and pies;
F for a farmer, rich, honest, and wise;
G for a gentleman, void of all care;
H for the hound, that ran down the hare;
I for an Indian, sooty and dark;
K for the keeper, that look'd in the park;
L for a lark, that soar'd in the air;
M for a mole, that ne'er could get there;
N for Sir Nobody, ever in fault;
O for an otter, that ne'er could be caught;
P for a pudding, stuck full of plums;
Q was for quartering it, see here he comes;
R for a rook, that croak'd in the trees;
S for a sailor, that plough'd the deep seas;
T for a top, that doth prettily spin;
V for a virgin, of delicate mien;
W for wealth, in gold, silver, and pence;
X for old Xenophon, noted for sense;
Y for a year, which for ever is green;
Z for the zebra, that belongs to the queen.[78]

« 614 »

A was an angler,
    Went out in a fog;
Who fish'd all the day,
    And caught only a frog.

B was cook Betty,
    A-baking a pie,
With ten or twelve apples
    All piled up on high.

C was a custard
    In a glass dish,
With as much cinnamon
    As you could wish.

No one ever seems to have been bothered by the fact that "H" and "I" are also missing.

73. This alphabet song did not make its appearance until William A. Wheeler collected it for his version of *Mother Goose's Melody* (1869).

74. This favorite rhyme for teaching the alphabet dates back at least to 1671, when it was quoted by John Eachard, an outspoken divine. In 1743 it was published by Mary Cooper in a spelling book, *The Child's New Play-thing*. Thereafter it appeared in numerous "Mother Goose" books, next in *Tom Thumb's Play Book*, published by A. Barclay of Boston in 1761.

"J" and "V" were omitted in these early alphabet rhymes: in the eighteenth century, "I" did duty for "J," "U" performed the same service for "V," and "W" often appeared as a "double U," "UU."

Obviously an offshoot of "A Was an Apple-Pie" is the alphabet rhyme usually headed, "A curious discourse about an Apple-pie, that passed between the Twenty-Five Letters at Dinner-time":

Says A, give me A good large slice.
Says B, a little Bit, but nice.
Says C, Cut me a piece of Crust.
Says D, it is as Dry as Dust.
Says E, I'll Eat now, fast who will.
Says F, I vow I'll have my Fill.
Says G, give it to me Good and Great.
Says H, a little bit I Hate.
Says J, I love the Juice the best.
And K the very same confessed.
Says L, there's nothing more I Love.
Says M, it makes your teeth to Move.
N noticed what the others said.
O Others' plates with grief surveyed.
P Praised the cook up to the life.
Q Quarrelled 'cause he'd a bad knife.
Says R, it Runs short, I'm afraid.
S Silent sat, and nothing said.
T thought that Talking might lose time.
U Understood it at meals a crime.
W Wished there had been a quince in.
Says X, these cooks there's no convincing.
Says Y, I'll eat, let others wish.
Z sat as mute as any fish.

While ampersand, he licked the dish.

75. There are many versions of this rhyming alphabet, sometimes called "Tom Thumb's Alphabet."

76. Later versions often give a couplet to each letter:

A was an Archer and shot at a frog,
But missing his mark shot into a bog.
B was a Butcher and had a great dog,
Who always went round the streets with a
*   clog . . . .*

77. The reference is probably to William I, William the Conqueror, who reigned from the battle of Hastings in 1066 to 1087, and not to his third son, Rufus, William II, who was killed by an arrow after a reign of thirteen years.

78. An alphabet rhyme which has appeared in many nursery rhyme books since James O. Halliwell first published it in the middle of the eighteenth century. Note that "U" is missing.

79. More commonly, in later versions, "Eleven, twelve, dig and delve . . . ."

80. This counting rhyme, common in one form or another to many countries, is said to have been "used in Wrentham, Massachusetts, as early as 1780." It may originally have gone up to thirty in some such form as this:

Twenty-one, charge the gun;
Twenty-two, the partridge flew;
Twenty-three, she lit on a tree;
Twenty-four, she lit down lower . . . .
Twenty-nine, the game is mine;
Thirty, thirty, make a kerchy.

81. This rhyme for remembering the Roman numerals is a later rather than an earlier creation; we found it first in a volume of *Mother Goose's Nursery Rhymes* published in 1886.

82. This is the first of many "Ride a Cock Horse" rhymes we shall encounter: rhymes to be sung while riding a rocking-horse or while "galloping"—dandling—a baby on one's knee.

A Cock Horse is perhaps a proud, high-spirited horse, perhaps the fifth horse once added to a coach-and-four when going up a hill. A writer to the *Times* of London (Novem-

D was fat Dick,
    Who did nothing but eat;
He would leave book and play
    For a nice bit of meat.

E was an egg,
    In a basket with more,
Which Peggy will sell
    For a shilling or more.

F was a fox,
    So cunning and sly;
Who looks at the hen-roost—
    I need not say why.

G was a greyhound,
    As fleet as the wind;
In the race or the course,
    Left all others behind.

H was a heron,
    Who lived near a pond;
Of gobbling of fishes
    He was wondrously fond.

I was the ice
    On which Billy would skate;
So up went his heels,
    And down went his pate.

J was Joe Jenkins,
    Who played on the fiddle;
He began twenty times,
    But left off in the middle.

K was a kitten,
    Who jumped at a cork,
And learned to eat mice
    Without plate, knife, or fork.

L was a lark,
    Who sings us a song,
And wakes us betimes
    Lest we sleep too long.

M was Miss Molly,
    Who turned in her toes,
And hung down her head

Till her knees touched her nose.

N was a nosegay,
   Sprinkled with dew,
Pulled in the morning
   And presented to you.

O was an owl,
   Who looked wondrously wise;
But he's watching a mouse
   With his large round eyes.

P was a parrot,
   With feathers like gold,
Who talks just as much
   And now more than he's told.

Q is the Queen
   Who governs the land,
And sits on a throne
   Very lofty and grand.

R is a raven
   Perched on an oak,
Who with a gruff voice
   Cries croak, croak, croak!

S was a stork
   With a very long bill,
Who swallows down fishes
   And frogs to his fill.

T is a trumpeter
   Blowing his horn,
Who tells us the news
   As we rise in the morn.

U is a unicorn,
   Who, it is said,
Wears an ivory bodkin
   On his forehead.

V is a vulture
   Who eats a great deal,
Devouring a dog
   Or a cat at a meal.

W was a watchman

ber 2, 1930) stated that "It was a customary sight during the latter half of the 18th century for travellers to Banbury and Birmingham to observe a group of children clustered at the foot of Stanmore Hill to witness the be-ribboned and rosetted fifth horse attached to the coach. As the gaily caparisoned jockey flourished his gilt-staff the boys and girls would chant 'Ride a cock-horse to Banbury Cross.'"

83. Banbury is a municipal borough in Oxfordshire, England, an area rich in nursery-rhyme locales. The editors of *The Oxford Dictionary of Nursery Rhymes* think that Banbury's many mentions may be due in part to the fact that J. G. Rusher, the printer of many juvenile publications c. 1840, worked there. Around 1843 Rusher published a book, *The Cries of Banbury and London*, which contained another "Banbury" rhyme that later found its way into "Mother Goose" books:

   As I was going to Banbury
   Upon a summer's day,
   My dame had butter, eggs, and fruit,
   And I had corn and hay;
   Joe drove the ox, and Tom the swine,
   Dick told the foal and mare,
   I sold them all—then home to dine,
   From famous Banbury fair.

84. Banbury Cross—described as a "goodly Crosse"—stood in the market place of the town—"Banbury fair" in the verse in Note 83 —until it was destroyed by the inhabitants of Banbury "far gone in Puritanism" who "so defaced it that they scarcely left one stone upon another." (The quotations are from the writings of an unnamed Jesuit priest, dated January 1601.) A modern cross, built in the nineteenth century, now stands in its place.

85. Banbury breads and pastries have been famous for centuries. "Banberrie cakes"—as they were referred to as early as 1586, were, and still are, made from mixed peel, biscuit crumbs, currants, allspice, eggs and butter, folded into a circle of puff pastry.

86. The line in later books usually reads: "And a twopenny apple pie." The editor of *Mother Goose's Melody* contributed to this rhyme the maxim: "There's a good boy, eat up your pye and hold your tongue; for silence is the sign of wisdom."

87. Better known today is the version of the above rhyme that goes:

> *Ride a cock-horse to Banbury Cross,*
> *To buy little Johnny a galloping horse;*
> *It trots behind and it ambles before,*
> *And Johnny shall ride till he can ride no*
> *   more.*

88. Variously identified as Queen Elizabeth I; the famous wife of the Earl of Mercia, Lady Godiva; and a lady named Celia Fiennes, who made many rides on horseback throughout England, from about 1697.

89. Perhaps a reference to the fifteenth-century custom of wearing a bell on the tapering toe of each shoe. These shoes in turn are said to have been designed to imitate the cloven hoof of a goat, and were worn by Satanists in open defiance of the Church. If this be a fact, the fad caught on, for the shoes were worn by many who were not Satanists.

90. There are so many versions of this favorite "Mother Goose" rhyme that we have given here the best known. Sometimes "Banbury Cross" is "Coventry Cross," sometimes the "fine lady" is "an old woman," sometimes the "white horse" is a "black horse." In another version (c. 1790), the "old woman" has

> *... a ring on her finger,*
> *A bonnet of straw,*
> *The strangest old woman,*
> *That ever you saw.*

Who guarded the street,
Lest robbers or thieves
    The good people should meet.

X was King Xerxes,
    Who, if you don't know,
Reigned over Persia
    A great while ago.

Y is the year
    That is passing away,
And still growing shorter
    Every day.

Z is a zebra,
    Whom you've heard of before;
So here ends my rhyme
    Till I find you some more.

« 615 »

One, two, buckle my shoe;
Three, four, open the door;
Five, six, pick up sticks;
Seven, eight, lay them straight;
Nine, ten, a big fat hen;
Eleven, twelve, I hope you're well;[79]
Thirteen, fourteen, draw the curtain;
Fifteen, sixteen, the maid's in the kitchen;
Seventeen, eighteen, she's in waiting;
Nineteen, twenty, my stomach's empty.
Please, Ma'am, to give me some dinner.[80]

« 616 »

X shall stand for playmates Ten;
V for Five stout stalwart men;
I for one, as I'm alive;
C for a Hundred, and D for Five;
M for a Thousand soldiers true;
And all these figures I've told to you.[81]

« 617 »

Ride a Cock Horse[82]
To Banbury[83] Cross,[84]
To see what

246

Tommy can buy,
A Penny White loaf,[85]
A Penny White cake,
And a Hugegy penny pye.[86]

« 618 »

Ride a cock-horse
To Banbury Cross
To buy Little Nancy
An ambling horse,
It gallops before,
And trots behind,
So Nancy may ride it
'Till it is blind.[87]

« 619 »

Ride a cock-horse to Banbury Cross,
To see a fine lady[88] upon a white horse;
Rings on her fingers and bells on her toes,[89]
And she shall have music wherever she goes.[90]

« 620 »

Ride away, ride away,
    Johnny shall ride,[91]
He shall have a pussy cat
    Tied to one side;[92]
He shall have a little dog
    Tied to the other,
And Johnny shall ride
    To see his grandmother.[93]

« 621 »

Cripple Dick upon a stick
    And Sandy on a sow,
Riding away to Galloway,
    To buy a pound o' woo'.[94]

« 622 »

See saw,[95] Margery Daw,[96]
    Jacky shall have a new Master;
Jacky must have but a penny a day,
    Because he can work no faster.[97]

[91]. Later, "Ride, baby, ride, Pretty baby shall ride . . . ."

[92]. Of his rocking-horse.

[93]. Some scholars believe this rhyme stems from a Scottish border song. But others deride this view, claiming that it is nothing more than a verse "chanted by nurses to divert their little ones."

[94]. Another version of this hobby-horse jingle goes:

Richard Dick upon a stick,
    Samson on a sow,
We'll ride away to Colley Fair
    To buy a horse to plough.

[95]. "Se saw" in the Melody and other older versions. Traditionally, a refrain repeated by children playing on a "see-saw." The Oxford English Dictionary tells us that the game of see-saw is not mentioned before 1700, but the word "see-saw" is much earlier. Originally, the rhyme may have been sung by sawyers to keep the rhythm of the two-handled saw; see-saw as a game would logically be played where wood was being sawed.

James O. Halliwell, describing the game of see-saw in 1849, gave as "a song of appropriate cadence" for the game:

Titty cum tawty,
    The ducks in water;
Titty cum tawty,
    The geese follow after.

[96]. The name "Margery," in the eighteenth and nineteenth centuries, was used almost exclusively by poor country people. "Daw" (Oxford English Dictionary) is "a lazy person, sluggard"—in Scotland, "an untidy woman, slut, slattern." The suspicion arises that Margery Daw, whoever she may have been, was no better than she should be.

[97]. The Newbery Melody adds the maxim: "It is a mean and scandalous practice in au-

247

thors to put notes to things that deserve no notice"—attributed to Grotius. Your present editors will try to keep this precept firmly in mind.

98. Or "sacradown" or "Sacch'ry-down" or "sacke a downe," an expression connected, as early as 1640, with sawyers. Like "See Saw, Margery Daw," this rhyme was probably first sung to keep up the rhythm of the saw, later by children playing see-saw.

99. The use of "Boston Town" here is taken by some to uphold Elizabeth Goose's claim to being "Mother Goose." But it is far more probable that the earliest version of the rhyme had "London Town" or some other English city.

100. "Or to any other town upon the face of the earth," added the editor of the Newbery *Melody* (a thought he attributed to Wickliffe), and various editors have altered the locality and the first line to rhyme with it:

See saw, Jack in a hedge,
Which is the way to London bridge?

Mother Goose's Quarto, published in Boston

« 623 »

See, saw, sacaradown,**98**
   Which is the Way to Boston Town?**99**
One Foot up the other Foot down,
   That is the Way to Boston Town.**100**

« 624 »

See Saw, Margery Daw,
Sold her Bed and lay on the Straw,
Was not she a dirty Slut,**101**
To sell her Bed and Lie in the Dirt.**102**

« 625 »

Die, pussy, die,
Shut your little eye;
When you wake,
Find a cake,
Die, pussy, die.**103**

« 626 »

One, two, three,
Four and five,
I caught a Hare alive;**104**
Six, seven, eight,
Nine and ten,
I let him go again.

Why did you let it go?
Because it bit my finger so.
Which finger did it bite?
The little finger on the right.**105**

« 627 »

One, two, three, four, five, six, seven,
All good children go to heaven,
    Penny on the water,
    Two pence on the sea,
    Threepence on the railway,
    Out goes she.**106**

« 628 »

One-ery, two-ery,
    Ziccary zan;
Hollow bone, crack a bone,
Ninery ten:
Spittery spot,
    It must be done;
Twiddleum twaddleum
    Twenty ONE.

Hink spink, the puddings stink,
    The fat begins to fry,
Nobody at home, but jumping Joan,
    Father, mother and I.
Stick, stock, stone dead,
    Blind man can't see,
Every knave will have a slave,
    You or I must be HE.**107**

« 629 »

One, two, three,
I love coffee,

c. 1825, held to that city, which had received her charter in 1822, and added the couplet:

Boston town's turned into a city,
But I've no time to change my ditty.

101. In Rudyard Kipling's "The Hill of Illusion," Captain Congleton, after hearing Mrs. Buzgago sing this verse, says, "I'm going to alter that to 'flirt.' It sounds better."

102. Both James O. Halliwell, in 1842, and Ray Wood, in 1938, collected a version of this old rhyme that goes:

Tommy Trot, a man of the law,
Sold his bed and lay upon straw;
Sold the straw and slept on grass,
To buy his wife a looking-glass.

The version in Wood's *American Mother Goose* was gathered from the "peckerwood" people of North Carolina.

103. A rhyme for stopping a swing.

104. In later versions, "a Hare" becomes "a fish."

105. This is a counting-out rhyme, used to designate which of a group of children shall be singled out as "It." Counting-out rhymes form a large section of nursery-rhyme literature, and we shall meet many more of them as we progress. The editor of the Newbery *Melody* appended to this rhyme the maxim: "We may be as good as we please, if we please to be good."

106. An English version of one of the best-known counting rhymes. American children in their play have sung:

One, two, three, four, five, six, seven,
All good children go to heaven,
    Some fly east,
    Some fly west,
    Some fly over the cuckoo's nest.

Or:

One, two, three, four, five, six, seven,
All good children go to heaven,
    When they die
    Their mothers cry,
One, two, three, four, five, six, seven.

107. These two counting-out rhymes come from *Gammer Gurton's Garland*, where they were titled "Telling Out." Books could, and have, been written on the counting-out rhyme alone. There are literally scores of versions of the two ancient formulas given above. It is said that the following version used to make Sir Walter Scott "roar with laughter" when he recited it to his seven-year-old friend, Marjorie Fleming:

Wonery, twoery, tickery, seven!
Alibi, crackaby, ten, and eleven;
Pin, pan, musky, dan;
Tweedle-um, twoddle-up, twenty-wan;
Erie, orie, ourie,
You—are—out.

An American version, first printed in 1814 by Jesse Cochran of Windsor, Vermont, in still another *Mother Goose's Melody*, goes:

Intery, mintery, cutery, corn,
Apple seed and briar thorn;
Wire, briar, limber lock,
Five geese in a flock,
Sit and sing by a spring,
O-U-T and in again.

Mother Goose's Quarto, c. 1825, gives:

One-ery, you-ery, ekery, Ann,
Phillisy, follysy, Nicholas, John,
Quee-bee, quaw-bee, Irish Mary,
Stinkle-em, stankle-em, buck.

James O. Halliwell contributed this variation:

Hickery, dickery, 6 and 7,
Alabone, crackabone 10 and 11,
Spin span muskidan;
Tweedle 'um twaddle 'um, 21.

Undoubtedly the best-known of all counting-out rhymes (in both the United States and Britain) is the comparatively recent:

Eena, meena, mina, mo,
Catch a nigger by the toe,
If he hollers, let him go,
Eena, meena, mina, mo.

108. Possibly another counting-out rhyme, this jingle may also be the forerunner of the comparatively recent:

I love coffee,
I love tea,
I love the girls
And the girls love me.

And Billy loves tea,
How good you be,
One, two, three,
I love coffee,
And Billy loves tea.**108**

« 630 »

I sent a letter to my love
And on the way I dropped it,
A little puppy picked it up
And put it in his pocket.
It isn't you, it isn't you,
But it is *you.*

« 631 »

As I went up the apple-tree,
All the apples fell on me;
Bake a puddin', bake a pie,
Did you ever tell a lie?
Yes, I did, and many times.
O-U-T, out goes she
Right in the middle of the deep blue sea.

« 632 »

As I went up the Brandy hill,
I met my father with good will;
He had jewels, he had rings,
He had many pretty things;
He'd a cat with nine tails,
He'd a hammer wanting nails.
Up Jock!
Down Tom!
Blow the bellows old man.**109**

« 633 »

We're three Brethren out of Spain
Come to court your Daughter Jane.

My Daughter Jane she is too young,
She has no skill in a flattering Tongue.

Be she young, or be she old,
It's for her Gold she must be sold;
So fare you well, my Lady gay,
We must return another Day.**110**

Turn back, turn back, thou Spanish knight,
And rub your spurs till they be bright.

My spurs are bright and richly wrought,
And in this town they were not brought;
Nor in this town will they be sold,
Neither for silver nor for gold,
So fare thee well, my lady gay,
For I must turn another way.

Turn back, turn back, thou scornful knight,
And take the fairest in thy sight.

The fairest maid that I can see
Is pretty Nancy—come to me.

Here comes my daughter safe and sound,
Every pocket with a thousand pound;
Every finger with a gay gold ring;
Please to take my daughter in.**111**

« 634 »

Round about, round about,
 Magotty Pye, **112**
My father loves good Ale,
 And so do I.**113**

« 635 »

Round about the rosebush,
 Three steps,
 Four steps,
All the little boys and girls
 Are sitting
 On the doorsteps.

« 636 »

Sally go round the sun,
Sally go round the moon,

109. Another counting-out rhyme.

110. The song as first given in the Newbery *Melody* ends here. The editor added the maxim: "Riches serve a wise man, and govern a fool."

111. This song, with its later additions, was used in a "choosing up sides" game, one child being selected on each repetition of the line "The fairest maid that I can see / Is pretty [child's name] come to me."

112. A sixteenth- and seventeenth-century word for the magpie. Later versions of the jingle have "gooseberry pie" and "applety pie."

113. This is a rhyme to be sung or recited by children as they join hands and dance around in a circle. It first appeared in *Mother Goose's Melody* c. 1765. The editor of the *Melody* (Goldsmith?) added his usual maxim: "Evil company makes the good bad and the bad worse."

114. The movements for this dance for little children, played for generations, are all self-explanatory.

115. This can be continued indefinitely with any movements of which little children are capable. In later years, this has come to be known as:

Here we go round the mulberry bush . . . .

And there is also the version of a similar dance game which begins:

Who will you have for your nuts and may,
 Nuts and may, nuts and may;
Who will you have for your nuts and may,
 On a cold and frosty morning?

This is followed by the selection of a child:

I'll have little [name of child] for my nuts
 and may . . . .

And then:

And who will you send to fetch him away,
 Fetch him away, fetch him away;
And who will you send to fetch him away,
 On a cold and frosty morning.

I'll send [name of child] to fetch him
 away . . . .

A classic ghost story has been written

around this version of the song. It is "A Visitor from Down Under," by L. P. Hartley.

116. As recently as November 1961, Mr. James Leasor was writing in his book *The Plague and the Fire* (New York: McGraw-Hill Book Co., Inc.) that this rhyme "had its origin in the [Great Plague]. Rosy [roses] refers to the rosy rash of plague, ringed to signify the tokens; the posies were herbs and spices carried to sweeten the air; sneezing [the third line is often given as "A-tishoo! A-tish-oo!"] was a common symptom of those close to death." And "We've all tumbled down" was in a way exactly what happened.

This is an interesting theory, but "If you consult *The Oxford Dictionary of Nursery Rhymes*" (as Charles Poore noted in his *New York Times* review of *The Plague and the Fire*), "you will find, in place of corroboration, the somewhat frosty notation that: 'The invariable sneezing and falling down in modern versions has given would-be origin-finders the opportunity to say that the rhyme dates back to the days of the Great Plague.'" Actually—surprising in a rhyme that has become the accompaniment to one of our most popular nursery games—"Ring-a-ring-a-roses" first appeared in print as late as 1881, in Kate Greenaway's *Mother Goose*.

117. There are so many versions of this famous song that we have thought it best to give here what amounts to still another version, combining and rearranging couplets from many sources. Those couplets which are printed in italics are those that appeared in the earliest existing recording of the song—that in *Tommy Thumb's Pretty Song Book*. In this case, however, we have modernized both the spelling and the punctuation. The opening couplet of the song, as given here, appeared for the first time in *Gammer Gurton's Garland,* where the song was titled "The Merry Bells of London."

118. One of our favorite books is *Walks in London*, by Augustus J. C. Hare (1834-1903). Our copy ("TWO VOLUMES IN ONE") was published in "New York / George Routledge and Sons, Limited / 9 Lafayette Place." No date is given, but the author states in his Preface: "Some of the chapters . . . have been already published, in a condensed form, in 'Good Words' for 1877."

Sally go round the chimney-pots
On a Saturday afternoon.

« 637 »
Now we dance looby, looby, looby,
Now we dance looby, looby light.

Shake your right hand a little,
And turn you round about.

Now we dance looby, looby, looby,
Now we dance looby, looby light.

Shake your right hand a little,
Shake your left hand a little,
And turn you round about.

Now we dance looby, looby, looby.
Now we dance looby, looby light.

Shake your right hand a little,
Shake your left hand a little,
Shake your right foot a little,
And turn you round about.

Now we dance looby, looby, looby,
Now we dance looby, looby light.
Shake your right hand a little,
Shake your left hand a little,
Shake your right foot little,
Shake your left foot a little,
And turn you round about.

Now we dance looby, looby, looby,
Now we dance looby, looby light.

Shake your right hand a little,
Shake your left hand a little,
Shake your right foot a little,
Shake your left foot a little,
Shake your head a little,
And turn you round about.
Now we dance looby, looby, looby,
Now we dance looby, looby light.**114**

« 638 »

Here we go round the bramble bush,
　The bramble bush, the bramble bush:
Here we go round the bramble bush,
　On a cold frosty morning!

This is the way we wash our clothes,
　Wash our clothes, wash our clothes:
This is the way we wash our clothes,
　On a cold frosty morning!

This is the way we clean our rooms,
　Clean our rooms, clean our rooms;
This is the way we clean our rooms,
　On a cold frosty morning![115]

« 639 »

Ring-a-ring-a-roses,
A pocket full of posies;
Hush! Hush! Hush! Hush!
We've all tumbled down.[116]

« 640 »

Gay go up and gay go down,
To ring the bells of London Town.[117]

Two sticks and an apple,
Say the bells at Whitechapel.[118]

Old Father Baldpate,
Say the slow bells at Aldgate.[119]

Maids in white aprons,
Say the bells at St. Catherine's.[120]

Oranges and lemons,
Say the bells of St. Clement's.[121]

Pancakes and fritters,[122]
Say the bells of St. Peter's.[123]

Bull's eyes and targets,
Say the bells of St. Margaret's.[124]

Brickbats and tiles,
Say the bells of St. Giles.[125]

A. RACKHAM

"*Whitechapel*" would here seem to mean the Church of St. Mary, of which Hare writes: "On the right of the main street [in Aldgate, 'now' in the poverty-stricken district of White- chapel] is the Church of St. Mary, which once occupied an important position, as before the time of railways most of the great roads into the eastern counties and all the coast lines on this side of London were measured from 'Whitechapel Church,' which 'shared with Shoreditch Church, Hick's Hall, Tyburn Turnpike, and Hyde Park Corner the position now occupied by the great railway-termini north of the Thames.' " Hare is here quoting from the *Saturday Review*, February 17, 1877. He continues:

"The church was rebuilt in 1876-77, with a spire two hundred and ten feet high in the place of the hideous building of Charles II's time. It is one of the few churches in which, as the churchyard had frequently been used for open-air preaching, an outside pulpit was added. . . ." Hare has much more to say about "Whitechapel Church," but he contributes nothing to our knowledge of its *bells*.

119. Aldgate—the name means Aeld or Old Gate—was the chief outlet from the City of London to the eastern counties from the time of the Romans to its destruction in 1760. The church of the Aldgate district referred to here would seem to be the Church of St. Botolph, built in 1744 on the site of an earlier church. Hare described it as "ugly."

253

120. Perhaps the Church of St. Catherine Coleman (Hare: "truly hideous")—but more likely the Church of St. Catherine Cree in Leadenhall Street. The latter replaced, in 1629, an older church in which Hans Holbein was buried.

121. Hare says the church referred to here is not the Church of St. Clement in Eastcheap but the Church of St. Clement Danes in Holywell Street, which was erected in 1680 under the superintendence of Christopher Wren. Hare wrote that its bells "chime merrily" and that they can play "the old Hundredth Psalm and other tunes." Other writers disagree with Hare and claim that the Church of St. Clement in Eastcheap is meant. The *"Oranges and lemons"* does not help to decide which church is meant: *both* churches are situated near the wharves at the foot of London Bridge, where citrus fruits from the Mediterranean are landed.

122. Or: "Old shoes and slippers. . . ."

123. This couplet probably does not refer to a London church at all but to St. Peter's in the town of Derby, where these words were chanted on Shrove Tuesday each year when one half of the town played the other half at football, using a giant ball.

124. Surely the Church of St. Margaret in Westminster. This is the special church of the House of Commons, and it was here that Dr. Sacheverell (see Note 63, Rhyme 28) preached his first sermon after his suspension, on Palm Sunday, 1713.

125. "The bells of St. Gile's are celebrated," Hare wrote of St. Giles, Cripplegate, and he quoted the lines:

Oh, what a preacher is the time-worn tower,
Reading great sermons with its iron tongue.

The church is celebrated for the burial of Milton and the marriage of Cromwell.

126. Perhaps the Church of St. Anne's (not "Ann's") is meant by this couplet. It stands in Macclesfield Street, Soho, with a tower made as Danish as possible to flatter the Danish husband of the Princess Anne. One of the first seat-holders in the church was Catherine Sedley, mistress of James II. The essayist, William Hazlitt, rests in the churchyard.

Kettles and pans,
Say the bells of St. Ann's.[126]

Pokers and tongs,
Say the bells of St. John's.[127]

Halfpence and farthings,
Say the bells of St. Martin's.[128]

You owe me ten shillings,
Say the bells of St. Helen's.[129]

When will you pay me?
Say the bells of Old Bailey.[130]

When I grow rich,
Say the bells of Fleetditch.[131]

Pray, when will that be?
Say the bells of Stepney?[132]

I am sure I don't know,
Say the great bell at Bow.[133]

When I am old,
Say the bells at St. Paul's.[134]

Here comes a candle to light you to bed,
Here comes a chopper to cut off your head.[135]

« 641 »
London Bridge
Is Broken down,[136]
Dance over my Lady Lee,[137]
London Bridge
Is Broken down,
With a gay Lady.

How shall we build
It up again,
Dance over my Lady Lee.
How shall we build
It up again,
With a gay Lady.

Build it up with
Gravel, and Stone,
Dance over my Lady Lee.

Build it up with
Gravel, and Stone,
With a gay Lady.

Gravel, and Stone
Will wash away,
Dance over my Lady Lee.
Gravel, and Stone,
Will wash away,
With a gay Lady.

Build it up with
Iron, and Steel,
Dance over my Lady Lee.
Build it up with
Iron, and Steel,
With a gay Lady.

Iron, and Steel,
Will bend, and Bow,
Dance over my Lady Lee.
Iron, and Steel,
Will bend, and Bow,
With a gay Lady.

Build it up with
Silver, and Gold,
Dance over my Lady Lee.
Build it up with
Silver, and Gold,
With a gay Lady.

Silver, and Gold,
Will be stoln away,
Dance over my Lady Lee.
Silver, and Gold,
Will be stoln away,
With a gay Lady.

Then we'll set
A Man to Watch,
Dance over my Lady Lee.
Then we'll set
A Man to Watch
With a gay Lady.[138]

127. Probably St. John's, Clerkenwell. The father and mother of John Wilkes Booth, the murderer of Abraham Lincoln, are buried in its graveyard, and its crypt once contained the coffin of "Scratching Fanny" Parsons, the girl who was supposedly haunted by the "Cock Lane Ghost."

128. "St. Martin's," say the editors of *The Oxford Dictionary of Nursery Rhymes*, "probably refers to St. Martin's Lane in the City, where the moneylenders used to live."

129. Surely the very famous St. Helen's, Bishopsgate, called by Hare "a kind of Westminister Abbey for the City."

130. Old Bailey is near the Fleet Prison where debtors were sent.

131. In most later versions, "Shoreditch." Shoreditch, where an old church once stood, is just outside the City walls. Once a district of theaters, considered centers of vice, the district has always had an immoral reputation. There is a tradition that Shakespeare stood at the doors of the Shoreditch playhouses and held horses for the spectators during the performance.

132. Stepney, too, is just outside the City. The bells are probably those of St. Dunstan Church, called by Hare "a beautiful green oasis amid the ugly brick houses" because of its great churchyard. There is a tradition that all children born at sea are parishioners of Stepney:

He who sails on the wide sea
Is a parishioner of Stepney.

133. St. Mary-le-Bow in Cheapside. "What child," Hare asked, "will not remember that it was Bow Bells which said to the poor runaway boy as he was resting on Highgate milestone—

"Turn again, Whittington,
Lord Mayor of London,

and that he obeyed them, and became the most famous of Lord Mayors?" Bow Bells have always been famous, and people born within sound of them are called Cockneys. Pope wrote:

Far as loud Bow's stupendous bells
resound . . . .

But Nazi bombs shattered the tower of St. Mary-le-Bow early in World War II, and the famous bells, silent since 1939, did not ring again until December 20, 1961. A generation of Cockneys had been born and passed without the traditional sounds.

134. The first important Protestant church raised in England. When Francis, fifth Earl of Bedford, commissioned the famous Inigo Jones to build it, he instructed that he would not go to any great expense about it—that it must be little better than a barn. "Then," said Jones, "it shall be the handsomest barn in England."

135. This song accompanies a game described by the editors of *The Oxford Dictionary of Nursery Rhymes* as follows:

" . . . two of the bigger players determine in secret which of them shall be an 'orange' and which a 'lemon'; they then form an arch by joining hands, and sing the song while the others in a line troop underneath. When the two players who form the arch approach, with quickening tempo, the climax of their recitation . . . they repeat ominously 'Chop, chop, chop, chop, chop!' and on the last *chop* they bring their arms down around whichever child is at that moment passing under the arch. The captured player is asked privately whether he will be an 'orange' or a 'lemon' . . . and he goes to the back of the player he finds he has chosen, and the game and singing recommence. As now usually played, the end comes when every child has been lined up on one or the other side of the arch, whereupon there is a tug of war to test whether the 'oranges' or the 'lemons' are the stronger . . . ."

136. Some writers claim that these lines reflect an actual occurrence—the destruction of London Bridge by King Olaf and his Norsemen in the early part of the eleventh century, after a battle with King Ethelred of England.

137. The idea here may be that where there is no walking it may still be possible to dance, but other scholars take the more practical view that one could both walk and dance over during a winter when the Thames was frozen, as it often used to be.

On the other hand, attempts have been

« 642 »

Here comes a poor woman from baby-land,
With three small children in her hand:
One can brew, the other can bake,
The other can make a pretty round cake.
One can sit in the garden and spin,
Another can make a fine bed for the king;
Pray ma'am, will you take one in?**139**

« 643 »

There is a girl of our town,
She often wears a flowered gown;
Tommy loves her night and day,
And Richard when he may,
And Johnny when he can:
I think Sam must be the man!**140**

« 644 »

Sally, Sally Waters, sprinkle in the pan,
Hie, Sally! Hie, Sally, for a young man!
Choose for the best,
Choose for the worst,
Choose for the prettiest that you like best.**141**

« 645 »

A dis, a dis, a green grass,
A dis, a dis, a dis,
Come all you pretty fair maids
And dance along with us.

For we are going a-roving,
A-roving in this land;
We'll take this pretty fair maid,
We'll take her by the hand.

You shall have a duck, my dear,
And you shall have a drake;
And you shall have a young prince,
A young prince for your sake.

And if this young prince chance to die,
You shall have another;
The bells will ring, and the birds will sing,
And we'll all clap hands together.

Tom, Tom, the piper's son,
He learnt to play when he was young,
He with his pipe made such a noise,
That he pleased all the girls and boys.

K.3

K. GREENAWAY

« 646 »

CHILDREN: To Beccles, to Beccles!
   To buy a bunch of nettles!
   Pray, old Dame, what's o'clock?
DAME: **142** One, going for two.
CHILDREN: To Beccles, to Beccles!
   To buy a bunch of nettles!
   Pray, old Dame, what's o'clock?
DAME: Two, going for three.**143**

made to connect the "Lady Lee" of the refrain here with the name "Leigh." Another suggestion is that the "Lee" is the river Lea, which runs into the Thames.

138. Here the earliest printed version of the rhyme ends, but later, more sophisticated versions continue:

> Suppose the man should fall asleep,
>   Fall asleep, fall asleep,
> Suppose the man should fall asleep?
>   My fair lady.
>
> Give him a pipe to smoke all night,
>   Smoke all night, smoke all night,
> Give him a pipe to smoke all night,
>   My fair lady.

The game that is played with this song as its accompaniment is both ancient and widespread. It may possibly go back to one played by Florentine children in the early fourteenth century. The editors of *The Oxford Dictionary of Nursery Rhymes* comment: "The builders have had to meet what has every appearance of being supernatural opposition . . . . All over the world stories of human sacrifice are associated with bridges, to the erection of which the rivers are supposed to have an especial antipathy."

139. Fragments from an old game called "The Lady of the Land."

140. James O. Halliwell gave this as a rhyme to be used for a game, undescribed, called "The Town Lovers."

141. This rhyme appeared in *Mother Goose's Nursery Rhymes* (1886), where it was given as a song for the game, "Kiss in the Ring," undescribed.

142. One child, called "the old Dame," sits on the floor, and the rest, joining hands, form a circle around her, and dancing, sing the "To Beecles" verse.

143. And so on until the old Dame reaches, "Going for twelve." After this the following questions are asked with these replies:

CHILDREN: Where have you been?
   DAME: To the wood.
CHILDREN: What for?
   DAME: To pick up sticks.

CHILDREN: What for?
DAME: To light my fire.
CHILDREN: What for?
DAME: To boil my kettle.
CHILDREN: What for?
DAME: To cook some of you chickens!

The children then all run away as fast as they can, and the old Dame tries to catch them. Whoever is caught first is the next to impersonate the old Dame.

144. Children stand in a circle, leaving a space between each. One child walks round the outside, and carries a glove in her hand, singing these words.

145. Repeating the last words very rapidly, the child with the glove drops it behind one of the children, and this child must overtake the other child, following her exactly in and out between the children until she catches her. If the pursuer makes a mistake in the pursuit, she loses, and the game is over; otherwise she continues the game with the glove.

James O. Halliwell later gave, as another rhyme for "Drop Glove" or "Drop Cap":

My hand burns hot, hot, hot,
And whoever I love best, I'll drop this
at his foot.

146. A rhyme for the grand old game of "Blind Man's Buff."

147. Two of the strongest children are selected *A* and *B*. *A* stands within a ring of children, *B* stands without.

148. *B* here strikes one of the children in the ring. The child struck leaves the ring and takes hold of *B* behind. In the same manner the other children, one by one, are taken by *B* and attached to his "tail," until he has them all. *A* then tries to get them back. *B* runs away with them. They try to shelter themselves behind *B*. *A* drags them off, one by one, setting them against a wall, until he has recovered all. Halliwell added: "A regular tearing game, as the children say."

149. James O. Halliwell was told that "green cheese" was cheese with sage and potato-tops added.

150. This was acted by two or more girls, who walked or danced up and down the room

« 647 »

I've a glove in my hand,
  Hittity Hot!
Another in my other hand,
  Hotter than that![144]
So I sow beans, and so they come up,
Some in a mug, and some in a cup,
I sent a letter to my love,
I lost it, I lost it![145]
I found it, I found it!
It burns, it scalds!

« 648 »

Blind man, blind man,
  Sure you can't see?
    Turn round three times,
      And try to catch me.
        Turn east, turn west,
          Catch as you can,
            Did you think you'd caught me?
              Blind, blind man![146]

« 649 »

A. Who is going round my sheepfold?[147]
B. Only poor Jack Lingo.
A. Don't steal any of my black sheep.
B. No, no more I will, only one by one. Up, says Jack Lingo.[148]

« 650 »

Green cheese,[149] yellow laces,
  Up and down the market-places,
    Turn, cheeses, turn![150]

« 651 »

I charge my daughters every one
To keep house while I am gone.
You and *you* but specially *you*,
Or else I'll beat you black and blue.[151]

« 652 »

A. Draw a pail of water,
   For my lady's daughter;
   My father's a king, and my mother's a queen,
   My two little sisters are dress'd in green,
   Stamping grass and parsley,
   Marigold leaves and daisies.
B and C. One rush, two rush,
   Pray thee, fine lady, come under my bush.[152]

« 653 »

Follow my Bangalorey Man;
Follow my Bangalorey Man;
I'll do all that ever I can
To follow my Bangalorey Man.
We'll borrow a horse, and steal a gig,
And round the world we'll do a jig,
And I'll do all that ever I can
To follow my Bangalorey Man.

« 654 »

Here we are on Tom Tiddler's ground,
Picking up gold and silver.[153]

« 655 »

Bat, bat,[154]
Come under my hat,
   And I'll give you a slice of bacon;
And when I bake
I'll give you a cake,
   If I am not mistaken.

« 656 »

One to make ready
   And two to prepare;
Good luck to the rider,
   And away goes the mare.[155]

« 657 »

Awake, arise, pull out your eyes,
And hear what time of day;

or street, turning when they said "Turn, cheese, turn!"

151. A rhyme for "Gypsy," a game similar to "Hide and Seek," in which one child is selected for the Gypsy, one for the Mother, and the others for the Children. The Mother begins the game by reciting this rhyme. During the Mother's absence, the Gypsy comes in, entices a child away, and hides her. The process is repeated until all the Children are hidden, when the Mother has to find them.

152. A string of children, hand in hand, stand in a row. *A* stands in front of them as leader, and two other children, *B* and *C*, form an arch, each holding both the hands of the other. *A*, reciting the first part of the rhymes, passes under the arch, followed by the whole string of children, the last of whom is taken captive by *B* and *C*, chanting the second part of the rhymes. This is repeated until all the children have been captured. Halliwell followed this with a somewhat similar rhyme which may indeed belong to the same game:

   Sieve my lady's oatmeal,
     Grind my lady's flour,
   Put it in a chestnut,
     Let it stand an hour;
   One may rush, two may rush,
   Come, my girls, walk under my bush.

153. "Tom Tiddler's Ground" is a children's game in which a space is marked off for the chief player—"Tom Tiddler." The other children then try to invade this space while Tom tries to keep them out of it. The child who successfully eludes Tom sings the above little rhyme. Hence, "Tom Tiddler's ground" has come to mean any place where pickings may be sought or had without effective interference.

154. Here the child who was hunting bats would clap hands.

155. A race-starting jingle, the forerunner of the modern:

   One for the money,
   Two for the show,
   Three to make ready
   And four to go!

156. A rhyme used to alert a player who was slow in taking his turn in a game.

157. The line "a hop and a scotch" might lead one to think that this is a rhyme to be chanted while playing the game hop-scotch, which gets its name from the word "scotch," a mark, and the hop-scotch diagram that is marked—or "scotched"—on the ground or sidewalk. But such is not the case: the title given to this rhyme in *Gammer Gurton's Garland* —"Water Skimming"—indicates the proper game in which it was recited: that of skipping or skimming flat stones across a small body of water at a mark. When the mark was hit, the boy skipping the stone scored, got "another notch on the scotch."

158. Two boys leave the group and privately arrange that the password shall be some implement of a particular trade. The trade is announced after this rhyme has been recited. The innocent player who correctly guesses the implement is then beaten with the other boys' caps until he reaches a fixed goal while all the other boys call out "plane him, hammer him, rasp him, solder him"—or whatever the selected implement may have been.

159. This rhyme, which has been printed in many "Mother Goose" books since its first appearance in *The Only True Mother Goose's Melodies*, seems to be an elaboration of a couplet from *Mother Goose's Quarto* (c. 1825):

Cat on the roof; bow, wow, says Towzer;
Don't hurt Puss, for she is a mouser.

Some of the phrases in the rhyme have now become part of the square-dance caller's repertoire; but even earlier this may have been a verse to be chanted triumphantly by one who has succeeded in "getting in free" in a game like "Run, Sheep, Run." Sometimes in such games, *one* getting in free entitles *all* the players to get in free. Your editors, Minnesota-reared, can well remember calling out: "Ole, Ole Olsen, all in free. . . ."

160. This rhyme is a five-hundred-year-old joke—said fast it sounds like Latin—which still had people laughing in 1943, when the last two lines formed the basis of the swing song "Mairzy Doats and Dozy Doats."

161. This ancient catch is still trapping innocents. Halliwell followed it with the similar:

1. I went up one pair of stairs.

And when you have done, pull out your tongue,
And see what you can say.**156**

« 658 »

A duck and a drake,
A nice barley cake,
With a penny to pay the old baker,
A hop and a scotch
A hop and a scotch
Slitherum, slatherum, take her.**157**

« 659 »

Two broken tradesmen,
Newly come over,
The one from France and Scotland,
The other from Dover.
What's your trade?**158**

« 660 »

Hogs in the garden, catch 'em, Towser;
Cows in the corn-field, run, boys, run!
Cats in the cream-pot, run, girls, run;
Fire on the mountain, run, boys, run!**159**

« 661 »

In fir tar is,
In oak none is,
In mud eels are,
In clay none are,
Goat eat ivy,
Mare eat oats.**160**

« 662 »

1. I am a gold lock.
2. I am a gold key.
1. I am a silver lock.
2. I am a silver key.
1. I am a brass lock.
2. I am a brass key.
1. I am a lead lock.
2. I am a lead key.

A. RACKHAM

1. I am a monk lock.
2. I am a monk key!**161**

« 663 »

A gaping wide-mouthed waddling frog.

Two pudding ends would choke a dog,
With a gaping wide-mouthed waddling frog.

Three monkeys tied to a clog,
Two pudding ends would choke a dog,
With a gaping wide-mouthed waddling frog.

Four horses stuck in a bog,
Three monkeys tied to a clog,
Two pudding ends would choke a dog,
With a gaping wide-mouthed waddling frog.·

Five puppies by our dog Ball,
Who daily for their breakfast call;
Four horses stuck in a bog,
Three monkeys tied to a clog,
Two pudding ends would choke a dog,
With a gaping wide-mouthed waddling frog.

2. *Just like me.*
1. *I went up two pairs of stairs.*
2. *Just like me.*
1. *I went into a room.*
2. *Just like me.*
1. *I looked out of a window.*
2. *Just like me.*
1. *And there I saw a monkey.*
2. *Just like me.*

Of course, the person who knows this old joke can turn the tables by going through everything right until he reaches the final sentence, which he changes to "Just like *you*. Ha, ha, ha! You didn't catch me that time!"

A third catch of the same kind is the venerable:

1. *I one it.*
2. *I two it.*
1. *I three it.*
2. *I four it.*
1. *I five it.*
2. *I six it.*
1. *I seven it.*
2. *I eight it.*
1. *Oh, so you* ate *the old dead horse.*
(Or something equally tasty.)

Another catch of this same kind goes:

Adam and Eve and Pinch-me
Went down to the river to bathe.
Adam and Eve got drownded,
Which one of the three was saved?

The innocent answers "Pinch me," and the diabolic propounder of the catch does just that.

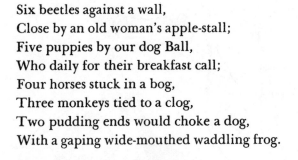

Six beetles against a wall,
Close by an old woman's apple-stall;
Five puppies by our dog Ball,
Who daily for their breakfast call;
Four horses stuck in a bog,
Three monkeys tied to a clog,
Two pudding ends would choke a dog,
With a gaping wide-mouthed waddling frog.

Seven lobsters in a dish,
As fresh as any heart could wish;
Six beetles against a wall,
Close by an old woman's apple-stall;
Five puppies by our dog Ball,
Who daily for their breakfast call;
Four horses stuck in a bog,
Three monkeys tied to a clog,
Two pudding ends would choke a dog,
With a gaping wide-mouthed waddling frog.

A. RACKHAM

Eight joiners in joiner's hall,
Working with their tools and all;
Seven lobsters in a dish,
As fresh as any heart could wish;
Six beetles against a wall,
Close by an old woman's apple-stall;
Five puppies by our dog Ball,
Who daily for their breakfast call;
Four horses stuck in a bog,
Three monkeys tied to a clog,
Two pudding ends would choke a dog,
With a gaping wide-mouthed waddling frog.

Nine peacocks in the air,
I wonder how they all came there,
I don't know, nor I don't care;
Eight joiners in joiner's hall,
Working with their tools and all;
Seven lobsters in a dish,
As fresh as any heart could wish;
Six beetles against a wall,
Close by an old woman's apple-stall;
Five puppies by our dog Ball,
Who daily for their breakfast call;

R. CALDECOTT

262

Four horses stuck in a bog,
Three monkeys tied to a clog,
Two pudding ends would choke a dog,
With a gaping wide-mouthed waddling frog.

Ten comets in the sky,
Some low and some high;
Nine peacocks in the air,
I wonder how they all came there,
I don't know, nor do I care;
Eight joiners in joiner's hall,
Working with their tools and all;
Seven lobsters in a dish,
As fresh as any heart could wish;
Six beetles against a wall,
Close by an old woman's apple-stall;
Five puppies by our dog Ball,
Who daily for their breakfast call;
Four horses stuck in a bog,
Three monkeys tied to a clog,
Two pudding ends would choke a dog,
With a gaping wide-mouthed waddling frog.

Eleven ships sailing o'er the main,
Some bound for France and some for Spain;
Ten comets in the sky,
Some low and some high;
Nine peacocks in the air,
I wonder how they all came there,
I don't know, nor I don't care;
Eight joiners in joiner's hall,
Working with their tools and all;
Seven lobsters in a dish,
As fresh as any heart could wish;
Six beetles on a wall,
Close by an old woman's apple-stall;
Five puppies by our dog Ball,
Who daily for their breakfast call;
Four horses stuck in a bog,
Three monkeys tied to a clog,
Two pudding ends would choke a dog,
With a gaping wide-mouthed waddling frog.

162. Like "The Twelve Days of Christmas" (Rhyme 424), "The Play of the Wide-Mouth waddling Frog, to amuse the Mind, and exercise The Memory," is a game of forfeits which was once very popular, especially at Christmastime. The success of this "Play" was such that it inspired many imitations, including "The Frisking, Barking Lady's Lap-Dog," "The Pretty, Playful Tortoiseshell Cat," and "The Noble, Prancing, Cantering Horse."

A tongue-twister which can be used—and was used—to play the same kind of game is the venerable:

One old Oxford ox opening oysters;
Two tee-totums totally tired of trying to trot
*   to Tadbury;*
Three tall tigers tippling tenpenny nails;
Four fat friars fanning fainting flies;
Five frippy Frenchmen foolishly fishing for
*   flies;*
Six sportsmen shooting snipes;
Seven Severn salmon swallowing shrimps;
Eight Englishmen eagerly examining Europe;
Nine nimble noblemen nibbling nonpareils;
Ten tinkers tinkling upon ten tin tinder-boxes
*   with tenpenny tacks;*
Eleven elephants elegantly upright;
Twelve topographical typographers typically
*   translating types.*

163. That is, the heart of the city, within walls.

164. Here the players, each giving a line in turn, must begin to reverse the sequence as shown in the second verse. He who misses pays a forfeit.

165. These words were to be repeated correctly, and as rapidly as possible, inserting the word "cother" after every word in the rhyme, on the pain of paying a forfeit.

166. The member of the company who can continue the bowl-bottle-table sequence the longest, in one breath, is the winner. The game has a modern counterpart (in reverse) in the well-known:

Ninety-nine beer bottles hanging on the wall;
Oh, what if one of those bottles should fall?
Ninety-eight beer bottles hanging on the
*   wall . . . .*

Twelve huntsmen with horn and hounds,
Hunting over other men's ground;
Eleven ships sailing o'er the main,
Some bound for France and some for Spain;
Ten comets in the sky,
Some low and some high;
Nine peacocks in the air,
I wonder how they all came there,
I don't know, nor I don't care;
Eight joiners in joiner's hall,
Working with their tools and all;
Seven lobsters in a dish,
As fresh as any heart could wish;
Six beetles against a wall,
Close by an old woman's apple-stall;
Five puppies by our dog Ball,
Who daily for their breakfast call;
Four horses stuck in a bog,
Three monkeys tied to a clog,
Two pudding ends would choke a dog,
With a gaping wide-mouthed waddling frog.**162**

« 664 »

This is the key of the kingdom.
In that kingdom there is a city.
In that city there is a town.**163**
In that town there is a street.
In that street there is a lane.
In that lane there is a yard.
In that yard there is a house.
In that house there is a room.
In that room there is a bed.
In that bed there is a basket.
In that basket there are some flowers.**164**

Flowers in a basket;
Basket on the bed;
Bed in the room;
Room in the house;
House in the yard;
Yard in the lane;
Lane in the street;

Street in the town;
Town in the city;
City in the kingdom—
And this is the key of the kingdom.

« 665 »

I went to the sea,
And saw twentee
   Geese all in a row:
My glove I would give
Full of gold, if my wife,
   Was as white as those.**165**

« 666 »

My father, he left me, just as he was able,
One bowl, one bottle, one table,
Two bowls, two bottles, two tables,
Three bowls, three bottles, three tables. . . .**166**

« 667 »

I love my love with an A, because
   he's Agreeable.
I hate him because he's Avaricious,
He took me to the sign of the Acorn,
And treated me with Apples.
His name is Andrew,
And he lives in Arlington.**167**

« 668 »

Buff says Buff to all his men,
And I will say Buff to you again;
Buff neither laughs nor smiles,
But carries his face,
With a very good grace,
And passes the stick to the very next place.**168**

« 669 »

Jack's alive and in very good health,
If he dies in your hand you must look to yourself.**169**

167. This exemplifies a beginning to the old game, "I Love My Love with an A," in which the players in turn must complete a line (in some versions, a complete stanza) using all the letters of the alphabet in turn.

168. Say the editors of *The Oxford Dictionary of Nursery Rhymes*: "An old forfeits game. The players seat themselves in a circle, and one, taking a wand, points it at a neighbour repeating the rhyme with mock solemnity. The player pointed at then becomes the one who points, and so on round the circle. 'It is a game,' remarks Chambers, 'in which the only art consists in keeping one's gravity while saying absurd things.' Those who laugh or smile must pay a forfeit."

169. Played with a stick, one end of which is burnt red-hot. The stick is passed in a circle from one player to the other. Each of those who passes the stick recites these lines. The player in whose hand the firebrand goes out loses the game and must pay a forfeit. Another rhyme for the same game goes:

Jack is alive, and likely to live,
If he dies in your hand, you've a forfeit to give.

Come riddle me riddle me riddle me ree,

None are so blind as they who won't see.

CHAPTER XIV

Mother Goose's Riddles and Tongue Twisters

Today the riddle is almost exclusively the property of children, but it was not always so.

Once grownups, especially at a holiday season, would vie with one another to see who could propound the most difficult riddles, and the losers would pay forfeits to the winners.

Properly, the "riddle" is an enigmatic description, often in verse; the "conundrum" is a question that is answered by a play on words. "As round as an apple, as deep as a pail; it never cries out 'till it's caught by the tail" is a riddle.[1] "When is a door not a door?" is a familiar conundrum.[2]

Riddle books were probably the first popular literature ever printed; certainly they were the first printed designed exclusively for entertainment. One of the earliest printed in English was Wynkyn de Worde's *Amusing Questions* (1511), and Shakespeare alludes to another in *The Merry Wives of Windsor*. This was *The Booke of Merry Riddles, together with proper Questions and witty Proverbs to make pleasant pastime,* and it contained "Two Legs Sat Upon Three Legs," which you will find in this chapter as Rhyme 709. An even more important

1. To which the answer is "a bell."

2. To which the traditional answer was "When it's a-jar" and the more modern answer is "When it's an egress" (a Negress).

3. James O. Halliwell included tongue twisters in his section on "Charms," on the grounds that a tongue twister, said as rapidly as possible three times in succession, was supposed to be a cure for the hiccoughs.

4. This is the way this favorite nursery rhyme first appeared in print, in *Gammer Gurton's Garland*, edition of 1810, but the version we know best today goes:

> Humpty Dumpty sat on a wall,
> Humpty Dumpty had a great fall.
> All the king's horses,
> And all the king's men,
> Couldn't put Humpty together again.

In the earliest appearance of this better-known version (as a manuscript addition to a copy of *Mother Goose's Melody* published about 1803) the last line reads:

> Could not set Humpty Dumpty up again.

The rhyme is certainly much older than that, however, and some scholars think that its age is "to be measured in thousands of years."

The answer to this riddle—for the rhyme *is* a riddle—is that Humpty Dumpty was an egg; and that explains why, having fallen and broken, he could not be put together again.

"Humpty Dumpty" is known as *boule, boule* in France, *Thille Lille* in Sweden, *Lille-Trill* in Denmark, *Hillerin-Lillerin* in Finland, *Annenadadeli* in Switzerland, and by many other names in various parts of Germany. The term "Humpty-Dumpty" is given in *The Oxford English Dictionary* as the name for an ale-and-brandy drink of the late seventeenth century, and also as "a short clumsy person of either sex." There is also a game for girls called "Humpty Dumpty."

"Humpty Dumpty" is one of the many nursery rhyme characters immortalized by Lewis Carroll in *Through the Looking-Glass*. There the last line of the rhyme is given as "Couldn't put Humpty Dumpty in his place again," which, as Alice observed, "is much too long for the poetry."

book, from the "Mother Goose" point of view, was the "Choice" collection of diversions by "Peter Puzzlewell, Esq." which was sponsored by Elizabeth Newbery c. 1790. A number of its "Riddles, Charades, Rebuses, etc." soon began to find their way into nursery-rhyme books.

In this chapter you will also find many examples of the tongue twister,[3] which Evan Esar, in his *Comic Dictionary*, defines as a group of words or phrases which gets your tang all tongueled up.

Perhaps the world's best-known tongue twister is "Peter Piper picked a peck of pickled pepper" (Rhyme 740), which Esar comments upon in another book (*The Humor of Humor*, New York: Horizon Press, 1952).

"The influence of Peter Piper was remarkable in several ways," he writes. "It led directly to the alliterative repeatism which has dominated the tongue twister ever since. . . .

"Another result of Peter Piper was its use as the title of the juvenile classic, *Peter Piper's Practical Principles of Plain and Perfect Pronunciation*. This in turn led to the flood of alliterative exercises by which children of a century ago were taught proper speech.

"A third consequence was its generation of a body of jokes. Like the story of the two Ubangi girls who met one hot day in the jungle. One of them stuck her disc-lipped face close to the other and repeated rapidly: 'Peter Piper picked a peck of pickled peppers! Now you fan me for awhile.'

"Or the story in which one young man said to another: 'I hear you took some lessons to overcome your stutter. Did they help?' 'N-n-not exactly,' stuttered the other. 'I l-l-learned to s-s-say "Peter Piper picked a peck of pickled peppers" b-b-but the t-t-trouble is, it d-d-doesn't c-c-come up m-m-much in c-c-conversation.' "

« 670 »

Humpty Dumpty sat on a wall,
Humpty Dumpty had a great fall;

Threescore men and threescore more,
Cannot place Humpty Dumpty as he was before.[4]

5. The answer is "a bed."

6. The answer is "a turnstile."

« 671 »

Formed long ago, yet made today,
I'm most enjoyed while others sleep;
What few would like to give away,
Nor any wish to keep.[5]

« 672 »

I'm in ev'ry one's way,
Yet no Christian I stop,
My four horns ev'ry day
Horizontally play,
And my head is nailed down at the top.[6]

Humpty Dumpty sat on a wall,
Humpty Dumpty had a great fall.

K. GREENAWAY

« 673 »

As I was walking in a field of wheat,
I picked up something good to eat;
Neither fish, flesh, fowl, nor bone,
I kept it till it ran alone.[7]

« 674 »

A shoemaker makes shoes without leather,
With all the four elements together,
Fire, Water, Earth, Air,
And every customer takes two pair.[8]

« 675 »

There was a thing a full month old
    When Adam was no more;
Before the thing was five weeks old,
    Adam was years four score.[9]

« 676 »

I went to the wood and I got it;
I sat me down, and I sought it;
I kept it still against my will
And so by force home I brought it.[10]

« 677 »

Arthur O'Bower has broken his band
And he comes roaring up the land;
The King of Scots with all his power
Cannot stop Arthur of the Bower.[11]

« 678 »

As I was going to St. Ives,
I met a man with seven wives,
Each wife had seven sacks,
Each sack had seven cats,
Each cat had seven kits;
Kits, cats, sacks, and wives,
How many were going to St. Ives?[12]

« 679 »

Apple-pie, pudding, and pancake,
All begins with an A.[13]

A. RACKHAM

7. As in "Humpty Dumpty," the answer is
"an egg." And here is perhaps an even better
riddle with the same answer:

  In marble halls as white as milk,
  Lined with a skin as soft as silk,
  Within a fountain crystal-clear,
  A golden apple doth appear.
  No doors are there to this stronghold,
  Yet thieves break in and steal the gold.

8. The "shoemaker" is a blacksmith.

9. The answer is "the moon."

10. The traditional answer to this riddle is
"a man with a thorn in his foot," but the an-

« 680 »

When V and I together meet,
They make the number Six compleat.
When I with V doth meet once more,
Then 'tis they Two can make but Four.
And when that V from I is gone
Alas! poor I can make but One.**14**

« 681 »

There was a girl in our towne,
Silk an' satin was her gowne,
Silk an' satin, gold an' velvet,
Guess her name, three times I've telled it.**15**

« 682 »

Hick-a-more, hack-a-more,
Hung on the kitchen door;
Nothing so long,
And nothing so strong,
As hick-a-more, hack-a-more,
Hung on the kitchen door.**16**

« 683 »

When I was taken from the fair body,
   They then cut off my head,
And then my shape was altered;
   It's I that make peace between king and king,
And many a true lover glad:
   All this I do and ten times more,
And more I could do still,
   But nothing can I do,
Without my guider's will.**17**

« 684 »

As I looked out my chamber window,
   I heard something fall;
I sent my maid to pick it up,
   But she couldn't pick it all.**18**

swer most often heard in the United States is "a briar." Homer, it is said, was so ashamed that he could not find the solution to a similar riddle that he died of his distress. The riddle that supposedly killed Homer goes: "All that we caught, we left behind, and carried away all that we did not catch." The answer here is "fleas."

11. There does not seem to be any historical significance to this curious rhyme. It is thought by most commentators to be a riddle, with "Arthur O'Bower" personifying the wind.

12. The answer to this famous riddle is probably known to everybody today: No "kits, cats, sacks, and wives" were going *to* St. Ives; they were coming *from* St. Ives. The only one going *to* St. Ives was *I*, the propounder of the riddle. There is a St. Ives in Huntington, but the town in the jingle is a fishing village of that name on the Cornish coast of England.

13. A kind of catch sentence. "All" of course does begin with an A.

14. It is necessary to remember that V once served as both V and U (you) to appreciate this pun of Stuart times.

15. This is the first in James O. Halliwell's collection of "Riddles." Of course, the answer is "Ann." The riddle containing its own answer seems to have been a favorite of our ancestors, and Halliwell gave several other examples.

16. A "hackamore" is a halter, usually of plaited horse-hair, used chiefly for breaking horses; but that is not the solution to this riddle. The answer here is "sunshine."

17. The answer is "a pen"—a quill pen of the kind used by our forefathers. Another version of this riddle goes:

I am become of flesh and blood,
*   As other creatures be;*
Yet there's neither flesh nor blood
*   Doth remain in me.*
I make kings to fall out,
*   I make them agree,*
And yet there's neither flesh nor blood
*   Doth remain in me.*

18. The answer is "a snuffbox."

19. Halliwell gave this as a riddle, and stated that the answer was "a tobacco pipe." It is not very easy to see how anyone ever arrived at this.

20. The answer is "a glove."

21. The answer is "a walnut on a tree."
And here is another version of the same riddle:

> There was a little green house,
> And in the little green house
> There was a little brown house,
> And in the little brown house
> There was a little yellow house,
> And in the little yellow house
> There was a little white house,
> And in the little white house
> There was a little heart.

22. This is a modernized wording of a riddle that dates back to the time of Henry VIII; the answer is "a bee." Two of the three kinds of bumblebees to be found in Scotland are supposed to be portrayed in this riddle:

> As I was going o'er Tipple Tine,
> I met a flock of bonny swine;
> Some yellow necked,
> Some yellow backed;
> They were the very bonniest swine
> That ever went over Tipple Tine.

And the answer to the following riddle is "a bee-hive:"

> Wee little house with the golden thatch,
> Twice I knocked and I lifted the latch:
> "And pray, is the mistress here?"
> "In black stuff gown and a yellow vest,
> She's busily packing her honey-chest;
> Will you taste a bit, my dear?"

23. The answer is "T-O-B-A-C-C-O."

24. The answer is that the men's names were both "King" and the dog's name was "Bin."

25. Halliwell gave no answer to this riddle but that generally accepted is "a plum pudding." On the other hand, Katherine Elwes Thomas has written that this rhyme was current at the time when Queen Mary of England was proposing to marry Philip II of Spain. If Mary was the "flour of England" and Philip the "fruit of Spain," the "Met together in a

« 685 »

I went into my grandmother's garden,
And there I found a farthing.
I went into my next door neighbour's;
There I bought a pipkin and a popkin,
A slipkin and a slopkin,
A nailboard, a sailboard,
All for a farthing.**19**

« 686 »

As I was going o'er London Bridge,
I met a cart full of fingers and thumbs!**20**

« 687 »

As soft as silk,
As white as milk,
As bitter as gall;
A thick wall,
And a green coat covers all.**21**

« 688 »

Little bird of paradise,
She works her work both neat and nice;
She pleases God, she pleases man,
She does the work that no man can.**22**

« 689 »

Make three-fourths of a cross,
And a circle complete,
And let two semi-circles
On a perpendicular meet;
Next add a triangle
That stands on two feet;
Next two semi-circles
And a circle complete.**23**

« 690 »

There was a king met a king
In a narrow lane;
Said the king to the king,
Where have you been?
I have been a hunting

The buck and the doe.
Will you lend me your dog?
Yes, I will do so;
Call upon him, call upon him.
What is his name?
I have told you twice
And won't tell you again.**24**

« 691 »

Flour of England, fruit of Spain,
Met together in a shower of rain;
Put in a bag, tied round with a string;
If you'll tell me this riddle,
I'll give you a ring.**25**

« 692 »

King Charles walked and talked
Seven years after his head was cut off.**26**

« 693 »

Every lady in this land
Has twenty nails upon each hand
Five and twenty on hands and feet
All this is true without deceit.**27**

« 694 »

Twelve pears hanging high,
Twelve knights riding by;
Each knight took a pear,
And yet left eleven there.**28**

« 695 »

Higher than a house,
Higher than a tree;
Oh, whatever can that be?**29**

« 696 »

Old Mother Twitchett has but one eye,
And a long tail which she can let fly,
And every time she goes over a gap,
She leaves a bit of her tail in a trap.**30**

shower of rain" would describe their first
meeting, which did take place in a downpour.
The last line might refer to the fact that
Queen Mary publicly gave Philip a ring.

26. Properly punctuated, this curious statement makes perfect sense:

> *King Charles walked and talked.*
> *Seven years after, his head was cut off.*

Several riddles of the same kind follow.

27. A riddle that is also an aid to teaching
punctuation. A similar exercise is:

> *I saw a peacock with a fiery tail,*
> *I saw a blazing comet drop down hail,*
> *I saw a cloud wrapped with ivy round,*
> *I saw an oak creep upon the ground,*
> *I saw a pismire swallow up a whale,*
> *I saw a sea brimful of ale,*
> *I saw a Venice glass fifteen feet deep,*
> *I saw a well full of men's tears that weep,*
> *I saw red eyes all of a flaming fire,*
> *I saw a house bigger than the moon and*
> *   higher,*
> *I saw the sun at twelve o'clock at night,*
> *I saw the man that saw this wondrous sight.*

Walter de la Mare pointed out that poets and
dreamers see nothing unusual in seeing "the
sun at twelve o'clock at night."
  Very like the above is:

> *I saw a fishpond all on fire*
> *I saw a house bow to a squire*
> *I saw a parson twelve feet high*
> *I saw a cottage near the sky*
> *I saw a balloon made of lead*
> *I saw a coffin drop down dead*
> *I saw two sparrows run a race*
> *I saw two horses making lace*
> *I saw a girl just like a cat*
> *I saw a kitten wear a hat*
> *I saw a man who saw these too*
> *And said though strange they all were true.*

28. Halliwell gave no answer to this riddle,
which perhaps involves a pun on "pears" and
"pairs" perhaps one knight named "Each-
knight."

29. The not too surprising answer is "a star,"
as it is to:

W. CRANE

I have a little sister, they call her Peep-Peep,
She wades the waters, deep, deep, deep;
She climbs the mountains, high, high, high,
Poor little creature she has but one eye.

30. The answer is "a needle and thread."

31. This is a charade rather than a riddle. "This very popular verse puzzle," explains The National Puzzlers' League in its *New Primer of Puzzledom* (1958), "uses a keyword which is broken up into two or more parts, each of which is a word." (There are also phonetic charades, enigmatic charades, and reversed charades.) Here the answer is "cur(r)-ants."

32. The traditional solution is that the man had one eye (which is not "no eyes"); there were two apples on the tree, he took one and left one (which is not "no apples"). But the editors of *The Oxford Dictionary of Nursery Rhymes* point out that "the illustrator of a modern nursery book solved the problem by drawing the tree with a board nailed to it marked APPLES."

33. Part rebus and part charade. The answer is "Cleopatra." The moon nine days old gives the C; Leo in the zodiac is the next sign to Cancer; "patra" is "pat rat without a tail."

« 697 »

Higgledy-piggledy
Here we lie
Picked and plucked,
And put in a pie.
My first is snapping, snarling, growling,
My second's hard-working, romping, and prowling.
Higgledy-piggledy,
Here we lie,
Picked and plucked,
And put in a pie.**31**

« 698 »

There was a man who had no eyes,
He went abroad to view the skies,
He saw a tree with apples on it,
He took no apples off, yet left no apples on it.**32**

« 699 »

The moon nine days old,
The next sign to Cancer;
Pat rat without a tail;—
And now, sir, for your answer.**33**

« 700 »

Little Nancy Etticoat
With a white petticoat,
And a red nose;
She has no feet or hands,
The longer she stands
The shorter she grows.**34**

« 701 »

Long legs and crooked thighs,
Little head and no eyes.**35**

« 702 »

There were three sisters in a hall,
There came a knight amongst them all;
Good morrow, aunt, to the one,
Good morrow, aunt, to the other,
Good morrow, gentlewoman, to the third,
   If you were aunt,
      As the other two be,
   I would say good morrow,
      Then, aunts, all three.**36**

A. RACKHAM

« 703 »

Congeal'd water and Cain's brother,
That was my lover's name and no other.**37**

« 704 »

Thirty white horses
Upon a red hill,
Now they tramp,
Now they champ,
Now they stand still.**38**

« 705 »

Black I am and much admired,
Men may seek me till they're tired;
I weary horse and weary men,
Tell me this riddle if you can.**39**

34. This famous riddle was at least two hundred years old when James O. Halliwell included it in his edition of 1842. The answer, as everybody no doubt knows, is "a lighted candle."

35. The answer is "a pair of tongs."

36. A moment's reflection will solve this riddle. The "gentlewoman" was the sister who had had a child. Unlike her two sisters, she was not an aunt but a mother. "Kinship" problems like this one form one of the largest, and to some, one of the most fascinating, class of puzzles. The best-known of all such problems is probably:

> Brothers and sisters have I none,
> Yet that man's father is my father's son.

37. The answer is "Ice-Abel," Isabel.

38. The answer is "the teeth and gums."

39. The answer is "coal."

40. "Old Noll" was the Royalists' nickname for Oliver Cromwell. The editors of *The Oxford Dictionary of Nursery Rhymes* believe that the composition of this riddle can be dated to the year 1648 because Cromwell did not come to power until June 1647 and "The king"—Charles I—was executed in January 1649.

41. The answer is "a rainbow."

42. The scholar's name was "Andrew."

43. The answer is "a chimney." There are many similar riddles, including:

> Red within and red without,
> Four corners round about.

Here the answer is "a brick."

> The land is white,
> The sea is black,
> It'll take a good scholar
> To riddle me that—

is answered by "paper and writing." And of course all of us remember that "a newspaper" is the answer to:

> Black and white
> And red [read] all over.

44. Perhaps the great-great-grandfather of all riddles was that posed to Oedipus by the

« 706 »

Purple, yellow, red, and green,
The king cannot reach it, nor yet the queen;
Nor can Old Noll, whose power's so great;[40]
Tell me this riddle while I count eight.[41]

« 707 »

As I was a-walking on Westminster Bridge,
I met with a Westminster scholar;
He pulled off his cap, an' drew off his gloves,
Now what was the name of this scholar?[42]

« 708 »

Black within and red without,
Four corners round about.[43]

« 709 »

Two legs sat upon three legs
With one leg in his lap;
In comes four legs
And runs away with one leg;
Up jumps two legs,
Catches up three legs,
Throws it after four legs,
And makes him bring one leg back.[44]

« 710 »

A riddle, a riddle,
As I suppose;
A hundred eyes,
And never a nose.[45]

« 711 »

As round as an apple,
As deep as a cup,
And all the king's horses
Cannot pull it up.[46]

« 712 »

As I went through the garden gap,
Who should I meet but Dick Red-cap!

A stick in his hand, a stone in his throat,
If you'll tell me this riddle, I'll give you a groat.**47**

« 713 »

Elizabeth, Elspeth, Betsy, and Bess,
They all went together to seek a bird's nest;
They found a bird's nest with five eggs in,
They all took one, and left four in.**48**

« 714 »

Highty, tighty, paradighty, clothed all in green,
The king could not read it, no more could the
    queen;
They sent for a wise man out of the East,
Who said it had horns, but was not a beast.**49**

« 715 »

See, see! what shall I see?
A horse's head where his tail should be.**50**

« 716 »

As I was going o'er London Bridge,
    And peep'd through a nick,
I saw four and twenty ladies
    Riding on a stick!**51**

« 717 »

Lives in winter,
Dies in summer,
And grows with its root upwards!**52**

« 718 »

When I went up Sandy-Hill,
I met a sandy-boy;
I cut his throat, I sucked his blood,
And left his skin a-hanging-o.**53**

« 719 »

Riddle me, riddle me, what is that?
Over the head and under the hat?**54**

Sphinx: What animal walks on four legs in the morning, two at noon, and three in the evening? Oedipus declared that the answer must be a man, for man walked on his hands and feet in the morning of life, strode erect on his two feet in his prime at noon, and in the evening of life supported his infirmities with a cane. "Leg" riddles have been popular ever since, and the nursery-rhyme version given here is a fine example. Of course it describes a man sitting on a three-legged stool with a leg of mutton in his lap. A dog comes in and steals the mutton; the man catches up the stool, throws it at the dog "and makes him bring one leg back."

Here is another "leg" riddle which involves a milkmaid, her stool, and her cow:

Two-legs sat on Three-legs by Four-legs.
One leg knocked Two-legs off Three-legs.
Two-legs hit Four-legs with Three-legs.

45. The usual answer is "a sieve," but if you said "a potato," we would not count you wrong.

46. Halliwell's version of a seventeenth-century riddle. The answer is "a well."

47. Squirrel Nutkin, in Beatrix Potter's tale, recites a similar riddle and gives away the answer by bobbing "up and down like *a red cherry*." There are many versions of this riddle, including:

Riddle me, riddle me, ree,
A little man in a tree;
A stick in his hand,
A stone in his throat,
If you read me this riddle
I'll give you a groat.

48. The answer, since "Elspeth, Betsy, and Bess" are all diminutives of Elizabeth, is that only one child went bird's-nesting.

49. This verse is said to portray "the holly tree."

50. The answer is "a horse with its tail tied to the manger."

"For a long time," the editors of *The Oxford Dictionary of Nursery Rhymes* write, "'The Wonderful Horse, With His Head Where His Tail Ought To Be' was a popular side-show at fairs. Those who paid their

277

money to see the wonder horse do not seem to have resented the trick, but to have persuaded their friends to see it too."

One is reminded of P. T. Barnum's sign, THIS WAY TO THE EGRESS.

51. The answer is "a firebrand with sparks upon it."

52. The answer is "an icicle."

53. The "sandy-boy" is "an orange."
  A similar riddle (with the answer "A bottle of something to drink") goes:

> Around the rick, around the rick,
> And there I found my Uncle Dick.
> I screwed his neck,
> I sucked his blood,
> And left his body lying.

54. The answer is "hair."

55. So how much did each one get? The question is complicated by the fact that the fiddler's wife may well have been the piper's mother. If this was the case, each of the three received one and three-quarters of a cake.

56. The answer is "an equal."

57. The answer is "a blackberry" (from blossom to full ripeness).

58. The answer is "smoke" or "mist."

59. This little rhyme is presumably a riddle, although no answer was given to it in *The Only True Mother Goose's Melodies*, c. 1843, where it first appeared in print. As in Rhyme 723, the solution may be "smoke" or "mist."

60. The answer is "ice."

61. The answer is "parchment, pen, and wax."

62. The answer is "a ship's nail."

63. The answer is "toys."

64. The answer is "dew."

65. The answer is "a pair of shoes."

66. The answer is "snow." Snow—as the "White bird featherless"—is also the poetic answer to the following riddle, in which "Lord Landless" is the sun which melts it:

« 720 »

The fiddler and his wife,
  The piper and his mother,
Ate three half-cakes, three whole cakes,
  And three-quarters of another.[55]

« 721 »

What God never sees;
What the king seldom sees;
What we see every day;
Read my riddle, I pray.[56]

« 722 »

As white as milk,
And not milk;
As green as grass,
And not grass;
As red as blood,
And not blood;
As black as soot,
And not soot.[57]

« 723 »

A house full, a hole full,
And you cannot gather a bowl full.[58]

« 724 »

Climb by rope
  Or climb by ladder,
Without either
  I'll climb higher.[59]

« 725 »

As I was going o'er London Bridge,
  I heard something crack;
Not a man in all England
  Can mend that![60]

« 726 »

The calf, the goose, the bee,
The world is ruled by these three.[61]

« 727 »

Over the water,
And under the water,
And always with its head down.[62]

« 728 »

The children of Holland
    Take pleasure in making,
What the children of England
    Take pleasure in breaking.[63]

« 729 »

A water there is I must pass,
A broader water never was,
And yet of all water I ever see,
To pass over with less jeopardy.[64]

« 730 »

Two brothers we are,
    Great burdens we bear,
All day we are bitterly pressed,
    Yet this I must say—
    We are full all the day,
And empty when we go to rest.[65]

« 731 »

Round the house and round the house,
And there lies a white glove at the window.[66]

« 732 »

Into my house came neighbor John,
With three legs and a wooden one;
If one be taken from the same,
Then just five there will remain.[67]

« 733 »

I saw a fight the other day;
A damsel did begin the fray,
She with her daily friend did meet,
Then standing in the open street,
She gave such hard and steady blows,

White bird featherless,
    Flew from Paradise,
Pitched on the castle wall;
    Along came Lord Landless,
    Took it up handless,
And rode away horseless to the King's white
    hall.

67. "Neighbor John" is "a four-legged stool," but to take away one and leave five, you must express "four" as a Roman numeral: IV.

R. CALDECOTT

279

He bled ten gallons at the nose;
Yet neither seem to faint nor fall,
Nor gave her any abuse at all.**68**

« 734 »

From house to house he goes,
    A messenger small and slight;
And whether it rains or snows,
    He sleeps outside at night.**69**

« 735 »

Four stiff-standers,
Four dilly-danders,
Two lookers, two crookers,
And a wig-wag.**70**

« 736 »

As I was going o'er yon moor of moss,
I met a man on a gray horse;
He whipp'd and he wail'd,
I ask'd him what he ail'd;
He said he was going to his father's funeral,
Who died**71** seven years before he was born.

« 737 »

Dreaming of apples on a wall,
    And dreaming often, dear,
I dreamed that, if I counted all,
    How many would appear?**72**

« 738 »

In Spring I look gay,
Decked in comely array,
In Summer more clothing I wear;
When colder it grows,
I fling off my clothes,
And in Winter quite naked appear.**73**

« 739 »

Two bodies have I,
Though both joined in one.
The stiller I stand,
The faster I run.**74**

A. RACKHAM

68. The "daily friend" is the town pump.

69. The answer is "a lane."

70. The answer is "a cow." It has been said (by Frederick Tupper, the late American authority on riddles) that this is a "world riddle" which can be "traced for thousands of years through the traditions of every people," but it seems first to have appeared in print, in English, in 1820.

71. The answer involves a play on words; the father was "a dyer."

72. The answer is "ten" ("dreaming of-ten").

73. The answer is "a tree."

« 740 »

Peter Piper picked a peck of pickled pepper;
A peck of pickled pepper Peter Piper picked;
If Peter Piper picked a peck of pickled pepper,
Where's the peck of pickled pepper Peter Piper
 picked?

« 741 »

When a twister a-twisting will twist him a twist,
For the twisting of his twist, he three twines doth
 intwist;
But if one of the twines of the twist do untwist,
The twine that untwisteth, untwisteth the twist.

Untwirling the twine that untwisteth between,
He twirls, with his twister, the two in a twine;
Then, twice having twisted the twines of the twine,
He twitcheth, the twice he twined, in twain.

The twain that, in twining, before in the twine
As twines were intwisted, he now doth untwine;
Twist the twain inter-twisting a twine more
 between,
He, twirling his twister, makes a twist of the
 twine.**75**

« 742 »

Robert Rowley rolled a round roll round,
A round roll Robert Rowley rolled round;
Where rolled the round roll Robert Rowley rolled
 round?

« 743 »

A thatcher of Thatchwood went to Thatchet
 a-thatching;
Did a thatcher of Thatchwood go to Thatchet
 a-thatching?
If a thatcher of Thatchwood went to Thatchet
 a-thatching,
Where's the thatching the thatcher of Thatchwood
 hath thatch'd?

74. The answer is "an hourglass."

75. Dr. John Wallis, mathematician and grammarian, included this grueling tongue twister in his *Grammatica Linguae Anglicanae*. It first appeared in juvenile literature in *Mother Goose's Quarto*, c. 1825.

« 744 »

My grandmother sent me a new-fashioned three cornered cambric country cut handkerchief. Not an old-fashioned three cornered cambric country cut handkerchief, but a new-fashioned three cornered cambric country cut handkerchief.**76**

« 745 »

Three crooked cripples went through Cripplegate, and through Cripplegate went three crooked cripples.

« 746 »

Vinegar, veal, and venison,
Are very good victuals, I vow.

« 747 »

Swan swam over the sea,
Swim, swan, swim!
Swan swam back again,
Well swum, swan!

A. RACKHAM

« 748 »

Theophilus Thistle, the successful thistle sifter,
In sifting a sieve full of unsifted thistles,
Thrust three thousand thistles through the thick of
    his thumb.
If Theophilus Thistle, the successful thistle sifter,
Can thrust three thousand thistles through the thick
    of his thumb,
See thou, in sifting a sieve full of unsifted thistles,
Thrust not three thousand thistles through the thick
    of thy thumb.

« 749 »

There was a man, and his name was Dob,
And he had a wife, and her name was Mob,
And he had a dog, and he called it Cob,
And she had a cat, called Chitterabob.
    Cob, says Dob,
    Chitterabob, says Mob,

76. Some readers will be reminded of Beatrice Lillie's difficulties, in a sketch in *At Home Abroad*, in trying to order "a dozen double damask dinner napkins."

Cob was Dob's dog,
Chitterabob Mob's cat.

« 750 »

Said Noble Aaron to Aaron Barron,
Oh, dear, my foot you put your chair on!
Said Aaron Barron to Noble Aaron,
O! you shall put your foot my chair on!

« 751 »

I need not your needles, they're needless to me,
    For kneading of needles is needless, you see,
But did my neat trousers but need to be kneed,
    I then should have need of your needles indeed.

« 752 »

How much wood would a woodchuck chuck
If a woodchuck could chuck wood?
He would chuck as much wood as a woodchuck
        could chuck
If a woodchuck could chuck wood.

« 753 »

Betty Botter bought some butter,
But, she said, the butter's bitter;
If I put it in my batter
It will make my batter bitter,
But a bit of better butter
Will make my batter better.
So she bought a bit of butter
Better than her bitter butter,
And she put it in her batter
And the batter was not bitter.
So 'twas better Betty Botter bought a bit of better
        butter.

« 754 »

Moses supposes his toeses are roses,
But Moses supposes erroneously;
For nobody's toeses are posies of roses
As Moses supposes his toeses to be.

A. RACKHAM

« 755 »

My dame hath a lame tame crane,
My dame hath a crane that is lame.
Pray, gentle Jane, let my dame's tame crane
Feed and come home again.

« 756 »

Three grey geese in a green field grazing,
Grey were the geese and green was the grazing.

« 757 »

The Leith police dismisseth us,
    I'm thankful, sir, to say;
The Leith police dismisseth us,
    They thought we sought to stay.
The Leith police dismisseth us,
    We both sighed sighs apiece,
And the sigh that we sighed as we said goodbye
    Was the size of the Leith police.

R. CALDECOTT

M. PARRISH

Of all the sayings in the world

　　The one to see you through

Is, Never trouble trouble

　　Till trouble troubles you.

CHAPTER XV

Mother Goose's Wise Sayings

The proverb has been called "a sage sentence," "a popular byword," "a pithy maxim"—and much else. We prefer to call it simply " wise saying" and to bring you here some of the many wise sayings in verse that have been attributed to Old Mother Goose.

« 758 »

Birds of a feather flock together,
    And so will pigs and swine;
Rats and mice will have their choice,
    And so will I have mine.

« 759 »

A cat may look at a king,
And sure I may look at an ugly thing.[1]

« 760 »

For every evil under the sun,
There is a remedy, or there is none.
If there be one, try and find it;
If there be none, never mind it.[2]

1. "An Answer to them that ask you, why you look at them, or what you look at," James Kelly wrote in his *Collection of Scottish Proverbs* (1721).

2. Or:

What can't be cured
Must be endured.

3. Or, as we would be more apt to say today: "A bird in the hand is worth two in the bush."

4. Or: High fences make good neighbors.

5. Commonly, today, taken as good advice to give to children, but probably, originally, a set of household rules for servants. Twentieth-century nursery-rhyme books sometimes put it (as Robert Louis Stevenson did):

A child should always say what's true
And speak when he is spoken to,
And behave mannerly at table;
At least as far as he is able.

Or:

Hold up your head,
Turn out your toes,
Speak when you're spoken to,
Mend your clothes.

« 761 »

A pullet in the pen
Is worth a hundred in the fen!**3**

« 762 »

A hedge between
Keeps friendship green.**4**

« 763 »

Wear you a hat or wear you a crown,
All that goes up must surely come down.

« 764 »

Give a thing, take a thing,
There's an old man's play thing.

« 765 »

Happy is the wooing
That's not long a-doing.

« 766 »

Scissors and string, scissors and string,
When a man's single he lives like a king.
Needles and pins, needles and pins,
When a man marries, his trouble begins.

« 767 »

A woman, a spaniel, and a walnut tree,
The more you beat them the better they be.

« 768 »

Ugly babies
Make pretty ladies.

« 769 »

Little ships must keep the shore;
Larger ships may venture more.

« 770 »

Come when you're called,
    Do what you're bid,
Shut the door after you,
    Never be chid.

Speak when you're spoken to,
    Come when one call;
Shut the door after you,
    And turn to the wall.⁵

« 771 »

Manners in the dining room,
    Manners in the hall,
If you don't behave yourself
    You shan't have none at all.

« 772 »

Of a little take a little
    You're kindly welcome, too;
Of a little leave a little
    'Tis manners so to do.

« 773 »

A boy that is good
  Will learn his book well;
And if he can't read
  Will strive for to spell.

« 774 »

Be always on time,
Too late is a crime.

« 775 »

Hearts, like doors, will ope with ease
To very, very little keys,
And don't forget that two of these
Are "I thank you" and "If you please."

« 776 »

All work and no play makes Jack a dull boy;
All play and no work makes Jack a mere toy.

« 777 »

Tommy's tears and Mary's fears
Will make them old before their years.

« 778 »

If wishes were horses
Beggars would ride;
If turnips were watches
I would wear one by my side.**6**

« 779 »

It costs little Gossip her income for shoes,
To travel about and carry the news.

« 780 »

The cock crows in the morn
To tell us to rise,
And he that lies late
Will never be wise:

M. PARRISH

6. James O. Halliwell seems to have been the first to publish this proverb in the form of a verse, but the thought itself dates back to the seventeenth century: "If wishes were butter-cakes, beggars might bite;" "If wishes were thrushes, then beggars would eat birds."

A similar proverb-in-verse is:

If ifs and an's were pots and pans,
There'd be no work for tinkers' hands.

7. Composed, probably, in the early nineteenth century from two old proverbs, and parodied ever since:

Early to bed and early to rise
And your girl goes out with other guys.

For early to bed,
And early to rise,
Is the way to be healthy
And wealthy and wise.**7**

« 781 »

Go to bed late,
Stay very small;
Go to bed early,
Grow very tall.

« 782 »

He that would thrive
Must rise at five;
He that hath thriven
May lie till seven;
He that will never thrive
May lie till eleven.

« 783 »

Eat at pleasure,
Drink by measure.

« 784 »

To sleep easy all night,
Let your supper be light,
Or else you'll complain
Of a stomach in pain.

« 785 »

The more rain, the more rest,
Fine weather's not always best.

A. RACKHAM

« 786 »

For want of a nail the shoe was lost,
For want of a shoe the horse was lost,
For want of a horse the rider was lost,
For want of a rider the battle was lost,
For want of a battle the kingdom was lost,
And all for the want of a horseshoe nail.**8**

8. This old proverb—a version of it appeared in Ben Franklin's *Poor Richard's Almanack* in 1758—does not seem to have been published in a "Mother Goose" book until 1898, when Andrew Lang included it in *The Nursery Rhyme Book*.

The Oxford Dictionary of Nursery Rhymes notes that a copy of it "was framed and kept on the wall of Anglo-American Supply Headquarters in London during the Second World War."

« 787 »

To make your candle last for a',
   You wives and maids give ear-o!
To put 'em out's the only way,
   Says honest John Bolde'ro.

« 788 »

He that hath and will not keep it,
He that wanteth and will not seek it,
He that drinketh and is not dry,
Shall want money as well as I.

« 789 »

Penny and penny
Laid up will be many;
Who will not save a penny
Shall never have many.

« 790 »

Wilful waste brings woeful want
   And you may live to say,
How I wish I had that crust
   That once I threw away.

« 791 »

A knight of Cales,9 and a gentleman of Wales,
And a laird of the north country—
A yeoman of Kent with his yearly rent
Could buy them out—all three.

« 792 »

In time of prosperity, friends will be plenty,
In time of adversity, not one in twenty.

« 793 »

When land is gone and money spent,
Then learning is most excellent.

« 794 »

Say well and do well
   End with one letter;
Say well is good,
   Do well is better.

M. PARRISH

« 795 »

Good, better, best;
Never rest
Till "good" be "better"
And "better" "best."

« 796 »

One thing at a time,
    And that done well,
Is a very good rule,
    As many can tell.

« 797 »

One, two, whatever you do,
Start it well and carry it through.
Try, try, never say die,
Things will come right, you know, by and by.

« 798 »

Little drops of water,
    Little grains of sand,
Make the mighty ocean
    And the pleasant land.[10]

« 799 »

Patience is a virtue,
    Virtue is a grace;
Both put together
    Make a very pretty face.

« 800 »

If you are not handsome at twenty,
Not strong at thirty,
Not rich at forty,
Not wise at fifty,
You never will be.

« 801 »

As foolish as monkeys till twenty and more,
As bold as a lion till forty and four;
As cunning as foxes till threescore and ten,
We then become asses, and are no more men.

[9.] Cadiz, in Spain, captured by Robert, Earl of Essex, in 1596, at which time he made knights of sixty of his retainers, some of them men of low fortune.

[10.] This "Mother Goose" rhyme is the opening of a poem by Julia A. Fletcher Carney (1823-1908) which continues:

So the little moments
    Humble though they be,
Make the mighty ages
    Of eternity.
Little deeds of kindness,
    Little words of love,
Help to make earth happy
    Like the heaven above.

Well, Mother Goose has written

A pretty book for you,

And filled it full of pictures fine,

And pretty verses, too.

MOTHER GOOSE'S MELODIES,
SELECTED AND ARRANGED BY
MY UNCLE SOLOMON, 1881

CHAPTER XVI

Nineteenth-Century Bouquet

In America, in the second half of the nineteenth century, the publishing houses of Boston, New York, and Philadelphia spilled out "Mother Goose" books in a steady stream.

With a few exceptions, they were cheaply produced and cheaply sold. This period saw the first appearance of books printed on linen, to withstand the wear and tear of many readings by children with sometimes careless hands. And Mother Goose, in America, retreated in the 1880's a full two hundred years: the old rhymes, first presented in coverless chapbooks, were once again printed in "paper-back." Behind the fly-specked windows of tiny shops, "Mother Goose" stood side by side with Nick Carter, Buffalo Bill, Frank Merriwell.

One handsome American book, first published in 1869, was William A. Wheeler's version of *Mother Goose's Melody*. Wheeler's publishers commissioned Henry L. Stephens and Gaston Fay to make steel engravings that crowded its pages, and in a later (1884) edition, illustrations in color by Alfred Kappes were added.

But the truly beautiful nursery-rhyme books of

A. RACKHAM

the 1870's-1890's were those published in Britain, thanks in large part to the shrewd picture publisher and printer Edmund Evans, who had developed a new process of color reproduction.

In 1877, Walter Crane, in *The Baby's Opera,* not only set many of the rhymes to music "by the Earliest Masters" but gave them "New Dresses" in the form of his own illustrations in color. The book was so well received that Crane followed it, in 1879, with *The Baby's Bouquet,* a companion volume.

Although the nineteenth-century master Randolph Caldecott died at the early age of thirty-nine, he left behind a whole shelf of books that he had illustrated after giving up an attempted career as a banker. His breezy, boyish drawings showed frogs in cutaways, babies in rabbitskins, and hard-blowing, pink-coated fox hunters—all in an atmosphere of bustle and good fun. "There Was an Old Woman Toss'd in a Blanket"—"There Were Three Jovial

Welshmen"—"A Frog He Would A-Wooing Go"—
these and many other nursery favorites achieved
their greatest popularity after Caldecott had illustrated them.

But the honors for the best-remembered nursery-
rhyme art of the nineteenth century must go to a
woman, a plump London artist-authoress named
Kate Greenaway.

Because spinster Greenaway had no family of her
own she regarded the grave little girls and proper
little boys of her drawings almost as if they were her
children, and designed their clothes with care and
taste. By doing so she unwittingly became an
extremely successful amateur dress designer, for
mothers in England, on the Continent, and in the
United States hastened to copy her styles for their
own children.

Indeed, the vogue for Kate Greenaway styles gives
no sign of dying out yet. In 1947 there began a strong
revival (sparked by L. Wohl and Company of New
York), and on the very Sunday that the introduction
to this chapter was written, a full-page advertisement
for present-day copies of Kate Greenaway's dresses
appeared in *The New York Times Magazine*.

Still, if it was the artists who held the center of the
stage in the second half of the nineteenth century,
writers and editors were busy in the wings.

William Miller (1810-72), sometimes called "The
Laureate of the Nursery," composed "Wee Willie
Winkie" (Rhyme 813). Eliza Follen (1787-1860), a
New England writer of children's books, produced
an important volume in *New Nursery Songs for All
Good Children* (c. 1843). "Three Little Kittens
They Lost Their Mittens" (Rhyme 815) is only one
of the many nursery poems ascribed to her. Septimus
Winter, an immensely successful American song
writer, created his most popular number, "Ten
Little Injuns" (Rhyme 818). The American poet
Henry Wadsworth Longfellow was credited with the
authorship of a nursery rhyme (Rhyme 827).

And in England, the Scottish scholar and man of
letters, Andrew Lang (1844-1912), edited, in 1898,

1. It is said that more than forty thousand copies of this children's classic, and its sequel, "The Peacock at Home," were sold in the first year, an unheard of record for that time.

2. There is an English phrase, "to play the Charlie Wag," meaning to play truant, but this comes, say the editors of *The Oxford Dictionary of Nursery Rhymes*, not from the rhyme, but from a "penny dreadful" of about 1860, *Charlie Wag, the Boy Burglar.*

3. A derisive rhyme employed against boys named Charley. Clifton Johnson, in *What They Say in New England: A Book of Signs, Sayings, and Superstitions* (Boston: Lee and Shepard, 1896), gives many similar examples, among them:

Joe, Joe,
Broke his toe
Riding on a buffalo.

Frank, Frank,
Turned the crank,
His mother come out and gave him a spank,
And knocked him over the sandbank.

Bert, Bert, tore his shirt
Riding on a lump of dirt.

My son John is a nice old man,
Washed his face in a frying-pan,
Combed his hair with a wagon-wheel,
And died with the toothache in his heel.

It is not to be thought that girls were exempt from such taunts:

Queen, Queen Caroline,
Washed her hair in turpentine;
Turpentine made it shine,
Queen, Queen Caroline.

4. The use of the word "humblebee" would seem to indicate that this rather unpleasant little rhyme is of English origin, but your editors have not encountered it in print before its appearance in the American *Only True Mother Goose Melodies*, published in Boston c. 1843 by Munroe and Francis.

5. The chimney sweep was a familiar figure in the streets of British cities from early to comparatively recent times. Shakespeare wrote

a volume that included, for the first time in a "Mother Goose" book, a version of a poem once as famous and as popular as anything in *Alice in Wonderland*: "The Butterfly's Ball and the Grasshopper's Feast" (Rhyme 832), written in 1807 by William Roscoe, a banker of Liverpool, to burlesque a city banquet for the amusement of his son.[1]

There are fewer of the best-loved rhymes in this chapter than in others, perhaps. But it is still a rich collection.

« 802 »

Charley Wag, Charley Wag,[2]
Ate the pudding and left the bag.[3]

« 803 »

There were two blind men went to see
    Two cripples run a race,
The bull did fight the humblebee
    And scratched him in the face.[4]

« 804 »

    Sweep, sweep,
    Chimney sweep,
From the bottom to the top,
    Sweep it all up,
    Chimney sweep,
From the bottom to the top.[5]

« 805 »

As I was going to Derby,
    Upon a market day,
I met the finest ram, sir,
    That ever was fed on hay.[6]

And if you think this is not so,
    For maybe you'll think I lie,
Oh you go down to Derby town
    And you'll see the same as I.

This ram was fat behind, sir,
    This ram was fat before,
This ram was ten yards high, sir,
Indeed he was no more.[7]

The wool upon his back, sir,
  Reached up into the sky,
The eagles built their nest there,
  For I heard young ones cry.

The wool on this ram's belly, sir,
  It grew down in the ground,
The Devil cut it off, sir,
  To make himself a gown.

The horns upon this ram, sir,
  They reached up to the moon,
A man went up them in January
  And didn't come down till June.

The space between the horns, sir,
  Was as far as a man could reach,
And there they built a pulpit,
  But no-one in it preached.

W. CRANE

R. CALDECOTT

This ram had four legs to walk upon,
    This ram had four legs to stand,
And every leg he had, sir,
    Stood on an acre of land.

And one of this ram's teeth, sir,
    Was hollow as a horn,
And when they took its measure, sir,
    It held a bushel of corn.

Now the man that fed this ram, sir,
    He fed him twice a day,
And each time that he fed him, sir,
    He ate a rick of hay.

The man that killed this ram, sir,
    Was up to his knees in blood,
And the boy that held the pail, sir,
    Was carried away in the flood.

The blood it ran for forty miles,
    I'm sure it was not more,
It turned the water wheels so fast
    It made the mill-stones roar.

The little boys of Derby, sir,
    They came to beg his eyes,
To roll around the streets, sir,
    They being of football's size,

The wool upon his tail, sir,
    Was very fine and thin,
Took all the girls in Derby town
    Full seven years to spin.

Indeed, sir, it's the truth, sir,
    For I never was taught to lie,
And if you go to Derby, sir,
    You may eat a bit of the pie.8

« 806 »

Once in my life I married a wife,
    And where do you think I found her?
On Gretna Green,9 in velvet sheen,
    And I took up a stick to pound her.
She jumped over a barberry-bush,

in *Cymbeline* (Act IV, Scene 2, lines 262-3):

Golden lads and girls all must,
Like chimney-sweepers, come to dust.

"Reader," Charles Lamb pleaded, "if thou meetest one of these small gentry in thy early rambles, it is good to give him a penny. It is better to give him two-pence. Better still—a basin of saloop, of which the chief ingredient is Sassafras; for it is a composition surprisingly gratifying to the palate of a young chimney-sweeper."

William Blake wrote a poem to "The Chimney Sweeper" (you will find it in Walter de la Mare's *Come Hither*)—but now he seems to have vanished almost as completely as Leerie, the old lamplighter in Stevenson's poem. It does seem rather a pity:

For we are very lucky, with a lamp before the
    door,
And Leerie stops to light it as he lights so
    many more;
And O! before you hurry by with ladder and
    with light,
O Leerie, see a little child and nod to him
    to-night!

6. It is a fact that rams have been closely associated with Derby for hundreds of years. "A ram is incorporated in the Borough coat-of-arms," says *The Oxford Dictionary of Nursery Rhymes*, "and in 1855 a fine ram was attached to the staff of the first Regiment of Derbyshire Militia."

And I jumped over a timber,
I showed her a gay gold ring,
And she showed me her finger.

« 807 »

The little black dog ran round the house,
And set the bull a roaring,
And drove the monkey in the boat,
Who set the oars a rowing,
And scared the cock upon the rock,
Who cracked his throat with crowing.

« 808 »

My little Pink,
I suppose you think,
I cannot do without you,
I'll let you know
Before I go,
How little I care about you.

« 809 »

Dear Sensibility, O la!
I heard a little lamb cry, baa!
Says I, "So you have lost Mamma?"

"Ah!"

The little lamb, as I said so,
Frisking about the fields did go,
And, frisking, trod upon my toe.

"Oh!"

« 810 »

Up in the green orchard there is a green tree,
The finest of pippins that ever you see,
The apples are ripe, and ready to fall,
And Reuben and Robin shall gather them all.

« 811 »

Milk-man, milk-man, where have you been?
In butter-milk channel up to my chin,
I spilt my milk and I spoilt my clothes,
And got a long icicle hung to my nose.

7. The narrator, in preparation for the verses to come—and few better tall tales in verse exist—is establishing his *bona fides*. He wishes to make it clear that, if anything, he is under-stating rather than overstating—a trait so characteristic of the English.

8. Only a few of the verses given here actually appeared in *The Only True Mother Goose Melodies*. The others have been added from numerous other sources in which "The Derby Ram" has appeared.

"The Derby Ram" is an American as well as a British classic—indeed, it is said to have been George Washington's favorite song—and there is a Cape Cod version which ends:

The man that owned this ram, sir,
Was counted very rich,
But the one that made this song, sir,
Was a lying son-of-a-bitch.

As might be expected, there are many other "naughty" verses.

9. A village in Dumfrieshire, Scotland, close to the English border, once the scene of many runaway marriages.

« 812 »
I like little pussy,
    Her coat is so warm,
And if I don't hurt her,
    She'll do me no harm.
So I'll not pull her tail,
    Nor drive her away,
But pussy and I
    Very gently will play.
She shall sit by my side,
    And I'll give her some food;
And pussy will love me
    Because I am good.**10**

R. CALDECOTT

« 813 »

Wee Willie Winkie runs through the town,
Upstairs and downstairs in his night-gown,
Rapping at the window, crying through the lock,
Are the children all in bed, for now it's eight
     o'clock?[11]

« 814 »

HEN: Cock, cock, cock, cock,
    I've laid an egg,
    Am I to go ba-are foot?

COCK: Hen, hen, hen, hen,
    I've been up and down,
    To every shop in town,
    And cannot find a shoe
    To fit your foot,
    If I'd crow my hea-art out.[12]

A. RACKHAM

« 815 »

Three little kittens they lost their mittens,
  And they began to cry,
Oh, mother dear, we sadly fear
  That we have lost our mittens.
What! lost your mittens, you naughty kittens!
  Then you shall have no pie.
Mee-ow, mee-ow, mee-ow.
No, you shall have no pie.

The three little kittens they found their mittens,
  And they began to cry,
Oh, mother dear, see here, see here,
  For we have found our mittens.
Put on your mittens, you silly kittens,
  And you shall have some pie.
Purr-r, purr-r, purr-r,
Oh, let us have some pie.

The three little kittens put on their mittens,
  And soon ate up the pie;
Oh, mother dear, we greatly fear
  That we have soiled out mittens.
What! soiled your mittens, you naughty kittens!
  Then they began to sigh,

10. The last four lines do not appear in *The Only True Mother Goose Melodies*, but were added in a chapbook of verses and hymns for children published a short time later.

11. "Wee Willie Winkie" was the nickname given to William Prince of Orange, later William III of England, but it is highly unlikely that William Miller, the author of this rhyme, intended it to have any political significance. The verse first appeared in a nursery rhyme book in *The Only True Mother Goose Melodies*, but its first appearance in print was in 1841 in a volume called *Whistle-Binkie; a Collection of Songs for the Social Circle*, published by David Robertson.

12. This rhyme usually carries the following instructions for reciting it:
  "To be said very quickly, except the last two words in each verse; which are to be 'screamed out.'"
This is one of the rhymes sometimes ascribed to the New England writer of children's books, Eliza Follen, and included in her collection, *New Nursery Songs for All Good Children*, c. 1843. There, however, she described it as "traditional."

13. The fact that these verses first appeared in print in *New Nursery Songs for All Good Children* has led to the rhyme being ascribed to Eliza Follen, but she herself described it as "traditional."

14. This catch from *The Pindar of Wakefield*, 1632, made its first appearance in a collection of nursery rhymes in Edward F. Rimbault's *Nursery Rhymes with the tunes to which they are still sung*, 1846.

15. The editors of *The Oxford Dictionary of Nursery Rhymes* note that "The origin of this . . . nursery rhyme presumably antedates 4 June 1561, when St. Paul's steeple was destroyed by lightning. The apple tree may even have been a real one for curious things happened on the steeple. Strutt in his *Sports and Pastimes* (1801) describes rope dancing on the steeple battlements (1553), a Dutchman standing on one foot on the weathercock (1546), and an acrobat killed while sliding down (1554)."

16. This immensely popular "nursery rhyme" was originally written by Septimus Winter as a song for the American minstrel shows of the 1860's. It was followed, in England, by the similar and equally popular "Ten Little Nigger Boys," written by Frank Green:

Ten little nigger boys went out to dine;
One choked his little self, and then there were nine.

Nine little nigger boys sat up very late;
One overslept himself, and then there were eight.

Eight little nigger boys travelling in Devon;
One said he'd stay there, and then there were seven.

Seven little nigger boys chopping up sticks;
One chopped himself in half, and then there were six.

Six little nigger boys playing with a hive;
A bumble-bee stung one; and then there were five.

Five little nigger boys going in for law;
One got in chancery, and then there were four.

Four little nigger boys going out to sea;
A red herring swallowed one, and then there were three.

Mee-ow, mee-ow, mee-ow,
Then they began to sigh.

The three little kittens they washed their mittens,
    And hung them out to dry;
Oh! mother dear, do you not hear
    That we have washed our mittens?
What! washed your mittens, then you're good kittens,
    But I smell a rat close by.
Mee-ow, mee-ow, mee-ow,
We smell a rat close by.[13]

« 816 »

The hart he loves the high wood,
    The hare she loves the hill;
The knight he loves his bright sword,
    The lady loves her will.[14]

« 817 »

Upon Paul's steeple stands a tree
As full of apples as may be;
The little boys of London town
They run with hooks to pull them down:
And then they go from hedge to hedge
Until they come to London Bridge.[15]

« 818 »

Ten little Injuns standin' in a line,
One toddled home and then there were nine;
Nine little Injuns swingin' on a gate,
One tumbled off and then there were eight.

    One little, two little, three little, four little, five
        little Injun boys,
    Six little, seven little, eight little, nine little, ten
        little Injun boys.

Eight little Injuns gayest under heav'n.
One went to sleep and then there were seven;
Seven little Injuns cutting up their tricks,
One broke his neck and then there were six.

Six little Injuns kickin' all alive,
One kick'd the bucket and then there were five;

Five little Injuns on a cellar door,
One tumbled in and then there were four.

Four little Injuns up on a spree,
One he got fuddled and then there were three;
Three little Injuns out in a canoe,
One tumbled overboard and then there were two.

Two little Injuns foolin' with a gun,
One shot t'other and then there was one;
One little Injun livin' all alone,
He got married and then there were none.[16]

« 819 »

A little pig found a fifty-dollar note,
And purchased a hat and a very fine coat,
    With trousers, and stockings, and shoes,
Cravat, and shirt-collar, and gold-headed cane,
Then proud as could be, did he march up the lane;
    Says he, "I shall hear all the news."

« 820 »

    A-milking, a-milking my maid,
    "Cow, take care of your heels," she said;
    "And you shall have some nice new hay,
    If you'll quietly let me milk away."

« 821 »

There was an old couple, and they were poor,
    Fa la, fa la la lee!
They lived in a house that had but one door,
    Fa la, fa la la la la lee!

The old man once he went far from his home,
    Fa la, fa la la lee!
The old woman afraid was to stay alone,
    O! what a weak woman was she.
The old man he came home at last,
    Fa la, fa la la lee!
And found the windows and door all fast,
    "O! what is the matter?" quoth he.

"O! I have been sick since you have gone,
    Fa la, fa la la lee!

*Three little nigger boys walking in the zoo;
A big bear hugged one, and then there were
    two.*
*Two little nigger boys sitting in the sun;
One got frizzled up, and then there was one.*
*One little nigger boy living all alone;
He got married, and then there were none.*

The "story line" of this version of the song inspired Agatha Christie's highly successful detective story, *And Then There Were None*, and the mystery play made from it, *Ten Little Indians*. The play does indeed end with a *little nigger boy (Injun)* getting married after the others have "kick'd the bucket" in a number of ingenious ways.

R. CALDECOTT

"If you'd been in the garden you'd heard me groan";
  "O, I am sorry for that," quoth he.

"I have a request to make unto thee,
  Fa la, fa la la lee!
"To pluck me an apple from yonder tree";
  "Ay, that will I, many," quoth he.

The old man tried to get up in the tree,
  Fa la, la la la lee!
But the ladder it fell, and down tumbled he;
  "That's cleverly done!" said she.

« 822 »

Oh, what have you got for dinner, Mrs. Bond?
There's beef in the larder, and ducks in the pond;
Dilly, dilly, dilly, dilly, come to be killed,[17]
For you must be stuffed and my customers filled!

Send us the beef first, good Mrs. Bond,
And get us some ducks dressed out of the pond,

Cry, Dilly, dilly, dilly, dilly, come to be killed,
For you must be stuffed and my customers filled!

John Ostler, go fetch me a duckling or two,
Ma'am, says John Ostler, I'll try what I can do,
Cry, Dilly, dilly, dilly, dilly, come to be killed,
For you must be stuffed and my customers filled!

I have been to the ducks that swim in the pond,
But I found they won't come to be killed, Mrs. Bond;
I cried, Dilly, dilly, dilly, dilly, come to be killed!
For you must be stuffed and my customers filled!

Mrs. Bond she flew down to the pond in a rage,
With plenty of onions and plenty of sage;
She cried, Dilly, dilly, dilly, dilly, come to be killed,
For you must be stuffed and my customers filled!

She cried, Little wag-tails, come and be killed,
For you must be stuffed and my customers filled!
Dilly, dilly, dilly, dilly, come to be killed,
For you must be stuffed and my customers filled!

« 823 »

Chan-wan, the good old man,
Kept a school by Yang-tse-Kiang,
His scholars sat upon the ground,
And learned their letters upside down,
Slippery, sloppery, snap and sneeze,
That's the way to learn Chinese!
And when the youngsters made a noise,
He, with his pig-tail, whipped the boys.
This all happened ages ago,
In the time of the good old emperor Fo.
Now, Chan-wan, the good old man,
Lies dead and buried by Yang-tse-Kiang.[18]

« 824 »

Ping-wing, the pieman's son,
Was the very worst boy in old Canton.
He stole his mother's pickled mice,
And threw the cat in the boiling rice,
And when they'd eaten her, said he,
"Me wonders where the mew-cat be?"

17. Country people all over England, like the hog callers of the American Midwest, had special cries with which to summon their birds and beasts.

For cows: Coop! Cush, cush! Or: Hoaf! Hobe! Mull! Proo! Proochy! Prut!

For calves: Moodie! Mog, mog, mog! Pui-hoi! Sook, sook!

For sheep: Co-hobe! Ovey!

For pigs: Check-check! Cheat! Dack, dack! Giss! Or: Gissy! Lix! Ricsic! Shug, shug, shug! Tantassa, tantassa pig, tow a row, a row! Tig, tig, tig!

For turkeys: Cobbler! Peet, peet, peet! Pen! Pur, pur, pur!

For geese: Fly-laig! Gag, gag, gag! Ob-ee! White-hoddy!

For pigeons: Pees! Pod!

For rabbits: Map!

18. This and the two following rhymes are taken from a handsome and curious collection of "Mother Goose's Melodies" published in Philadelphia by Porter & Coates during the 1870's. The introduction states that "The original drawings of the series of chromo illustrations of 'dear Old Mother Goose' . . . were not designed for the public eye, but as a birthday gift from a loving daughter to her father, who occupies one of the highest positions in the United States Government."

It is highly probable that this "loving daughter" was a versifier as well as a talented artist, for these three rhymes bear a family resemblance, and none of them, so far as we can discover, has ever appeared in any other "Mother Goose" book.

19. About this rhyme there is great scholarly disagreement. No one is really sure whether it is British or American, and there is no certainty about the medium in which it first appeared in print, although this is generally supposed to be a book called *Sugar and Spice, And All That's Nice*, published in 1885.

The authorship of the rhyme has been attributed to Thomas Bailey Aldrich, but a more popular theory has it that Henry Wadsworth Longfellow created the first stanza, if not the second and third, in a baby-talk version written about his daughter Edith on a day when she refused to have her hair curled. The editors of *The Oxford Dictionary of Nursery Rhymes* seem to lean toward the idea that Longfellow *did* write the poem. They point out that Longfellow (in *Table Talk*) admitted that "When I recall my juvenile poems and prose sketches, I wish that they were forgotten entirely. They, however, cling to one's skirt with a terrible grasp." According to Blanche Roosevelt Tucker Macchetta's *The Home Life of Henry W. Longfellow,* published two months after the poet's death in 1882, Longfellow would acknowledge the authorship of the rhyme when sufficiently taxed with it.

20. This is the earliest version of this nursery rhyme that we have been able to find in a Mother Goose book—in *Gems from Mother Goose Melodies* (1898). Its original wording, however, was:

> *If I had a donkey wot wouldn't go*
> *I never would wollop him—no, no, no;*
> *I'd give him some hay and cry gee O!*
> *And come up Neddy.*

This is the chorus of a music-hall song written by Jacob Beuler and published in 1822. It was intended to poke fun at the Prevention of Cruelty to Animals Act sponsored in England by Richard "Humanity" Martin, one of the founders of the Royal Society for the Prevention of Cruelty to Animals. *The Oxford Dictionary of Nursery Rhymes* states that the first two lines of Beuler's chorus "were already traditional" when he wrote it, and quotes him as saying: "These two lines were given to me, to work upon by a friend, for which I return thanks; for the song has proved one of the most popular I have ever written." The song is mentioned by Dickens in his *Old Curiosity Shop.*

« 825 »

Old Tuskummik, Medicine Man,
Lived on goose and pickled clam.
Goose and clam was all his diet,
Nothing else would keep him quiet.
He lived on a tree as high as the moon,
And fed himself with a silver spoon.
All the Indians miles around
Squatted themselves upon the ground,
Warriors, squaws and little papooses,
To see him feed on clams and gooses.
Naughty Indian, Old Tuskummik,
Naughty man to spoil his stomach!

« 826 »

We're all jolly boys,
And we're coming with a noise.
Our coats shall be made
With fine lace brocade,
Our stockings shall be silk
As white as the milk,
And our tails shall touch the ground.

« 827 »

There was a little girl, and she had a little curl
Right in the middle of her forehead;
When she was good, she was very, very good,
But when she was bad she was horrid.

One day she went upstairs, while her parents, unawares,
In the kitchen down below were occupied with meals;
And she stood upon her head, on her little truckle bed,
And she then began hurraying with her heels.

Her mother heard the noise, and thought it was the boys
A-playing at a combat in the attic;
But when she climbed the stair, and saw Jemima there,
She took and she did whip her most emphatic.[19]

308

« 828 »

The old woman must stand at the tub, tub, tub,
The dirty clothes to rub, rub, rub;
But when they are clean, and fit to be seen,
I'll dress like a lady, and dance on the green.

« 829 »

There was an old soldier of Bister,
Went walking one day with his sister;
    When a cow at a poke,
    Toss'd her into an oak,
Before the old gentleman miss'd her.

« 830 »

If I had a donkey, and he wouldn't go,
Do you think I would whip him?
    Oh, no, no!
I'd give him a carrot, and cry, "Gee whoa,
    Gee up, Neddy!"**20**

« 831 »

There was a little woman, as I've been told,
Who was not very young, nor yet very old,
Now this little woman her living got,
By selling codlins,**21** hot, hot, hot.

« 832 »

Come, take up your hats, and away let us haste,
To the Bullfrog's ball, and the Grasshopper's feast;
The trumpeter, Gad-fly, has summoned the crew,
And the revels are now only waiting for you.
On the smooth-shaven grass, by the side of a wood,
Beneath a broad oak which for ages has stood,
See the children of earth and the tenants of air,
To an evening's amusement together repair.
And there came the Beetle, so blind and so black,
Who carried the Emmet, his friend, on his back;
And there came the Gnat and the Dragon-fly too,
With all their relations, green, orange, and blue.
And there came the Moth, with her plumage of
    down,

The rhyme has appeared frequently in twentieth-century "Mother Goose" books, with varying endings. Here are two of them:

*... Oh, no, I'd give him oats and hay,
And let him stand there all the day.*

*... I'd put him in a barn and give him some corn,
The best little donkey that was ever born.*

*Little Jack Horner sat in the corner,
Eating a Christmas pie;
He put in his thumb, and pulled out a plum,
And said, oh! what a good boy am I.*

K. GREENAWAY

309

21. Or "codlings"—cooking apples, hard at the core, served stewed or baked.

22. Or:

> Cry-baby, cry,
> Take your little shirt-tail
> And wipe your little eye
> And go and tell your mammy
> To give you a piece of pie.

Jeers like these have been repeated for well over a hundred years at least—as has this taunt:

> Cowardy cowardy custard,
> Eat your father's mustard.

A. RACKHAM

And the Hornet with jacket of yellow and brown;
And with him the Wasp, his companion, did bring,
But they promised that evening to lay by their sting.
Then the shy little Dormouse peeped out of his hole,
And led to the feast his blind cousin the Mole;
And the Snail, with her horns peeping out of her
shell,
Came, fatigued with the distance, the length of an
ell.
A mushroom the table, and on it was spread
A water-dock leaf, which their table-cloth made.
The viands were various, to each of their taste,
And the Bee brought the honey to sweeten the feast.
With steps most majestic the Snail did advance,
And he promised the gazers a minuet dance;
But they all laughed so loud that he drew in his head,
And went to his own little chamber to bed.
Then, as evening gave way to the shadows of night,
Their watchman, the Glow-worm, came out with his
light,
So home let us hasten, while yet we can see,
For no watchman is waiting for you or for me.

« 833 »

When the wind blows,
Then the mill goes,
And our hearts
Are light, and are merry.

« 834 »

Cry, baby, cry,
Put your finger in your eye
And tell your mother it wasn't I.**22**

M. PARRISH

Oh, Pillykin, Willykin, Winky Wee!

How does the President take his tea? . . .

CHAPTER XVII

Modern Old Mother Goose

"The infants and children of the nineteenth century have not deserted the rhymes chanted so many ages since by the mothers of the north," James O. Halliwell wrote in 1853.

Nor have the infants and children of the twentieth century.

And Old Mother Goose has kept step with the times: in this chapter you will find a nursery rhyme about an aviator (Rhyme 874), and another that inquires into the President's preferences in tea (Rhyme 875).

The century opened with "the Old Familiar Rhymes and Jingles of Mother Goose" edited and illustrated by W. W. Denslow, then riding high on a wave of popularity generated by the fact that he was the original illustrator for L. Frank Baum's *The Wonderful Wizard of Oz*. The rhymes and jingles in *Denslow's Mother Goose* are familiar indeed, but the man who first pictured the Scarecrow and the Tin Woodman and the Cowardly Lion produced a gay and charming book, with every verse in it hand-lettered by Fred W. Goudy, the distinguished type designer.

Few popular illustrators of the early years of our own century failed to try to depict "Little Miss Muffet" and "Simple Simon" and "Tom, Tom, the Piper's Son" in his or her own distinctive way. They included Ethel Franklin Betts, Charles Robinson, Blanche Fisher Wright, Grace G. Drayton, the creator of the "Campbell Kids"; Jessie Wilcox Smith, known for her *Good Housekeeping* covers.

And, in 1913, that classic illustrator of children's literature, Arthur Rackham.

Some of Rackham's Mother Goose pictures are as cheerful as his celebrated illustrations for *The Night Before Christmas*; others—with their hobgoblins and mischievous fairies hiding in gnarled and elfin trees—are as spooky as his equally celebrated illustrations for *Peter Pan and Wendy*.

The Mother Goose books of the twentieth century are perhaps too well known to most of us—as children, and then as the parents of children—to require much comment here.

The chapter that follows brings you the rhymes, but for many of the delightful pictures that so often

A. RACKHAM

accompanied them, you must turn to the books
themselves.

« 835 »

There once were two cats of Kilkenny,
Each thought there was one cat too many,
So they fought and they fit,
And they scratched and they bit,
Till, excepting their nails
And the tips of their tails,
Instead of two cats, there weren't any.

« 836 »

Poor Dog Bright
Ran off with all his might,
Because the cat was after him—
Poor Dog Bright!

Poor Cat Fright
Ran off with all her might,
Because the dog was after her—
Poor Cat Fright!

A. RACKHAM

« 837 »

"Will you walk into my parlor?" said the spider to
    the fly—
" 'Tis the prettiest little parlor that ever you did spy.
The way into my parlor is up a winding stair;
And I have many curious things to show you when
    you're there."
"Oh, no, no," said the little fly; "to ask me is in vain;
For who goes up your winding stair can ne'er come
    down again."

"I'm sure you must be weary, dear, with soaring up
    so high;
Will you not rest upon my little bed?" said the spider
    to the fly.
"There are pretty curtains drawn around; the sheets
    are fine and thin;
And if you like to rest awhile, I'll snugly tuck you
    in!"
"Oh, no, no," said the little fly; "for I've often heard
    it said,
They never, never wake again, who sleep upon your
    bed!"

Said the cunning spider to the fly—
"Dear friend, what can I do
To prove the warm affection I've always felt for
    you?"
"I thank you, gentle sir," she said, "for what you're
    pleased to say,
And bidding you good-morning now, I'll call
    another day."
The spider turned him round about, and went into
    his den,
For well he knew the silly fly would soon come back
    again;
So he wove a subtle web in a little corner sly,
And set his table ready, to dine upon the fly.
Then he came out to his door again, and merrily
    did sing—
"Come hither, hither, pretty fly, with the pearl and
    silver wing;
Your robes are green and purple—there's a crest

upon your head!
Your eyes are like the diamond bright but mine are
dull as lead!"

Alas! alas! how very soon this silly little fly,
Hearing his wily, flattering words, came slowly
flitting by.
With buzzing wings she hung aloft, then near and
nearer drew;
Thinking only of her brilliant eyes, her green and
purple hue—
Thinking only of her crested head—poor foolish
thing! At last,
Up jumped the cunning spider, and firmly held her
fast!
He dragged her up his winding stair, into his dismal
den,
Within his little parlor—but she ne'er came out
again!

And now, dear little children, who may this story
read,
To idle, silly, flattering words, I pray you ne'er give
heed;
Unto an evil counselor close heart, and ear and eye,
And take a lesson from this tale of the Spider and
the Fly.[1]

« 838 »

Alas! alas! for Miss Mackay!
Her knives and forks have run away;
And when the cups and spoons are going,
She's sure there is no way of knowing.

« 839 »

Corporal Tim
   Was dressed so trim,
He thought them all afraid of him;
    But sad to say,
      The very first day,
      He had a fight,
        He died of fright,
And that was the end of Corporal Tim.

A. RACKHAM

[1]. The author of this poem was Mary Howitt.
Here is a much shorter nursery rhyme that
says much the same thing:

At early morn the spiders spin,
And by and by the flies drop in;
And when they call, the spiders say,
Take off your things, and stay all day!

317

M. PARRISH

« 840 »

The giant Jim, great giant grim,
Wears a hat without a brim,
Weighs a ton, and wears a blouse,
And trembles when he meets a mouse.

« 841 »

My learned friend and neighbor Pig,
Odds bobs and bills, and dash my wig!
'Tis said that you the weather know;
Please tell me when the wind will blow.[2]

« 842 »

Little Miss Donnet
She wears a big bonnet;
And hoops half as wide
As the mouth of the Clyde.

318

« 843 »

Polly, Dolly, Kate and Molly,
All are filled with pride and folly.
Polly tattles, Dolly wriggles,
Katy rattles, Molly giggles;
Who'er knew such constant rattling,
Wriggling, giggling, noise, and tattling.

« 844 »

Here's Sulky Sue;
    What shall we do?
Turn her face to the wall
    Till she comes to.
If that should fail,
    A smart touch with the cane,
Will soon make her good,
    When she feels the pain.

« 845 »

Cackle, cackle, Mother Goose,
Have you any feathers loose?
Truly have I, pretty fellow,
Half enough to fill a pillow.
And here are quills, take one or ten,
And make from each, pop-gun or pen.**3**

« 846 »

Hoddley, poddley, puddles and fogs,
Cats are to marry poodle dogs;
Cats in blue jackets and dogs in red hats,
What will become of the mice and the rats?

« 847 »

Three young rats with black felt hats,
Three young ducks with white straw flats,**4**
Three young dogs with curling tails,
Three young cats with demi-veils,
Went out to walk with two young pigs
In satin vests and sorrel wigs.
But suddenly it chanced to rain
And so they all went home again.**5**

A. RACKHAM

2. Some country people think that pigs are
sensitive to dampness and that when they
stack up straw to sleep on, they are trying to
avoid getting wet in an approaching storm.
There is no truth to the belief.

3. Or:

> *. . . Here are quills, take one or two,*
> *And down to make a bed for you.*

4. " 'Flats' are probably sandals," say the editors of *The Oxford Dictionary of Nursery
Rhymes*, but Leonard Weisgard, in his illustration for this rhyme in *The Family Mother
Goose: Little Goose* (1951), chose to show the
"three young ducks" in flat straw sailor hats—
"boaters," as the English call them.

5. Folklorists have traced this rhyme back for
several generations, although it seems to have
appeared in print for the first time in 1932, in
The Land of Nursery Rhyme.

« 848 »

A famous old woman was Madam McBight,
She slept all the day, she slept all the night,
One hour was given to victuals and drink,
And only a minute was taken to think.

« 849 »

The Brown Owl sits in the ivy-bush,
  And she looketh wondrous wise,
With a horny beak beneath her cowl,
  And a pair of large round eyes.

« 850 »

Mr. East gave a feast;
Mr. North laid the cloth;
Mr. West did his best;
Mr. South burned his mouth
With eating a cold potato.

« 851 »

Mr. Ibister, and Betsy his sister,
Resolved upon giving a treat;
  So letters they write,
  Their friends to invite,
To their house in Great Camomile Street.

A. RACKHAM

« 852 »

Oh, my pretty cock, oh, my handsome cock,
  I pray you, do not crow before day,
And your comb shall be made of the very beaten
    gold,
  And your wings of the silver so gray.

« 853 »

There dwelt an old woman at Exeter,
When visitors came it sore vexed her,
  So for fear they should eat,
  She locked up all her meat,
That stingy old woman of Exeter.

« 854 »

There was an old woman of Gloucester,
Whose parrot two guineas it cost her,
  But its tongue never ceasing,
  Was vastly displeasing,
To the talkative woman of Gloucester.

« 855 »

There was an old woman of Harrow,
Who visited in a wheelbarrow,
  And her servant before,
  Knocked loud at each door,
To announce the old woman of Harrow.

R. CALDECOTT

Jack and Jill
Went up the hill,
To fetch a pail of water;
Jack fell down
And broke his crown,
And Jill came tumbling after.

K. GREENAWAY

6. And little boys in America sing:

It's raining, it's pouring,
The old man is snoring;
He got into bed
And bumped his head
And couldn't get up in the morning.

7. These lines stem from a highly successful music-hall song composed by John Stamford and first published in 1877.

« 856 »

The greedy man is he who sits
And bites bits out of plates,
Or else takes up an almanac
And gobbles all the dates.

« 857 »

Wash the dishes, wipe the dishes,
Ring the bell for tea;
Three good wishes, three good kisses,
I will give to thee.

« 858 »

Jerry Hall
He is so small,
A rat could eat him,
Hat and all.

« 859 »

Little Miss Lily, you're dreadfully silly
To wear such a very long skirt:
If you take my advice, you would hold it up nice,
And not let it trail in the dirt.

« 860 »

I bought a dozen new-laid eggs,
Of good old farmer Dickens;
I hobbled home upon two legs,
And found them full of chickens.

« 861 »

It's raining, it's raining,
There's pepper in the box,
And all the little ladies
Are holding up their frocks.[6]

« 862 »

Three times round goes our gallant ship,
And three times round goes she,
Three times round goes our gallant ship,
And sinks to the bottom of the sea.

« 863 »

Jeremiah, blow the fire,
Puff, puff, puff!
First you blow it gently,
Then you blow it tough.[7]

« 864 »

Gregory Griggs, Gregory Griggs,
Had twenty seven different wigs.
He wore them up, he wore them down,
To please the people of the town;
He wore them east, he wore them west,
But he never could tell which he loved the best.

323

« 865 »

Tom tied a kettle to the tail of a cat,
Jill put a stone in a blind man's hat,
Bob threw his grandmother down the stairs—
And they all grew up ugly, and nobody cares.

« 866 »

Here lies old Fred.**7A**
It's a pity he's dead.
We would have rather
It had been his father;
Had it been his sister,
We would not have missed her;
If the whole generation,
So much better for the nation,
But since it's only Fred
Who was alive, and is dead,
There's no more to be said.

« 867 »

Don't Care didn't care,
    Don't Care was wild:
Don't Care stole plum and pear
    Like any beggar's child.

Don't Care was made to care
    Don't Care was hung:
Don't Care was put in a pot
    And boiled till he was done.

« 868 »

Calico Pie,**7B**
The little birds fly
Down to the Calico tree.
Their wings were blue
And they sang "Tilly-loo"
Till away they all flew,
    And they never came back to me,
        They never came back,
        They never came back,
    They never came back to me.

7A. A garbled version of a contemporary rhyme about Frederick, Prince of Wales, who died in 1751 after being hit on the head by a tennis ball.

7B. This "nursery rhyme" is part of the well-known poem by Edward Lear.

324

« 869 »

The dogs of the monks
    Of St. Bernard go
To help little children
    Out of the snow.

Each has a rum-bottle
    Under his chin,
Tied with a little bit
    Of bobbin.

« 870 »

The herring loves the merry moonlight,
    The mackerel loves the wind;
But the oyster loves the dredging song,
    For she comes of a gentle kind.

« 871 »

High in the pine-tree
    The little turtle-dove
Made a little nursery,
    To please her little love.
"Coo," said the little turtle-dove,
    "Coo," said she;
In the long shady branches
    Of the dark pine tree.

« 872 »

Up and down the City Road,
    In and out of the Eagle,
That's the way the money goes,
    Pop goes the weasel!

Half a pound of tuppenny rice,
    Half a pound of treacle,[8]
Mix it up and make it nice,
    Pop goes the weasel!

Every night when I go out
    The monkey's on the table;
Take a stick and knock it off,
    Pop goes the weasel![9]

8. "Treacle"—molasses.

9. The popular explanation of this music-hall-song-cum-nursery-rhyme is that "the weasel" is an implement used in the cobbler's trade. To "pop" was to pawn the weasel on a Friday night—in order to get the money to go "Up and down the City Road" and enjoy one's self at such public houses as "the Eagle."

« 873 »

Oh where, oh where has my little dog gone?
Oh where, oh where can he be?
With his ears cut short and his tail cut long,
Oh where, oh where is he?[10]

« 874 »

"Flying-man, Flying-man,
    Up in the sky,
Where are you going to,
    Flying so high?"

"Over the mountains
    And over the sea—!"
"Flying-man, Flying-man,
    Can't you take me?"

« 875 »

Oh, Pillykin, Willykin, Winky Wee!
How does the President take his tea?
He takes it with melons, he takes it with milk,
He takes it with syrup and sassafras silk;
He takes it without and he takes it within,
Oh, Pinky-doodle and Jollapin!

« 876 »

Fishy, fishy in the brook,
Daddy catch him on a hook,
Mommy fry him in a pan,
Johnny eat him like a man.

« 877 »

His angle rod was made of a sturdy oak,
His line was a cable which in storms ne'er broke;
His hook he had baited with a dragon's tail,
And he sat upon a rock and bobbed for whale.

« 878 »

Tally-Ho! Tally-Ho!
A hunting we will go!

A. RACKHAM

10. The American song writer, Septimus Winter, who gave the nursery "Ten Little Injuns" (Rhyme 818), also contributed this. Originally, it was "Der Deitcher's Dog," first published in 1864.

11. P. A. Ditchfield, in his book *Old English Customs*, states that this jingle is thirteen hundred years old, and that it was first recorded in a book of sixth-century jests compiled by one Hierocles. There is a similar rhyme for boys:

Father, may I go to war?
    Yes, you may, my son;
Wear your woollen comforter,
    But don't fire off your gun.

We will catch a fox
And put him in a box
And never let him go, oh!

« 879 »

Mother, may I go out to swim?
    Yes, my darling daughter,
Hang your clothes on a hickory limb
    And don't go near the water.[11]

« 880 »

There was once a fish.
    (What more could you wish?)
He lived in the sea.
    (Where else would he be?)
He was caught on a line.
    (Whose line if not mine?)
So I brought him to you.
    (What else should I do?)

« 881 »

Chook, chook, chook, chook, chook,
    Good morning, Mrs. Hen.
How many chickens have you got?
    Madam, I've got ten.
Four of them are yellow,
    And four of them are brown,
And two of them are speckled red,
    The nicest in the town.

« 882 »

Fishes swim in water clear,
Birds fly up into the air,
Serpents creep along the ground,
Boys and girls run round and round.

« 883 »

Who's that ringing at my door bell?
    A little pussy cat that isn't very well.
Rub its nose with a little mutton fat,
    That's the best cure for a little pussy cat.

« 884 »

Three little ghostesses,
Sitting on postesses,
Eating buttered toastesses,
Greasing their fistesses,
Up to their wristesses,
Oh, what beastesses
To make such feastesses!

A dillar, a dollar,
A ten o'clock scholar ;
What makes you come so soon ?
You used to come at ten o'clock,
But now you come at noon !

K. GREENAWAY

327

No, no, my melodies will never die,

While nurses sing and babies cry.

ONLY TRUE MOTHER GOOSE MELODIES, C. 1843

CHAPTER XVIII

Mother Goose Tomorrow

In the year 1846, an American publisher, Theodore Bliss of Philadelphia, brought out a sharply abridged edition of James O. Halliwell's *The Nursery Rhymes of England* which he waggishly titled *The Book of Nursery Rhymes Complete from the Creation of the World to the Present Day*.

It would be arrogant, not to say rash, to call *The Annotated Mother Goose* as "definitive" a collection.

We make no such claim—but we do believe that most readers, young or old, will find here all the familiar rhymes, scores that are not so familiar, some once known and since forgotten, and others that are completely new to them.

This is not to say that *every* rhyme that some may consider a nursery rhyme is to be found in these pages. It was the custom, especially in America, and especially in the early years of the present century, for publishers to "pad" Mother Goose books to make them seem of greater value. They did this in two ways. First, they included many staff-written rhymes that were usually mere paraphrases of such old favorites as "Bah, Bah, Black Sheep," "Little Boy Blue," and "Bo-peep"—and very amateurish paraphrases, at that. Second, such publishers often included some exceedingly well-known poems by quite celebrated authors—Sir Walter Scott's "The Pibroch of Donnel Dhu," and Lewis Carroll's "The Walrus and the Carpenter," and William Cowper's "The Diverting History of John Gilpin" and William Allingham's "The Fairies," ("Up the airy mountain,/Down the rushy glen,/We daren't go a-hunting/For fear of little men").

It would be unthinkable, of course, to produce a "Mother Goose" collection that left out "Old Mother Hubbard" or "Mary Had a Little Lamb," although their authors are known. But we have done without the poems listed above, and others like them —Eugene Field's "Wynken, Blynken and Nod," for example—even though these poems have been published, often anonymously, in many "Mother Goose" books, and may, in another generation or so, be considered "true" nursery-rhyme literature.

The "true" nursery or "Mother Goose" rhyme, then, is generally, but not always, of anonymous authorship.

What other rules have we been guided by in deciding what should, and should not, be included here?

M. PARRISH

There are only three of them:

First, it seems to us that while a nursery rhyme can certainly be *read*, it is primarily a song to be sung or a jingle to be *said*. It follows that genuine nursery rhymes are most often learned from a person rather than from a book; they are "orally transmitted," as the folklorists say—passed along by word of mouth from the older to the younger generation, as are folk ballads and tales. Eventually, of course, most if not all of these nursery rhymes do find their way into books, and from them pass once again into the "oral stream" to begin a whole new life.

Second, a nursery rhyme is generally short, sometimes only a couplet or a quatrain in length. There are rhymes much longer than that in this book, but we have deliberately excluded most tales-in-verse, of which "The History of Tom Thumb"—found in several nursery rhyme collections, including Boyd Smith's—is a lengthy (and very tedious) example.

Third, and most important, a nursery rhyme by definition is a rhyme intended to lull an infant or amuse a somewhat older child. A certain number of "school rhymes"—mostly those collected by James O. Halliwell—do appear here, but in general we have left these rhymes to such splendid collections as Carl Withers's *Rocket in My Pocket*, Ray Woods's *American Mother Goose* and *Fun in American Folk Rhymes*, and especially to Iona and Peter Opie's *I Saw Esau* and *The Lore and Language of Schoolchildren*.

* * * *
* * *
* * * *

Every parent knows how much small children resent any deviation from a song or story as they first heard it. "But that's not the way it *goes*!" they complain. Once the form is fixed, it tends to stay that way, often over several centuries.

Yet the nursery rhyme is not entirely static. From generation to generation the old rhymes *do* change, take on such new dresses that sometimes they are hardly recognizable. And, from generation to generation, entirely new rhymes *are* born.

Is it important to record and preserve these variations, these new rhymes?

We believe that it is, because we believe, with many others, that the nursery rhyme is an important part of our English-American heritage of "folk-lore" —the traditional tales, songs, dances, customs, beliefs and sayings that have come to us, for the most part, from the countries of northern Europe.

We echo the thought expressed by Richard Chase in his book, *American Folk Tales and Songs* (New York: New American Library, 1956), when he says:

"Every song, ballad, hymn, carol, tale, singing game, dance tune, set of dance figures, or even bit of dramatic dialogue that comes from unwritten, unpublished, word-of-mouth sources may contribute immeasurably to the future culture of our nation. It is conceivable that some readers of this book may have preserved in their own family, songs, tales, games or other traditions that have hitherto never been recorded, or important variants of those that are known. We urge these readers to share their traditions with others. It is hoped that this book may reawaken memories of half-forgotten songs or tales, and make more and more people aware of the importance of preserving these 'old ways.'"

You, too, can be a "Mother Goose" collector!

W. CRANE

There was an old Man,

　And he had a Calf,

And that's Half;

　He took him out of the Stall,

And put him on the Wall. . . .

And that's all.

THE END

Bibliography

A Chronological Listing of Some Important Books of
Nursery Rhymes
(and Books About Them)

Acknowledgment is due to the many editors, from Oliver Goldsmith to Marguerite de Angeli, who have gathered and preserved the old rhymes —and especially to Iona and Peter Opie for their pioneering, monumental, and always-fascinating collections.

Songs for the Nursery, or Mother Goose's Melodies, *Boston: Thomas Fleet,* 1719.
> The putative first Mother Goose.

Tommy Thumb's Pretty Song Book, *Vol. ii. London: Mary Cooper,* c. 1744.
> The earliest existing book of nursery rhymes. A single copy of the second volume is in the library of the British Museum.

The Child's New Play-thing, *London: Mary Cooper, Second edition,* c. 1744.

Nurse Truelove's New-Year's Gift; or, the Book of Books for Children, *London: John Newbery,* 1755.

The Famous Tommy Thumb's Little Story-Book, *London: Stanley Crowder and Benjamin Collins,* c. 1760.

The Top Book of All, for Little Masters and Misses, *London: Crowder, Collins, and R. Baldwin,* c. 1760.

Simple Simon, *London: Cluer Dicey and Richard Marshall,* 1764.

Mother Goose's Melody: or, Sonnets for the Cradle, *London: John Newbery,* c. 1765.
> Probably the first "Mother Goose" book, perhaps edited by Oliver Goldsmith. No copies of the first printing have survived.

The Fairing: or a Golden Toy for Children, *London: John Newbery,* 1765.

Tom Thumb's Play Book, *Boston: A. Barclay,* 1771.

Mirth Without Mischief, *London: C. Sheppard,* c. 1780.

Nancy Cock's Pretty Song Book for All Little Misses and Masters, *London: John Marshall,* c. 1780.

Gammer Gurton's Garland or The Nursery Parnassus, *London: R. Christopher,* 1784.
> Enlarged editions: Christopher and Jennett, c. 1799; R. Triphook, London, 1810.

Mother Goose's Melody: or, Sonnets for the Cradle. *Worcester, Mass.: Isaiah Thomas,* 1786.

A republishing of the Newbery edition (c. 1765), and probably the first American Mother Goose. No complete copy of the 1786 edition has been found. The earliest known perfect copy of a later edition (1794), in the library of the American Antiquarian Society at Worcester, was used to produce facsimile editions by William H. Whitmore (1889), W. F. Prideaux (1904), and Frederic G. Melcher (1954).

Tommy Thumb's Song Book for all Little Masters and Misses, *Worcester, Mass.: Isaiah Thomas,* 1788.

The Tom Tit's Song Book, *London: C. D. Piguenit,* c. 1790.

A Choice Collection of Riddles, Charades, Rebuses, &c, *by Peter Puzzlewell, Esq. London: Elizabeth Newbery,* 1792.

Christmas Box, *London: A. Bland and Weller,* 1797.

The Newest Christmas Box, *London: Longman and Broderip,* c. 1797.

Christmas Box, Volumes II and III. *London: A Bland and Weller,* 1798.

Life and Death of Jenny Wren, *London: T. Evans,* c. 1800.

The Comic Adventures of Old Mother Hubbard and Her Dog, *London: John Harris,* 1805.

Songs for the Nursery Collected from the Works of the Most Renowned Poets, *London: Benjamin Tabart and Co.,* 1805.
Enlarged edition, published 1818 by William Darton.

Original Ditties for the Nursery, *London: John Harris,* c. 1805.

Rhymes for the Nursery, *London: Darton and Harvey,* 1806.

The Happy Courtship, Merry Marriage and Pic-nic Dinner of Cock Robin and Jenny Wren, *London: John Harris,* 1806.

Little Rhymes for Little Folks, *London: John Harris,* 1812.

Nursery Songs, *London: G. Ross,* c. 1812.

Mother Goose's Melody, *Windsor, Vt.: Jesse Cochran,* 1814.

The Old Woman and Her Three Sons, *London: John Harris,* 1815.

Mother Goose Melody, *London: John Marshall,* 1817.

The History of Sixteen Wonderful Old Women, *London: John Harris,* 1821.
The earliest known book of limericks.

Anecdotes and Adventures of Fifteen Gentlemen, *London: John Marshall,* c. 1822.

Grandmamma's Nursery Rhymes, *London: J. Fairburn,* c. 1825.

Mother Goose's Quarto: Or Melodies Complete, *Boston: Munroe and Francis,* c. 1825.

Nursery Rhymes for Children, *London: J. Fairburn,* c. 1825.

Sara Josepha Hale: Poems for Our Children, 1830.

Nurse Lovechild's Ditties for the Nursery, *London: D. Carvalho,* c. 1830.

Nursery Rhymes, *London: James Catnatch,* c. 1830.

New Year's Gift, *London: James Catnatch,* c. 1830.

John Bellenden Ker: An Essay on the Archaeology of Popular English Phrases
   and Nursery Rhymes, 1834.
   Expanded in 1837 and again in 1840.

London Jingles, *Banbury: J. G. Rusher,* c. 1840.

Poetic Trifles, *Banbury: J. G. Rusher,* c. 1840.

Nursery Poems, *Banbury: J. G. Rusher,* c. 1840.

Nursery Songs, *Banbury: J. G. Rusher,* c. 1840.

Nursery Rhymes from the Royal Collections, *Banbury: J. G. Rusher,* c. 1840.

James O. Halliwell: The Nursery Rhymes of England, *London: Published
   for the Percy Society by T. Richards,* 1842.
   Revised and enlarged, 1843, 1844, 1846, 1853, and c. 1860.

Eliza Follen: New Nursery Songs for All Good Children, c. 1843.

The Only True Mother Goose Melodies, *Boston: Munroe and Francis,*
   c. 1843.
   Reprinted, 1905, by Lothrop, Lee and Shepard, Boston, with an introduction
   by the Reverend Edward Everett Hale, D.D.

The Book of Nursery Rhymes Complete from the Creation of the World to
   the Present Day, *Philadelphia: Theodore Bliss & Co.,* 1846.

Edward F. Rimbault: Nursery Rhymes With the Tunes to Which They Are
   Still Sung, 1846.

James O. Halliwell: Popular Rhymes and Nursery Tales, *London: John
   Russell Smith,* 1849.
   Revised and enlarged edition, c. 1860.

The Mother Goose: Containing All the Melodies the Old Lady Ever Wrote,
   Philadelphia: G. S. Appleton, 1851.
   "Edited by Dame Goslin."

Charles Bennett: Old Nurse's Book of Rhymes, Jingles and Ditties, 1858.

Mother Goose's Melody, or Songs for the Nursery, *edited by William A.
   Wheeler. Boston and New York: Houghton Mifflin Company,* 1869.
   Without credit to Mr. Wheeler, his collection was re-issued in 1872 as *Mother
   Goose's Melodies for Children,* with illustrations by Henry L. Stephens and
   Gaston Fay. It was again reissued, under its original title, but again with no
   credit to Mr. Wheeler, in 1884. This edition added illustrations in color by
   Alfred Kappes.

Mother Goose and Her Son Jack and Other Rhymes, *New York: McLoughlin
   Bros,* 186-.

Mother Goose's Melodies, *New York: McLoughlin Bros,* 186-.

The Baby's Opera: A Book of Old Rhymes with New Dresses, *by Walter Crane. The Music by the Earliest Masters. London and New York: Frederick Warne & Co., Ltd,* 1877.

The Baby's Bouquet: A Fresh Bunch of Old Rhymes and Tunes, *arranged and decorated by Walter Crane. London and New York: Frederick Warne & Co., Ltd.,* 1879.

Mother Goose's Melodies, Containing All That Have Ever Come to Light of Her Memorable Writings, *Philadelphia: J. B. Lippincott Co.,* 1879.

Mother Goose's Melodies, *Philadelphia: Porter & Coates,* 187-.

Mother Goose; or the Old Nursery Rhymes, *London and New York: G. Routledge and Sons,* 1881.
    The earliest edition with the famous illustrations by Kate Greenaway. Re-issued, 1910?, by Frederick Warne & Co., Ltd.

Mother Goose's Melodies, Selected and Arranged by My Uncle Solomon, *New York: Hurst & Company,* 1881?

William Wells Newell: Games and Songs of American Children, *New York: Harper & Brothers,* 1884.
    Revised and enlarged edition, 1903.

Mother Goose's Nursery Rhymes: A Collection of Alphabets, Rhymes, Tales, and Jingles, *New York: Williams Company,* 1886.
    With 220 illustrations by Sir John Gilbert, John Tenniel, Harrison Weir, Walter Crane, and others.

Old King Cole Mother Goose Melodies, *New York: McLoughlin Bros,* 1886.

Mother Goose Melodies, *New York: McLoughlin Bros,* 1887.

The Original Mother Goose's Melody, *Albany: J. Munsell's Sons,* 1889.
    The facsimile of the Isaiah Thomas printing in 1794, with introductory notes by W. H. Whitmore. Re-issued with *The Fairy Tales of Mother Goose* added, by Damrell and Upham, Boston, 1892.

G. F. Northall: English Folk-Rhymes: A Collection of Traditional Verses Relating to Places and Persons, Customs, Superstitions, etc., *London: K. Paul, French, Trübner & Co.,* 1892.

Alice Bertha Gomme: Traditional Singing Games of England, Scotland, and Ireland. *In two volumes. London: David Nutt,* 1894-8.

Sabine Baring-Gould: A Book of Nursery Songs and Rhymes, *London: Methuen & Co.,* 1895.
    With illustrations by members of the Birmingham Art School under the direction of A. J. Gaskin.

Clifton Johnson: What They Say in New England: A Book of Signs, Sayings, and Superstitions, *Boston: Lee and Shepard,* 1896.

Gems from Mother Goose Melodies, *New York: McLoughlin Bros,* 1898.

The Nursery Rhyme Book, *London,New York:Frederick Warne & Co.,Ltd.,*1898.

Edited by Andrew Lang. Illustrated by L. Leslie Brooke.

Mother Goose's Quarto of Nursery Rhymes, *New York: McLoughlin Bros,*
18--.

Mother Goose's Chimes, Rhymes and Melodies, *Philadelphia: Henry B.*
Ashmead, 18--.

Denslow's Mother Goose: Being the Old Familiar Rhymes and Jingles of
Mother Goose Edited and Illustrated by W. W. Denslow, *New York:*
McClure, Phillips & Company, 1901.
Each rhyme is hand-lettered by Fred W. Goudy.

Robert Ford: Children's Rhymes, Children's Games, Children's Songs,
Children's Stories: A Book for Bairns and Big Folk, *Paisley: A. Gardner,*
1904.

Frank Kidson: 75 British Nursery Rhymes, *London: Augener, Ltd.,* 1904.
"With the melodies which have always been associated with them."

The Complete Mother Goose, *New York: Frederick A. Stokes Company,* 1909.
Illustrated by Ethel Franklin Betts.

Mother Goose's Nursery Rhymes, *New York: A. L. Burt,* 190-.
With 240 illustrations by Gordon Browne, R. Marriott Watson, L. Weedon,
and others.

The Big Book of Nursery Rhymes, *London: Blackie and Son, Ltd.,* 190-.
Edited by Walter Jerrold. Illustrated by Charles Robinson.

The Hey Diddle Diddle Picture Book, *London and New York: Frederick*
Warne & Co., Ltd., 190-.
One of the many "Mother Goose" books illustrated by the celebrated Randolph
Caldecott.

The Panjandrum Picture Book, *London and New York: Frederick Warne &*
Co., Ltd., 190-.
Also with pictures by Randolph Caldecott.

Old Mother Goose's Nursery Rhymes, *London: E. Nister,* 1910.
Illustrated by E. Stuart Hardy.

Lina Eckenstein: Comparative Studies in Nursery Rhymes, *London:*
Duckworth and Co., 1911.

Jolly Mother Goose Annual, *Chicago and New York: Rand McNally &*
Company, 1912.
"With new pictures by Blanche Fisher Wright."

Mother Goose's Nursery Rhymes, *Philadelphia: David McKay,* 1912.
With ten full-colored plates and four hundred and twenty-four woodcuts by
Sir John Gilbert, John Tenniel, Harrison Weir, Walter Crane, W. McConnell,
J. B. Zuecker, and others.

Mother Goose: The Old Nursery Rhymes, *London: William Heinemann;*
New York: The Century Co., 1913.
This is the edition with the famous illustrations by Arthur Rackham.

The Little Mother Goose, *New York: Dodd, Mead & Company*, 1914.
   Illustrated by Jessie Wilcox Smith. Reissued in 1918.

Nurse Lovechild's Legacy: Being a Mighty Fine Collection of the Most Noble,
   Memorable and Veracious Nursery Rhymes, *London: The Poetry
   Bookshop,* 1916.
   The rhymes in this interesting collection were obtained from eighteenth- and
   early nineteenth-century chapbooks. Illustrated by C. Lovat Fraser. Reissued,
   1924, by Henry Holt and Company, New York.

Nursery Rhymes, *New York: Charles Scribner's Sons,* 1916.
   Illustrated by Grace G. Drayton, the creator of the "Campbell Kids."

Nursery Rhymes, *London: T. C. and E. C. Jack,* 1919.
   With pictures by C. Lovat Fraser. Reissued, 1946, by Alfred A. Knopf, New
   York.

The Boyd Smith Mother Goose, *New York and London: G. P. Putnam's Sons,*
   1919.
   "With numerous illustrations in color and in black and white, from original
   drawings by E. Boyd Smith; the text carefully collated and verified by Lawrence
   Elmendorf."

Come Hither: A Collection of Rhymes and Poems for the Young of All Ages,
   New York: Alfred A. Knopf, 1923.
   "Made by Walter de la Mare. Embellished by Alec Buckels." New and revised
   edition, 1928.

Henry Bett: Nursery Rhymes and Tales: Their Origin and History, *London:
   Methuen & Co.; New York: Henry Holt and Company,* 1924.

Mother Goose's Nursery Rhymes, *New York: The Macmillan Company,* 1925.
   Edited by L. Edna Walter. Illustrated by Charles Folkard.

The Less Familiar Nursery Rhymes, *London: Ernest Benn, Ltd.,* 1926.
   Edited by Robert Graves. One of the Augustan Books of English Poetry
   (Series 2).

Jack Horner's Pie: A Book of Nursery Rhymes, *New York: Harper & Brothers,*
   1927.
   Selected and illustrated by Lois Lenski.

Willy Pogány's Mother Goose, *New York: T. Nelson & Sons,* 1928.

Henry Bett: The Games of Children: Their Origin and History, *London:
   Methuen & Co., Ltd.,* 1929.

Vincent Starrett: All About Mother Goose, *Glen Rock, Penn.: Appelicon
   Press,* 1930.

Katherine Elwes Thomas: The Real Personages of Mother Goose, *Boston:
   Lothrop, Lee & Shepard Co.,* 1930.
   "The nursery rhymes, jingles and ditties, connected with the name of Mother
   Goose, are here for the first time presented in their correct historical perspec-
   tive."

Rhymes from Mother Goose, *New York: D. C. Heath and Company. Revised
   edition,* 1930.

Compiled by Charles Welch.

The Land of Nursery Rhyme, *London: J. M. Dent & Sons, Ltd.; New York: E. P. Dutton & C.,* 1932.
"As seen by Alice Daglish [Dalgeish?] and Ernest Rhys, with a map and pictures by Charles Folkard."

Mother Goose, *New York: The Heritage Illustrated Bookshelf,* 1936.
"A Comprehensive Collection of the Rhymes Made by William Rose Benet, Arranged and Illustrated by Roger Duvoisin." Reissued in 1938, 1940, 1943.

The Romney Gay Mother Goose, *New York. Grosset & Dunlap, Inc.,* 1936.

Four & Twenty Blackbirds, *New York: Frederick A. Stokes Company,* 1937.
"Nursery Rhymes of Yesterday Recalled for Children of To-Day. Collected by Helen Dean Fish. Illustrated by Charles Lawson."

The Gay Mother Goose, *New York and London: Charles Scribner's Sons,* 1938.
Selected by Alice Dalgleish. With drawings by Francoise.

Ray Wood: The American Mother Goose, *Philadelphia and New York: J. B. Lippincott Co.,* 1938.
With a foreword by John A. Lomax. Illustrated by Ed Hargis.

J. B. MacDougall: The Real Mother Goose: The Reality Behind the Rhymes, *Toronto: The Ryerson Press,* 1940.

The Tenggren Mother Goose, *Boston: Little, Brown and Company,* 1940.

Mother Goose Rhymes, *New York: Platt & Munk Co.,* 1940.
Edited by "Watty Piper." Illustrated by Margot Austin.

Ride a Cock Horse and Other Nursery Rhymes, *London: Chatto and Windus,* 1940.
Illustrated by Mervyn Peake.

A Book of Nursery Rhymes, *London: Chatto and Windus,* 1941.
Illustrated by Enid Marx.

The Tall Book of Mother Goose, *New York and London: Harper & Brothers,* 1942.
Pictured by Feodor Rojankovsky.

Mother Goose: Seventy-Seven Verses with Pictures by Tasha Tudor, *New York: Oxford University Press,* 1944.

A Rocket in My Pocket: The Rhymes and Chants of Young America, *New York: Henry Holt and Company,* 1946.
Collected by Carl Withers. Illustrated by Susanne Suba.

English Nursery Rhymes, *Linz-Urfahr "Länderverlag,"* 1946.
Title and text in both English and German. Collected and translated by Mary Schachinger.

The Mother Goose, Gathered from Many Sources, *Mount Vernon, N.Y.: The Peter Pauper Press,* 1946.
Illustrated by Sonia Roetter.

Iona and Peter Opie: I Saw Esau: Traditional Rhymes of Youth, *London: Williams and Norgate, Ltd.,* 1947.

Lewis Spence: Myth and Ritual in Dance, Game and Rhyme, *London: Watts & Co.,* 1947.

The Real Mother Goose, *New York: Rand McNally & Co.,* 1947.
Illustrated by Blanche Fisher Wright.

Iona and Peter Opie: The Oxford Dictionary of Nursery Rhymes, *New York: Oxford University Press,* 1951.

The Family Goose: Little Goose, Mother Goose, Father Goose, *New York: Harper & Brothers,* 1951.
Three attractive little volumes with pictures by Leonard Weisgard.

Ray Wood: Fun in American Folk Rhymes, *Philadelphia and New York: J. B. Lippincott Co.,* 1952.

Lavender's Blue: A Book of Nursery Rhymes, *n.p.: Franklin Watts,* 1953.
Compiled by Kathleen Lines. Pictured by Harold Jones.

Marguerite de Angeli's Book of Nursery and Mother Goose Rhymes, *Garden City, N.Y.: Doubleday & Company, Inc.,* 1954.

Iona and Peter Opie: The Oxford Nursery Rhyme Book, *New York: Oxford University Press,* 1955.

Nursery Rhymes for Certain Times, *London: Faber and Faber, Ltd.,* 1956.
With drawings by Elinor Darwin and Moyra Leathem and an introduction by Walter de la Mare.

Nursery Rhymes, *London: J. M. Dent & Sons, Ltd.; New York: E. P. Dutton & Co. Inc.,* 1958.
Collected and illustrated by A. H. Watson.

Touch Blue, *New York: Thomas Y. Crowell Company,* 1958.
Compiled by Lillian Morrison. Illustrated by Doris Lee.

The Lore and Language of Schoolchildren, *Oxford: Clarendon Press. Iona and Peter Opie,* 1960.

Index of First Lines

NOTE

The page number follows each first line. Definite and
indefinite articles are included as part of the first line.